PRAISE FOR
ONLINE EDUCATION

"Before the US Senate investigation, Rob MacArthur virtually alone crusaded against a massive government-supported corporate scam in our college system. It wasn't that for-profit education was inherently wrong, it was the way it was funded and regulated that led to wholesale abuse and the financial ruin of so many aspiring students...leaving us tax payers on a trillion dollar hook. *Online Education Fraud: The Diary of a Short Seller* is the story of a little known stock analyst who embarked on more than a decade of forensic research and advocacy, taking on and exposing the greed of an industry and the corruption of Washington. His only ally was the truth."

—Parker Quillen former hedge fund manager

"Rob MacArthur's exhaustive 15-year investigation of the for-profit education industry details how hard the industry fought to cover up student loan fraud. Had it not been for MacArthur's tenacity, especially in his pursuit of Apollo Group, you can't help wonder if the fraud would still be going on today."

—Herb Greenberg, journalist

"The term 'equity analyst' covers a wide spectrum of rigor relating to research, insights and due diligence. A great analyst comes at almost every issue with a healthy dose of skepticism but knows there will be a leap of faith moment where the cost (time and otherwise) of incremental information is challenging. The best analyst will selectively go that extra distance in situations where the range of outcomes warrants the investment in additional research. Then there is Rob. Until he could personally verify and triangulate a data point, it was nothing more than someone's thesis. There are no leaps of faith moments because facts can be verified and outputs can be measured, personally! I have had the pleasure of working with and for some of the best in the business but the standard that Rob held himself to, was simply another league. "

—Rick Shea President of Vardon Capital, LLC

"Rob MacArthur's book does an excellent job saying things that our government should be saying, but will not do so due to the power of campaign contributions. These for-profit organizations are stealing billions of dollars per year from taxpayers and are ruining the lives of tens of thousands of individuals who are stuck with non-dischargeable student loans for the rest of their lives. The government needs to: (a) fully support recovery of the stolen billions of tax payer dollars; (b) permanently debar the corporate entities and their individual executives from ever again engaging in work paid for with Higher Education Act Title IV funds."

—Dan Bartley, Attorney at Law

"During the 1990's many managers invested in rapidly growing companies with accelerating earnings and price momentum. The for-profit sector displayed those traits. However, after CLCX, and throughout the 2000's momentum managers realized the for-profit sector's earnings were based on false information and bad business practices. Rob was way out in front of that inflection, making a lot of money for his clients."

—Steven R. McNally President, SRM Capital Management

"MacArthur's knowledge and scrutiny of the for-profit education sector are boundless. Neither the companies, nor the regulators escape his critique. The book outlines the tactics that public companies deployed over 15 years. MacArthur followed the money through FOIA requests, government reports and lawsuits. Using shoe-leather reporting, he reads between the lines providing an example for investigative journalists to follow."

—Chris Nolter, Senior Writer, *The Deal*

Online Education
FRAUD

Online Education

FRAUD

The Diary of a Short Seller

ROBERT MACARTHUR

Alternative Research Services, Inc.

ISBN-13: 978-0-9905706-0-8

LCCN: 2014918115

Cover Design by Alan Pranke

Typeset by Mary K. Ross

Printed in the United States of America

DEDICATED TO RAY DIRKS[1]

CONTENTS

PREFACE

What you are about to read is true: an exposé dedicated to the hundreds of thousands of students exploited by the publicly traded for-profit education companies gaming the student loan program. This book is the culmination of my fifteen-year quest to expose fraud at online education companies.

Short selling is the art of predicting stocks that go down instead of up, a research service I provided to hedge funds for the last 20 years. I specialized in for-profit education research starting in 1998. In the early 2000s, under the Bush Administration, there was little or no enforcement activity of for-profit schools. In fact, at one point, a lobbyist working for Apollo Group, Inc. was recruited to work at the U.S. Department of Education (ED) as the assistant secretary for postsecondary education. Despite the screams from the Office of the Inspector General (OIG) through various investigative reports, the OIG's pleas for better enforcement fell on deaf ears. However, in January 2009, the new Obama Administration closed certain regulatory loopholes and began to enforce existing laws.

The book covers the legal and regulatory history of the industry, starting in the late 1990s through 2008, followed by a more detailed look at 2009 and 2010. I track, by month and date, events that led to the sharp decline in share prices across the sector, and how management fought back. All of the stocks in the group, of which there are roughly a dozen, fell by 50% or more from January 2009 through December 2010.

On Wall Street it is common to receive contradictory information, sometimes simultaneously, which could move a stock or many stocks in a very short period of time. By presenting the information in the sequence in which it was received, the reader is now able to see what we saw, feel what we felt, and understand the drama that plays out on a daily basis in the stock market. As an investor, one must weigh each piece of information, in real time, figuring out which detail is most important. Guessing wrongly can be costly. To accentuate that struggle, I have inserted "****" to indicate new and sometimes imperfect information. The stock market is not dictated by infallible scientific laws, like math or physics. Hopefully, the reader will enjoy seeing seasoned hedge fund managers wrestle with volatile information flow.

There were several issues that, while not having a direct correlation to the stock prices at a given moment, had serious consequences for the industry in the long-term. I am referring to the federal government, via various agencies, but primarily the Department of Education's response to the fraud they uncovered at the companies involved.

Parts of the book come from my research reports to clients. I am indebted to my assistant, Prashant Rao, who tolerated working for me for seven years. I truncated many news articles, lawsuits, personal recordings, Street analyst comments, as well as lengthy interviews of current and former employees alleging various forms of fraud. In trying to manage the level of details I left out a lot of evidence proving fraud across the sector. All of the italics were added by me.

I have a responsibility to protect some sources I developed over the years. I have interviewed many former employees, mostly at University of Phoenix, a division of Apollo Group, Inc. I either address these sources as "source" or use a system of letters to hide their identities. Where possible, I have left the real names of the players. Upon learning about the publication of this book, the publicly traded for-profit companies will immediately seek to distance themselves by discrediting me and suggesting the book only discusses past behavior, not present goings-on. I stopped covering the industry in December 2012. At its peak in 2010, UOP had 470,000 students and $4.7 billion of revenue. By August of 2013, they had revenue of $3.3 billion and only 269,000. However, given the magnitude of the issues plaguing the industry, such as the low quality of education, I am not confident they can be turned around—*ever*. While revenue has continued to fall, as of this writing, some stocks in the group have nearly doubled in price from the end of 2013 to early 2014. Yet it is not obvious that their business practices have changed. I guess the market has a short memory.

According to a *Wall Street Journal* article written on January 13, 2014, there were 32 state attorneys-general investigating for-profit education companies. The Consumer Financial Protection Bureau filed suit against ESI on April 30, 2014. And on May 24, 2014, it traded down 20% due to weaker than expected revenues and more fear of regulatory entanglements. Then on June 12, 2014, Corinthian College (COCO) received a letter from the Department of Education that imposed a 21-day delay in the Company's processing of student loan funds, which will likely put them out of business. The announced they were closing school thereafter and the stock fell from $1.10 to $.20. So there has been movement by the regulators as of this writing in the summer of 2014. The problem is they are late by at least 5 years. And that's five years worth of students suffering at the hands of industry.

When I talk about for-profit schools in the book, I am mainly talking about the publicly traded for-profit schools, not several thousand privately owned for-profit companies that run their business more responsibly, in theory. In fact, the demise of the public companies, has created an opportunity for private for-profit school, to fill the void left by publicly traded for-profits. You can follow me on Twitter under the name "Fraudauthor" or via my website, www.altresearch.com. At some point I expect to post relevant documents in the footnotes or other important documents that didn't make into the book.

INTRODUCTION

*F*raud: the crime of using dishonest methods to take something valuable from another person; a person who pretends to be what he or she is not in order to trick people.[1] Similar to subprime mortgage lending, widespread systemic fraud in the for-profit education industry over the last decade is creating a wave of defaults. Publicly traded for-profit schools in their current form are a menace to society. They have the highest dropout rate, highest default rates, lowest graduation rates, and lowest loan repayment rates. In 2009, 54% of students in these institutions dropped out, an increase of 20 percentage points from 2001.[2] Nearly 600,000 students who enrolled in 2009 left without a degree or certificate by mid-2010. And few people realize that student loans are guaranteed by the federal government. Often students do not realize that personal bankruptcy is not a means of shedding student loan debt, forcing indebted students to live under financial stress for years.

For-profit education companies have an annual enrollment of approximately 1.9 million students and generate approximately $32 billion of revenue per year from the federal student loan program, also known as the Title IV. In early 2009, I wrote letters to the SEC Chairwoman and the new incoming Secretary of Education warning them of the pending avalanche of defaulting student loan debt on the horizon caused by predatory recruiting by for-profit schools. Just like the subprime lending

1   "Definition of Fraud, *Merriam-Webster.com*," http://www.merriam-webster.com/dictionary/fraud, accessed July 8, 2014.

2   "Degreeless Debt," *Education Sector*, http://www.educationsector.org/publications/degreeless-debt-what-happens-borrowers-who-drop-out, Feb. 23, 2012.

crisis where mortgages were given to people who were not creditworthy, so too, has it been the case with college loans. Many students who are not really college capable are being given access to loan funds that will never be repaid, causing taxpayers to carry those financial losses.

In 2011-12, the average bachelor graduate from a for-profit school had $40,038 of debt compared to $32,308 at private non-profit schools and only $25,640 at public schools. For associate degree students the debt burden was $24,684 and $13,970 for public colleges.[3] Only one-quarter to one-third of borrowers at for-profit and public two-year institutions were making timely payments on their loans, and more than half of all borrowers were delinquent or had already defaulted.

In 2011, the government reported outstanding student loan debt at $914 billion, with approximately $122 billion of that in default.[4] By 2013, outstanding student loan balances guaranteed by the government increased to over $1 trillion. About 11.5% of student loan balances were more than 90 days delinquent or in default, totaling $124 billion. According to a National Center for Education Statistics study, 23% of students who attended for-profit schools in 2008-9 were unemployed and seeking work.[5]

Many bad loans from for-profit education recruiting have made their way upstream to Sallie Mae, a quasi-governmental organization set up by the government to provide support to the loan program, just like Fannie Mae with the mortgage business. As of December 2009, charge-offs for "non-traditional" loans were 28.5% while traditional charge-offs were 5.1%. Delinquencies for non-traditional loans were 32% compared to only 9% for traditional loans. The average FICO score for a traditional loan was 725, while it was only 623 for non-traditional students.[6]

In September 2009, at the peak of for-profit education's growth, Sallie

3   Ben Miller, "The Student Debt Review," *New America,* http://education.newamerica. net/sites/newamerica.net/files/policydocs/TheStudentDebtReview_2_18_14.pdf,   Feb. 2014.

4   Tyler Durden, "The Next Subprime Crisis is Here," *Zero Hedge,* http://www.zerohedge. com/news/2012-09-28/next-subprime-crisis-here-over-120-billion-federal-student-loans-default, Sept. 28, 2012.

5   "Student Loan Debt Statistics," *American Student Assistance,* http://www.asa.org/pol-icy/resources/stats/

6   "Form   10K: SLM   Corporation," http://www.sec.gov/Archives/edgar/da-ta/1032033/000095012310018176/w76911e10vk.htm, accessed July 8, 2014.

had $4.8 billion of "non-traditional" private loans. SLM CEO Al Lord told investors at an analyst conference on September 16, "There are a variety of reasons for these high charge-offs...Loans that we, for the most part, call non-traditional loans, which are basically loans that were made to students at schools, largely for-profit schools and with low FICO scores." Eventually, SLM figured out this was not a great business proposition. They cut back their support of for-profit education companies, which forced the schools to make loans directly to their students. This obvious conflict of interest is creating even bigger problems.

"According to Sallie Mae CEO Albert Lord, 'we were just not very good at saying no.' Through its "nontraditional" loan program, Sallie Mae lent billions to students who had little prospect of being able to pay the money back. Knowing it could securitize the loans and sell off the risk, Sallie Mae was unconcerned since it knew that, no matter how predatory and unfair the loan terms, students generally cannot discharge private student loan debt in bankruptcy."[7]

SLM disclosed new federal probes on October 13, 2013, targeting possible violations of consumer protection laws—a sign that Washington is pressing the nation's largest student loan company. Sallie Mae, the top recipient of Department of Education contracts, told investors in a quarterly report that the Consumer Financial Protection Bureau launched an investigation into how the company processes borrowers' payments on student loans last month. Sallie Mae said it expects to pay penalties to the government and restitution to affected customers, though it didn't specify possible amounts. The FDIC informed SLM it plans to publicly accuse it of violating numerous federal laws.[8]

Many low-income students benefit from the Pell grant program. However, it deteriorated into a get-rich-quick scheme as prospective students who frequently applied to for-profit schools gained the Pell money and then never showed up for class. Some students were using

7   "Sallie Mae Doesn't Deserve More Taxpayer Money," *Consumer Warning Network,* http://www.consumerwarningnetwork.com/2008/12/16/sallie-mae-doesn%E2%80%99t-deserve-more-taxpayer-money/, Dec. 16, 2008

8   Shahien Nasieripour, "Sallie Mae Faces Additional Government Probes as Scrutiny Increases," *Huffington Post,* http://www.huffingtonpost.com/2013/10/28/sallie-mae-inves-tigations_n_4172169.html, Oct. 28, 2013

Pell money to buy cars, TVs, and other consumer goods that had nothing to do with education. These "Pell Runners" as they were called, created a huge pool of students who dropped out of for-profit colleges and often fell into a debt situation. One former VP of Academic Affairs from Apollo Group put it this way: "This was, in many ways, a willing conspiracy by both enrollment 'counselors' and 'students.' Lax regulation and weak oversight in the best of circumstances fueled the mini-boom." Enrollment counselors knowingly facilitated this practice of borrowing more money than was needed. Pell grants flowing to for-profit colleges increased from $1.1 billion in the 2000-1 school year to $7.5 billion in the 2009-10 school years. At its peak, the University of Phoenix (UOP) alone received roughly $1 billion of Pell money each year. At approximately $4,000 per student, that's just over 250,000 students. This has left the government to clean up the mess for years to come, sometimes seizing tax refunds and other property from defaulted students. As long as for-profit schools get their money upfront, they have no incentive to care if that student stays enrolled. These students were the easiest to recruit using aggressive marketing.

Amidst the backdrop of the post-subprime lending environment, the growth in student loans happened when access to credit was greatly diminished, especially for people at the low end of the economic scale. Gone were the days of using one's home as an ATM through refinancing. Gone were the days of loose credit cards and easy car loans. This liquidity crunch elevated demand for student loans as an alternative source of credit. The for-profit schools benefited from this as student loan funds became the next ATM for the lower class, which they targeted.

For-profit colleges have also been raiding the GI Bill program. They receive the largest share of military educational benefit programs: 37% of post-9/11 GI Bill benefits and 50% of Department of Defense Tuition Assistance benefits flowed to for-profit colleges. Eight of the top ten recipients of Department of Veterans' Affairs post-9/11 GI Bill funds have been for-profit education companies.[9]

In the book, I cite many lawsuits and government reports. Given

---

9   "Harkin: Report Reveals Troubling Realities, *U.S. Senate,* http://www.help.senate.gov/ newsroom/press/release/?id=45c8ca2a-b290-47ab-b452-74d6e6bdb9dd, July 30, 2012

their size it is impractical to track each lawsuit to its outcome. Instead, I offer many egregious allegations in the lawsuits so the reader can see the patterns of misbehavior across the industry. I tried to footnote many cases, allowing the reader to follow my trails of crumbs.

That is where we have been. Let's see how we got here and what can be done to fix the problem.

CHAPTER 1

History of For-profit Education Fraud

August 1998

M y career in the investment industry as a short seller started in 1994; however, it wasn't until 1998 that I was asked by a client to investigate a for-profit college called Computer Learning Centers, Inc. (CLCX). CLC was a for-profit education chain specializing in computer hardware and network equipment repair, with roughly 25 schools nationwide and just over $100 million of revenue and a 50% growth rate.

I am a digger. I love turning over rocks looking for fraud and other misbehavior by public companies. Short sellers predict stocks that go down. We find public information that management doesn't necessarily want the general public to know. Wall Street analysts can get lazy, getting all of their information from management, which is fine for a reputable company. But it's a problem if the management can't be trusted and is doing things they shouldn't be doing and concealing them to jack up their stock price. That means the analysts on the Street are going to be the last to know, not the first when something goes awry. As a short seller I wanted to be first to know the bad news before the market reacts to it.

Proprietary data is highly value-added to the investment community, especially for short-sellers, who are willing to bet against the corporate line, realizing at some point the market will figure it out and price the negative news into the stock. The management of a corrupt company often accuses short sellers of manipulating their stocks down with false or misleading information. Of course, they forget to mention they, too, have a financial incentive to get their stock up. This is where management sometimes follows the wrong path. When there are problems and they start to grow larger and larger, it becomes harder and harder to hide them. Then, one day, the truth comes out and the stock goes down—in theory. And a real telltale sign of corrupt or crooked management is when they come out, vocally attacking the short sellers as CLC did.

Some brief mechanics on the basic concept of short selling: The typical investment strategy, on the "long" side, is "buy low / sell high." If one buys a stock at $20, and it trades up to $30, and the stock is sold, the investor makes $10 of profit. The short seller does the trade in reverse order, "sell high / buy low." Imagine selling a stock short at $30, then watching it fall to $20, and buying it back, thus gaining a profit of $10. The short seller borrows stock he doesn't own and gives it back to the owner later when he closes the position. If the stock price is *higher* than where he borrowed it, he loses money. If he buys back the shares borrowed at a *lower* price, he profits. The short seller must predict the price of a stock will decline over time to survive.

I started my work on CLC by calling the state agencies responsible for regulating the company. In Virginia, I found several disgruntled students wrote letters to the state complaining about the quality of education at CLC. The Virginia regulator had a box of complaints that were being ignored. CLC had three schools plus its corporate headquarters in the Washington, DC metro area, within earshot of federal regulators. It was well known that educational institutions were forbidden, by law, from paying commission to employees for recruiting students. This was a practice the for-profit sector fought hard to prevent; however, it was fairly obvious that incentives to recruit students would lead to recruiting unqualified students. Through the late 1980s and early 1990s, the U.S. Department of Education (ED) shuttered many schools due to predatory recruiting practices. These practices later emerged in the larger number of students defaulting on loans.

As I dug deeper into the story, I found many students who were upset about their treatment by CLC. I found out CLC lost its eligibility to participate in student financial aid programs in their Chicago and Philadelphia facilities. I uncovered several ED reports as well as state agency reports that expressed strong concerns about CLC's accounting and compliance with the loan program. Issues around incorrect or late refunds were big no-no's with the ED.

What I realized was that both the ED and several states have regulatory authority over colleges, although the states are kind of spotty in their enforcement. The regional offices for the ED were not sharing their findings from their audits with each other or the states, which had similar findings. Had they done so, CLC would've been in a lot of trouble earlier on, saving students and taxpayers a lot of aggravation and expense.

My initial work was very innocent as I routinely took one federal or state report and showed it to another state regulator. To say the least, several were upset that they had not seen the reports earlier because it would have been a guide for their own investigations of CLC in their region. Once the pieces of the puzzle were assembled, the pattern of abuse became apparent. Although almost no one in the ED regional offices gave me the same answer regarding how they would apply their findings. Some regulators would say, no big deal about one finding; others said they would have broadened the audit and alerted the Inspector General. The violations were not meaningful taken separately, at least, in terms of dollars. But taken together, pretty soon we were talking real money and moreover systemic abuse. One finding suggested the school kept students' financial aid when it should've been returned, for example.

In January of 1998, with the stock at $35, I started to accumulate several incriminating documents. CLC had four or five schools in California so there was some communication among the state and federal regulators within California that allowed them to see the trends. However, both were unaware of what federal and state regulators were finding in other states where CLC had schools. With my audit of CLC from Pennsylvania in hand, I asked the California regulators for their interpretation. In the Pennsylvania report they found, "The review sample of borrows contained

8 students who had withdrawn from their programs. An error in the input of data into the refund calculation and the incorrect application of unpaid charges was found in 8 of the 8 withdrawn students." That sounded fishy, then this, "This examination revealed that the refunds may have been incorrectly calculated as the school's calculation of the total scheduled hours completed by 7 of the students may be incorrect."[1] That sounded like they were charging students that dropped out or didn't show up.

In another review performed in San Francisco in December of 1997, regulators found, that in 30% of the CLC files reviewed the cost of attendance was overstated. Also, there were concerns during the audit as to the record keeping of entrance exams and retakes and the school was informed during the exit conference that the admissions testing process should be reviewed. It went on to say that students were admitted that did not meet the enrollment requirements and would not have been eligible for Title IV. I asked Pennsylvania to interpret the California documents and so on, cross-referencing as a reality check in several states.

This all sounded bad for CLC, but how was I going to make money recommending CLC as a short, given that it seemed to be going up every day in early 1998? Clearly, these abuses had been recurring without consequence over a long period of time. On March 9, 1998 with the stock in the high $30s, Jerry Knight of the *Washington Post* wrote an article in which he stated that there was a multi-million dollar mud-wrestling match under way to control ("control" is a bad choice of words) the price of CLC. On the one side are CLC executives who have made millions of dollars over the last two years as the stock has rallied from $3 to $40. On the other side are a half-dozen Wall Street traders who are highly skeptical of CLC's success and are betting the stock will fall. Short sellers have sold short four million of the 11 million shares freely tradable to investors, an extremely high percentage.

CEO, Reid Bechtel, stated in Jerry's article, "Every dollar the stock goes up is $4 million the shorts take out of their own bank accounts." Bechtel made no bones about trying to fight the shorts. "After the stock jumped $4.50 a share one day last month, Bechtel exulted and vowed to do it again, 'We've already gone through Hiroshima and it's time for Nagasaki,'

---

1   U.S. Department of Education *CLC Anaheim Program Review*," April 1997.

he told an investor." This only antagonized the shorts and validated their arguments, instead of scaring them. Man, was I starting to hate this guy.

That comment followed an earnings report, which launched the stock into the low $40s. I had one client, an aggressive growth momentum mutual fund and a big holder of the stock, who threatened to buy the stock recklessly to scare the short sellers into buying back the stock, thus closing their short positions and taking a loss. That is what is known as a "short squeeze," when everyone runs for the door to close their short position at roughly the same time. The stock price increase in these circumstances can be extreme. Short sellers can get trapped if average volume of the stock is low. Sometimes, Wall Street is the Wild West. It's a contact sport not for the faint of heart. With the stock up almost 10% after their positive earnings release, I was in a world of hurt.

What no one knew at the time, however, was that the Illinois Attorney General had filed suit against them for fraudulent practices, seeking full tuition financial aid refunds. Just as the stock ripped up to new highs in the low $40s, it suddenly started to reverse and reverse hard. Someone knew about it because the stock dropped from up $3 to down $3 in about ten minutes. The exchange halted trading. Once the market reopened, the news cratered the stock down $13 points. And it fell another $7 in the weeks after that. By late April, CLC fell to $10. Bechtel got "Hiroshima" all right, but I don't think that's what he had in mind.

There is something about being a short seller that is addicting. There is a pride that comes with defeating bad guys, and these *were* bad guys. True short sellers live for frauds. And you can make a lot of money in a very short period time when negative information comes out. To "fight" the shorts, CLC announced a share buyback leading to a minor squeeze into the mid-teens. It's not the best use of the company's capital; however, sleazy management tends to lose sight of what's in the company's long-term interest and is more interested in the short-term stock price.

By the summer of 1998, I was giving and getting a lot of information from several state and federal regulators. I had more information than they did. I began supplying them with research gathered from lawsuits, Street analyses, and various public documents from around the country.

One day, I received a call from three senior regulators on speaker from the ED. They were very curious about why I was calling officials around the country regarding CLC. They told me they were aware of CLC's behavior, but hadn't quite caught them with their hands in the cookie jar (their phrase, not mine). That didn't make me feel too good. Rather than being relieved I was disappointed by their lack of action to date, given the evidence. How long had they known about CLC? I explained the job function of a short seller, suggesting they should think of me as an investigative reporter. I implied that several hedge funds believed CLC's accounts receivables were too high, that it represented late refunds not yet made back to the government, which implied the financial statements were, in reality, weaker than what was being reported to the public.

Unfortunately for the short sellers, on June 9 CLC settled the suit with the Illinois AG for a mere $500,000, despite previous claims that they weren't going to settle. Several clients had locked in their gains when the stock was down. I had a lot of my own money invested, too, so I got killed. The AG proclaimed the settlement a success, but the stock rallied from $17 to $24, more than anyone I knew expected. Yet $500,000 was a rounding error compared to the revenue CLC gained from those students.

My clients and I were upset with what seemed a measly settlement. However, it did set an interesting precedent because it allowed us to assign a potential liability for other cases where tuition refunds were being sought. Investors ignored the fact that $500,000 covered tuition refunds for only 55 students. So what if that number was 10,000 students? The numbers get large fast. The schools didn't want that precedent to be established. I mention this because it may be relevant for the present day 2014 investigations occurring across the U.S.

While we had to suffer through the pain of the stock doubling from the low teens to the high 20s, it gave us another opportunity to short it for another leg down. I continued to get my hot little hands on some very incriminating information to bolster my short thesis.

Management attended an industry conference sponsored by a Wall Street firm in San Francisco. Usually, they have "break-out" sessions where management can meet with investors. Unfortunately for CLC, they were in a room full of short sellers asking them about their accounting practices. Most of them were MBAs from top-level schools. CLC's CFO had a hot temper and became angry that money managers would ask about their accounting and their accounts receivables. This was clearly an "ah-ha" moment for the shorts. On the next conference call management said the short sellers don't understand accounting. We had a good laugh over that one.

I also obtained a letter from the Office of the Inspector General (OIG) detailing CLC's pattern of making incorrect and late refunds, citing the fact that many refunds were up to nine months late. At the bottom of the letter in bold type, it said, "CLC should ensure that its independent auditors include specific steps in their next compliance audit to test for the weaknesses noted above and comment on these issues in their report." Where was that comment in their audit? None of the SEC filings had a comment referencing specific "weaknesses!"

During the summer I received a random call from a producer at the local ABC affiliate, *WJLA*, in Washington, DC. In their coverage of the issue, they interviewed several disgruntled students. Then they posed as students and went into CLC schools with hidden cameras. There, they surreptitiously recorded enrollment counselors guaranteeing a $100,000 salary after coming out of their computer program, which was illegal to do, I was told. The hidden camera footage embarrassed the firm and pressured the ED to act. The exposed employee was fired the next day despite the fact that many of the recruiters were making similar misleading comments to secure enrollments, which was unfortunate.

After that, the ED had just about had enough. They organized a "raid," a loosely held term when thinking about a federal agency. They gave CLC one week's notice before they were coming to inspect the books. Typically, they give schools a month or two, so this situation was different. I did a real data dump on the ED office in Philadelphia, the office in charge of the Washington, DC area. Armed with the knowledge from the documents I obtained, they should've been well prepared for their visit to the company.

Milberg Weiss, a large shareholder class action law firm, had filed suit against CLC following the IL suit. It didn't take long for them to find me through the grapevine. I really wasn't interested in helping their case, but I gave them a few government reports from my FOIAs.

However, one night I made a phone call to one of their attorneys that I will never forget. It went something like this:

Darren, Rob MacArthur, I am calling to tell you that Computer Learning Centers, at this very minute, is shredding documents at their main campus in Virginia. The Department of Education sent the for-profit education company a letter last week giving them only a few days' notice that they are coming to investigate the main campus. These are documents that pertain to the illegal use of commissions for enrollment counselors.

How do you know this?

Several custodians that hate the management are carrying the shredded documents to the dumpster. They called a former employee. That employee called a short seller I know and that short seller called me and I am calling you. Turnaround time? About an hour!

Soon, their actions would come to light. On August 11, 1998 Bloomberg News reported: "Computer Learning Centers, Inc. allegedly discarded student records in a dumpster after federal auditors asked the company for them, according to court papers filed by lawyers for shareholders suing the company."[2] The stock dropped $5.75, to $16.87.

Rodger Murphy, a spokesman for the U.S. Department of Education, responded, "Unless they have a unique filing system we're not aware of, those records should not have been in the dumpster." Private investigators hired by Milberg found documents, including "original student applications and registration forms," in the trash, according to the amended complaint. The Department of Education's May 4 letter sought access to, among other things, "registration and attendance records." William Lerach of Milberg Weiss said, "We believe such behavior is incriminating and highly

---

2   Dave Evans, "Computer Learning Centers Dumped Files Pre-Audit, Suit Says" *Bloomberg News*, Aug. 11, 1998.

suggests the defendants knew and committed a fraud and wanted to destroy the evidence."

On August 17 1998, *The Washington Post* published a similar article. "Less than 48 hours before Education Department auditors arrived at the Fairfax headquarters of Computer Learning Centers, Inc. for a special examination in May, company officials discarded thousands of pages of student records in a trash bin." A private detective "dipped into the dumpster," pulling student applications, rosters of students who dropped out, and other records sought by investigators handling the student aid funds.

Bechtle attempted to justify the practice. "'It's just waste in the normal operations of our business,' Bechtle said. 'We threw out our trash every day . . . 10, 12 bags. That includes trash from wastebaskets, things students throw away. He must have been climbing through pizza boxes and coffee cups.'" Then, the stock climbed back to $19.68 after two analysts issued reports downplaying the importance of the discarded documents and recommending purchase of the shares. 'There is nothing of significance that was revealed,' said Scott Soffen, an analyst with Legg Mason Wood Walker in Baltimore"[3]

After the *Post* article appeared, I decided to call a senior official at the ED with whom I had corresponded numerous times over the prior year. The first thing she said to me was, "I can no longer talk to you." Then she hung up. I briefly polled my hedge fund clients about what they thought was the reason for her response. The survey came out nine to one (me being the lone dissenter) that the odds are that the criminal investigation in the Inspector General's office had now begun and that they were shutting down the lines of communication to the media and other outsiders.

But I sensed a rift inside the Department of Education between those regulators eager to investigate CLC and those who wanted to bury it. It sent chills down my spine that somehow ED officials were already making plans to distance themselves from the controversy and embarrassment around CLC. My contact went from being very friendly to very hostile. No matter, I wasn't aiming to win a popularity contest.

---

3   Jerry Knight, "Suit Says School Dumped Records Sought in Probe," by *Washington Post*, Aug. 13, 1998.

On August 28, Bloomberg reported, "Computer Learning Centers, Inc. fell 55 percent after the operator of computer schools warned its second-quarter earnings will be less than expected because of lower enrollment."[4]

"(The earnings warning) is not the disaster that the market is showing," said Scott Soffen, an analyst at Legg Mason Wood Walker, Inc."

"Charles Cosgrove, Computer Learning's financial chief, said analysts' estimates will have to come down for the third and fourth quarters. Computer Learning had $8 million in cash and cash equivalents at the end of the second quarter. 'I have no idea what we have in the bank today,' said Cosgrove in a conference call. Cosgrove said the company has begun a turnaround and August is 'looking very good.'"

"Reid Bechtle, the company's chief executive, said in a conference call that he was not aware anything was found by investigators in 'Garbagegate' except pizza boxes and plastic cups."

On September 15 Bloomberg published an article referencing the program review that the ED published. While the report does not indicate that any other adverse action is contemplated as a result of the Department's review, it does warn that a recurrence of these findings in a future program review or audit may result in departmental action. In spite of the dumpster incident, they evidently almost let them go. One would think there should've been a criminal investigation, not simply a warning.

On September 16 1998, *The Washington Post* stated, "The ED yesterday reported widespread violations of federal student aid regulations… [The school] gave federal loans and grants to students who weren't eligible, received government grants for students who *never* attended classes and collected federal aid for students even after they dropped out."They found extensive "improper disbursements of federal funds." It can't get any more fraudulent than that.

In a final act of desperation, CLC issued a subpoena to me and other short sellers in the shareholder class action suit filed against them by Milberg Weiss. Grasping at straws, they tried to argue that short sellers had manipulated their stock. I simply parried with my Freedom of Information Act (FOIA) requests, telling the judge all I did was redistribute

---

4   Dave Evans, "Computer Learning Centers Falls 55% on Earnings Warning," *Bloomberg News*, Aug. 28, 1998.

incriminating government documents. The judge expressed annoyance with the company for dragging me into the case and dismissed me in about five minutes. Thank God for FOIA. I've made good use of it over the years.

CLC was my first foray into the rapidly growing "for-profit" education sector, which in 1998 was still in its infancy. CLC put me on the map in the hedge fund community as a proficient short seller. Pouring over regulations, legalese, and the like had made me an expert. Thereafter, hedge fund managers followed my work over the next several years, hoping for another good short idea.

Eventually, CLC was found guilty of violating Title IV regulations by giving incentive compensation to its enrollment counselors. The ED won their case and sent CLC a bill for $187 million, which put the company out of business, as they had almost no cash.

Even before the CLC debacle, in the late 1980s and early 1990s, the Department of Education started to crack down on schools they deemed to be operating illegitimate businesses. Many schools were closed because of high student default rates, often in excess of 40%. Often these were massage school or beauty schools. In that time, the ED implemented regulations to prevent schools from paying commission to enrollment counselors. Justifiably, they were concerned about the quality of students who would be recruited under any type of commission-based quota system.

After CLC, I was worn out and swore I would never become involved in such a scandal again. In the end, the aggravation wasn't worth the money or my sanity. I had made and lost a lot of money for clients and myself. I continued to track CLC's liquidation proceedings. Unfortunately, there wasn't much left for the government to recapture. Everyone had his or her hands out looking for money but the government was slow, so taxpayers took the hit.

In the years following the collapse of CLC, the remaining public companies began to flourish. Currently, there are about 12 public competitors in the industry.[5] Apollo Group performed the best, as their programs focused on the online arena, and the company was thus uniquely positioned to take advantage of the growing popularity and ease of access to the Internet and the ease of access to student loans—the Title IV program. From 1995 through 2004, Apollo's stock rose from $1 to $98 per share, post-splits. Career Education increased from $3 in 2000 to $67 in 2004. Other for-profit education companies, including DeVry (DV), ITT Education (ESI), Strayer University (STRA), and Corinthian College (COCO), also experienced similar moves. Doesn't it seem strange that a publicly traded college would have such a monumental rise? I didn't know that college education had such a strong underlying growth rate.

While I recommended Apollo as a short from $95 to $33 from 2004 to 2007, my real involvement was when it moved from $90 in 2009 to $16 in 2012. By then, exposing the fraud for several public companies in the sector became my obsession. Hundreds of thousands of poor, unsuspecting students were having their lives and credit ratings destroyed by the industry, stuffing them with loans that would never be paid back, and all for naught, given the minimal odds of graduating from these institutions.

---

5   I say about because as of 2014 several of the companies are close to bankruptcy, for example, COCO is $.16.

My crusade for justice was for both the student victims who suffered dearly at the hands of for-profit schools gaming the system, and for taxpayers, who deserved protection from companies that live in regulatory no-man's land between securities laws and Department of Education regulations. And of course I want to make money for clients.

CHAPTER 2

For-profit Education 2002 through 2008

In the early 2000s, the Office of the Inspector General's office tried to do its job of overseeing the ED, publishing several scathing reports that exposed the lack of proper enforcement by the Office of Post-Secondary Education. Under Bush, the enforcement was very lax, which benefited the for-profit sector; site visits were being conducted less frequently, fines for violations were negligible, etc. The Inspector General was largely being ignored by the agency over which they had oversight.

In October of 2002, Bill Hansen, then a Deputy Secretary of Education, effectively re-wrote the way the incentive compensation ban would be enforced. In a memo dated October 30, 2002, Hansen wrote: "After further analysis, I have concluded that the preferable approach is to view a violation of the incentive compensation prohibition as not resulting in monetary loss to the Department. Improper recruiting does not render a recruited student ineligible to receive student aid funds for attendance at the institution on whose behalf the recruiting was conducted. Accordingly, the Department should treat a violation of the law as a compliance matter for which remedial or punitive sanctions should be considered… [h]owever, much more commonly, the appropriate sanction to consider will be the imposition of a fine." CLC would still be in business under this application.

Hansen left the Department in June 2003 to work for ACS, a subcontractor of Apollo's, where he served as managing director. After that, in 2005, Hansen joined Apollo's lobbying firm, the Chartwell Group.

On March 20, 2002, another important development came when Sally Stroup was sworn in as assistant secretary for postsecondary education. Sally had served on Capitol Hill as the former director of industry and government affairs at Apollo prior to her appointment.[1] She clearly had a conflict of interest working at the ED probably on Apollo's behalf. Unsurprisingly, at every turn she testified on Capitol Hill in favor of policies that directly benefited for-profit schools. For example, at the time, Sally Stroup was reporting to the House Post-Secondary Education Committee that default rates were going down for online education companies. She touted low default rates as an indicator of the program's success, but this was a total lie.

The OIG had issued a scathing report about the loopholes in the default rate calculation and lack of enforcement. The loophole was that if students ask for a "deferment" for their student loans, they are dropped from the default rate calculation.[2] Employees of for-profit schools later told me the financial aid counselors routinely told students to ask for a deferment right away, when certain loans required payment while still in school, thus automatically removing them from the default calculation.

Meanwhile, Sally was receiving highly critical letters and audits from the Inspector General and the General Accountability Office (GAO) about the ED's lack of proper enforcement. In September of 2004, Sally received sharp criticism of the distance education program suggesting her reports to Congress "contained unsupported, incomplete and inaccurate statements."[3]

In April 2005, she testified on Capitol Hill about the success of online education. The ED started an online education "pilot" program. The eight participants, including Apollo and CECO, had enrollment growth of nearly 700%, with the total number of students increasing from 7,930 in 1998-99 to 63,350 in 2003-04. The pilot program, which lasted for five years, waived many of the rules that impeded growth into online education. Similarly, enrollment of seven other online schools showed growth of 400%, from 45,997 students in 2000-01 to 223,404 in 2003-04. That precipitous growth should've been a red flag.

---

1   Sally Stroup testimony, *Dept. of Education,* http://www2.ed.gov/about/offices/list/ope/stroup.html, modified April 17, 2006.

2   "Letter addressed to Sally Stroup," OIG audit A30-C0017, Dec. 22, 2003.

3   "U.S. Department of Education's Administration of the Distance Education Demonstration Program" OIG audit A09-D0010, September 2004

On May 26, 2005, John Higgins, the Inspector General from the ED, testified in Congress on the dangers of for-profit education: "Violations of this requirement occur when refunds are not paid timely, when incorrect calculations result in returning insufficient funds, and when institutions fail to pay refunds at all, which is a *criminal offense under the HEA.*" Higgins declared, "Historically, fraud and abuse predominantly involves proprietary schools. In fact, over the last six completed fiscal years the majority—approximately *74 percent*—of our institutional fraud cases involved proprietary schools."

* * * *

I was amazed at how quickly the rest of the stocks in the group recovered after CLC. Much later I would learn from the former CEO of ITT that the remaining for-profit companies went out of their way to hire all the CLC people they could find. One would think given all of the issues of enforcement and oversight of Title IV money, the industry would be somewhat tainted. The remaining players should have been fearful lest they become the next CLC. The opposite was true. Periodically, I would glance at the reported earnings per share, amazed at the strength of their growth. All of them, particularly APOL, consistently beat the earnings estimates by a wide margin, thus attracting institutional investors. I was certainly skeptical of the reality underlying the numbers, but knew in my heart that being short could be hazardous to one's financial health.

Seeing what happened to CLC in November 2002, the industry sought "clarification" of the ban on incentive compensation. That same month, the so-called "Safe Harbor" provisions went into effect. The Safe Harbor regulations inserted the word "solely" into the language of the regulations banning commission for enrollment counselors in an effort to soften the ban. Under the new provisions, incentive compensation was deemed legal, so long as an enrollment counselor's income wasn't "solely" derived from a quota system. The Safe Harbor regulations were re-written to run contrary to the legislation over incentive compensation, thus creating a loophole around the intention of the law. As one might expect, the publicly traded for-profit schools began to exploit this loophole by saying, in name only, that they did not have enrollment counselors earning income "solely" based on a quota system.[4] So as long as the schools could prove just 1% of an enrollment counselor's income came from something other than a quota, the school was in compliance. The industry would argue they were given the green light by ED to change their recruiting activities. Had they not abused it, they probably would've been ok.

Once everyone figured out the "solely" loophole would work, they all wanted in on it. Suddenly, in the early 2000s, investors saw tremendous growth across the sector. Apollo had always been the biggest for-profit school. Later, several of the senior executives of Apollo left to work for its competitors. This led to several initial public offerings by companies run by former Apollo executives. I affectionately refer to those companies as the "Apollo children": Bridgepoint Education (BPI), Education Management (EDMC), and Grand Canyon (LOPE).[5] I was most anxious to follow these companies and recommend them as shorts, too, knowing they were likely to be as corrupt as Apollo. Over time, listening to their conference calls and reading the SEC filings, I was able to corroborate my suspicion. My short sale recommendation of Apollo quickly evolved into a short recommendation of the sector, but particularly the Apollo children. The rest of the schools were more legitimate prior to the Safe Harbors, but they, too, followed suit, although somewhat begrudgingly at first. They didn't want to miss out on the money they could make since the loophole worked and the ED stopped enforcing the ban on incentive compensation.

Bridgepoint Education had 84.4% of associate students dropped. Students who attended a for-profit college accounted for 47% of all federal student loan defaults, but they enrolled just 13% of students nationally.[6] Nine companies had associate degree programs with withdrawal rates over 60%.[7]

---

4   34 C.F.R. § 668.14(b)(22)(ii)(A)

5   Bridgepoint came public in April of 2009, EDMC in October of 2009, and LOPE in November of 2008.

6   "New Data Confirm Troubling Student Loan Default Problems," *Institute for College Access and Success*, http://www.ticas.org/files/pub//CDR_2013_NR.pdf, Sept. 30, 2013

7   "Executive Summary from the Senate HELP Committee," *U.S. Senate*, July 2012.

* * * *

On August 29, 2003, Apollo was notified that a *qui tam* "whistleblower" lawsuit action (*Hendow*) had been filed against it by two employees on behalf of themselves and the federal government.[8] A whistleblower is a lawsuit by private individuals on behalf of the federal government. The action is often filed under seal and remains under seal until the U.S. Department of Justice decides whether to intervene in the litigation. I was lucky because a lot of the *Hendow* documents showing UOP's behavior were made public in subsequent years. If the government declines to intervene in a whistleblower action, as it did in this case, the "Relators," as plaintiffs are called, may elect to pursue the litigation on behalf of the government and, if they are successful, receive a portion of the federal government's recovery.[9] Over time, nearly all of the publicly traded for-profits became the target of whistleblower suits similar to *Hendow*.

In several court cases and government reports, particularly in the *Hendow* whistleblower suit versus Apollo Group, as well as the *McKinney* suit filed against Apollo, it was alleged that the company had intentionally sought to circumvent the incentive compensation ban (i.e. showing how enrollment counselors were paid based on factors other than enrollment quotas). However, the DOJ's decision to not intervene was taken as a green light by the industry and off they went like a rapacious predator to raid the Title IV program.

* * * *

During the early 2000s, one of the more egregious cases of fraud in the

---

8   *United States ex rel Hendow vs. University of Phoenix, et al.*, Eastern District of California, case number 2:03-cv-00457; *McKinney vs. Apollo Group et al.*, Southern District California, case number 3:07-cv-02373.

9   The whistleblower action alleges, among other things, violations of the False Claims Act 31 U.S.C. § 3729(a)(1) and (2), by University of Phoenix for submission of a knowingly false or fraudulent claim for payment or approval, and knowingly false records or statements to get a false or fraudulent claim paid or approved in connection with federal student aid programs, and asserts that University of Phoenix improperly compensates its employees.

sector was Career Education (CECO).[10] Following CLC, the California legislature created what became known as the Bureau of Private Post-Secondary Education, as part of the Attorney General's office. That office was receiving multiple complaints from students about for-profit schools. Career Education had merged a couple of some small for-profit companies, assimilating many schools over a short period of time. Several schools were in California. CECO quickly developed a bad reputation in the industry for its shady recruiting practices. However, they were able to show strong growth. From 2000 to 2004, the company's stock price went from $5 to $75, turning the CEO into a billionaire.

On December 3, 2003 CECO's shares were halted in response to an article that claimed, "Many staff members have been asked by management to commit forgery, fraud, perjury or whatever else is necessary to pass audit inspections," according to Cam Van Wingerden, the former registrar of Career Education's Brooks Institute of Photography in Santa Barbara, California, in the local newspaper, the *News-Press*. Van Wingerden filed a complaint with the Accrediting Council for Independent Colleges and Schools, accusing the school of forging student signatures and altering student records to pass accreditation auditor inspections. When the stock reopened, the shares fell from $55 down to $39. "A thorough investigation of allegations raised by a disgruntled former employee of Brooks Institute of Photography has shown that the allegations are false, malicious and possible libelous."[11] This set into motion investigations by several accreditors CECO was using. Under threat that they may lose their accreditation, and thus, the ability to enroll students, the shares fell further.

The next day, it tumbled to $31! The stock had nearly tripled over the prior twelve months. Other companies suffered from the fallout as well. APOL went from $73 to $62 on this news over the next few days. Corinthian (COCO) went from $65 to $53, ITT Education (ESI) from $56 to $44. It was a nice chain reaction—if you are a short seller. "Despite media reports to the contrary, no specific allegations of accounting irregularities

---

10   See also *Laronda Sanders vs. Career Education; Skelton vs. American Intercontinental University;* and *Millio et al vs. Career Education; Anika Meade-Welton vs. Career Education.* There are many more with allegations of fraud.

11   http://www.businesswire.com/news/home/20031203005624/en/Statement-Career-Education-Corporation#.U7_lHsLQfAw.

were made by the former employee," said John M. Larson, CEC chairman, president, and CEO. "The allegations, which are generally focused on the handling of student information and personnel issues, have been investigated and found to be without merit." CEC said they are not aware of any lawsuit filed by this former employee against the school. The school claims to have strict internal controls over employees, saying company policy as outlined in the Employee Handbook "prohibits falsification of any company records or submissions to government agencies."[12]

This tainted the stocks in the group that summer. Amongst other things, this later prompted the company's accreditor to suspend CEC's ability to recruit students for its online division, but the company simply set up shop in another part of country and enlisted a different and less restrictive accreditor—The Higher Learning Commission (HLC), which accredits most of the shady publicly traded for-profit schools.

In early 2004, CECO rallied all the way back to $70 from $40. It took a year to complete, as the Street and management sold investors on the idea that the problems were isolated to one school, but it would soon become evident that that wasn't the case. But when the *Taubenfeld* amended complaint was filed against the company, in June 2004, it caused the stock to drop from $70 back to $45.[13] The lawsuit quoted over two-dozen former

---

12   http://www.businesswire.com/news/home/20031204005213/en/Career-Educa-tion-Corporation-Comment-Brooks-Institute-Photography.

13   *David Taubenfeld vs. Career Education* 03-C8884, Northern District of Illinois.

employees across the company attesting to the fraudulent behavior at CECO. This was a rich source of evidence regarding things to come at other companies. On June 23, the stock fell 17% after the company said it received a formal investigations order from the SEC.[14] The stock dropped $8.76 to $49.82. The company said it "intends to continue to fully co-operate with the SEC." The news of the inquiry came less than a week after an amended shareholder lawsuit. Here are just two paragraphs from the amended complaint, which is 67 pages, and almost every paragraph reads similarly.

Paragraph 42 of the *Taubenfeld* amended complaint reads, "In addition, according to Witness 2, it was a 'CEC invention' to provide loans to students who were otherwise unable to obtain sufficient financing from other sources to pay for their complete tuition. For example, if the total cost of tuition was $30,000, and the student only obtained $13,000 in financial aid, CEC would arrange for the student to pay $100 per month throughout the student's attendance at school…Witness 2 indicated that CEC would recognize revenue throughout the term of the student's enrollment even when the tuition was being paid from a loan extended by CEC. Witness 2 referred to this as 'make believe money' because CEC was essentially recognizing revenue (and a receivable) based on money it had lent to its students."

Paragraph 43: "Witness 2 also indicated that she had been instructed to falsify student records. On numerous occasions when a student dropped out of school, the school would notify the government agency so that the *school would continue to receive government funds*…Witness 2 confirmed that the school would falsify student records to show as still enrolled a student who had dropped…CEC did this in order to obtain the financial aid to cover the student's tuition."

I made about a dozen FOIA requests for information from the ED regarding 12 different CECO schools. Their reports read similarly to *Taubenfeld*, but yet there was no serious enforcement activity. Since CECO is based in Illinois, the ED's Illinois office would be responsible for the whole chain should they take action against the company. The Illinois IG

---

14   There were several suits but *James Stellato vs. Career Education* filed in Northern District of Illinois was also a good example of allegations of wrongdoing.

said they were aware of the CECO case (unlike the Attorney General, by the way). They have been following the case and responded to certain allegations that have been brought forth on an individual basis at the regional level, specifically, in New Jersey and California. As of now the CECO issue has not been "assigned" to the IL office, but that could be subject to change as events unfold (that's close to being a direct quote). They didn't sound in any hurry.

The California Attorney General wasn't going to wait; they went after CEC aggressively after receiving many complaints from students. "Brooks Institute of Photography violated the Reform Act by willfully misleading, falsifying, and omitting critical information that persuaded prospective students to enroll in educational programs that were advertised and promoted in preparation for a high paying career in their respective fields of study…Further, required data submitted by Brooks Institute to the Bureau was found to be inaccurate, incomplete, and misleading, fraudulent and deceptive."[15]

June 24, 2004: Also in June, a division of the U.S. Department of Education has uncovered violations in obtaining federal loans at Corinthian College, Inc.'s Bryman College campus in San Jose, California. As a result, the department revoked the school's ability to receive advance payments on its student loans, these individuals said. Corinthian gets 82% of revenue from student loan program and has about 150 schools mostly in California and Florida. The company did not comment on the matter as it was regarded as normal and non-material.

In August 2004, a negative report was published by the ACCJC, an accreditor CECO used for a couple of schools in California. This scathing 59-page document contributed to the move down in the stock from $45 to the low $20s. The school stated 90% placement rates; however, their accreditor calculated that only 38% of students ever complete their program of study.

On August 2, 2004, COCO reported that their earnings were less than expected. They said last month a review by the ED found the company's

---

15   "Brooks Institute of Photography Notice of Conditional Approval from the California Bureau of Private Post-Secondary and Vocational Education." I filed an open record request. The letter is dated July 11, 2005.

San Jose campus failed to comply with student aid requirements. Shares fell *39%*, $7.37, to $11.35. I know some of my clients had shorted some in the mid $30s, but I don't think anyone stayed short to catch the move. Career Education fell another 19% to $33.84 and APOL fell 13% to $72.56.

On August 19, Herb Greenberg publishing a scathing article about a new lawsuit filed against ITT Education. In the amended class action suit filed in the US District Court of Indiana, it was alleged the company was destroying documents. "According to the suit, 'ITT Institutes in California and Memphis both carried out systematic and orchestrated document destructions, undoubtedly to conceal the fraudulent activities from government investigators.'"

According to a "corroborated" account by a former student recruiter, the suit alleges that several ITT employees "spent an entire Saturday in October 2003" at ITT's Anaheim, Calif. campus "removing and destroying financial aid documents and records related to student attendance and grades before an impending review by California state auditors concerning student financial aid matters.[16]

On December 12, 2004, *The Chicago Tribune* published a scathing article about CECO, which is based in Illinois. The reporter and I had several conversations about the civil lawsuits filed against the company. Several investigations were focused on where so-called "admissions advisers" use the same high-pressure tactics employed by telemarketers. A Senate investigation report in 1991 found student loan volume doubled between fiscal years 1983 and 1989, while loan defaults more than tripled to nearly $2 billion a year due in part to the growth of for-profit schools. One company involved in the scandal was Phillips Colleges, Inc., where Career Education founder and Chief Executive John M. Larson was an executive prior to 1993.

The *Tribune* article continues: "Phillips was banned from participating in federal student aid programs and fined $107 million by the Department of Education. The company eventually sold or closed all of its schools as part of a settlement with the government... In 1994, Larson founded Career Education, which bought some of Phillips' former schools." Larson

---

16   By Herb Greenberg, "Suit alleges ITT document destruction Commentary: Cites 'corroborated' account of shredding" *CBS MarketWatch.com* Aug. 19, 2004

was never held accountable and quit CECO worth more than $1 billion. A zebra can't change the color of its stripes.

The CA Bureau report was published regarding CECO's Brooks Institute of Photography in December of 2004.[17] CECO was now trading in the mid-$20s, down from the $70s in June 2004. The state required CECO to set up a fund for tuition refunds going all the way back to 1999. Inspectors discovered that school officials had helped students manipulate financial aid documents to obtain the maximum possible towards tuition fees— breaching Title IV of the Higher Education Act. They found admissions officers assisted students in claiming extra dependents to obtain additional financial aid, according to the legal sources. According to the ED web page that school has 2100 students. At 2100 students, five years of attendance and approximately $20,000 in tuition, that would be $200 million if the state sought total refunds for the students. I heard that through heavy lobbying efforts by the industry, the Bureau was dismantled.

March 15, 2005: shares of Career Education took flight, rallying from $32.74 to $38. Jefferies came out and reaffirmed his stance that "policies and procedures in place do ensure that the company's financial integrity and school quality are consistent with the company's mandates and standards that have contributed to its success over the years." He put a price target of $45 on CECO's shares.[18]

Buried within the 10-K filed on March 16, 2005, CECO reported that its "special committee has informed us that it has substantially completed its investigation and that it has evaluated the preliminary results of that investigation. At the conclusion of its investigation, the special committee intends to make a final report of its findings, and any proposed recommendations, to our Board of Directors." The CECO 10-K included language in the auditor's letter (Ernst & Young) expressing *concern about revenue recognition* and internal control policies. Shortly after at an analyst conference, management indicated that their internal review board found no evidence of fraud. Further, a First Boston analyst made comments to the effect that since the CECO management signed the 10-K, therefore,

---

17   They cite California consumer protection regulations 948.16 and 948.32 and several others.

18   Richard Close, "CECO Stock Soars After 10-K Filed" Jefferies & Co., March 17, 2005

there must not be any fraud. A combination of those two events caused a massive short squeeze rallying the stock from $26 to $42. I pressed my clients to short the stock on the way up.

By April 2005, there were several separate suits against CECO, seeking tuition refunds for all students at those three schools going back to California's statutory maximum of four years. They are estimating that AIU Los Angeles will be $90 million. I am guessing in aggregate it could be closer to 200 million for all three schools. The law firm was concerned that the company might go out of business prior to them actually getting the money for their plaintiffs. I had several discussions with the attorney about the 10-K, the ESI 10-K and the recent allegations in COCO lawsuits. The patterns of abuse across the sector looked the same.

* * * *

Backtracking a little, in February 2004, we meet University of Phoenix. On February 4, 2004, the ED's office in San Francisco, which oversees Arizona and UOP, published a 45-page "program review." Donna Wittman was the author of the document. She is a senior enforcement professional in the ED's California office in San Francisco. The opening salvo read, "This report contains a serious finding regarding the school's substantial breach of its fiduciary duty; specifically that the University of Phoenix (UOP) systematically engages in actions designed to mislead the Department of Education and to evade detection of its improper incentive compensation system for those involved in recruiting activities. The finding of noncompliance is referenced to the applicable regulators, and specifies the action required to comply with the regulations and statutes."

"ED investigators interviewed more than 60 present and former enrollment counselors of students (called 'enrollment counselors' by UOP) prior to, during and after the site visit. Most of the enrollment counselors said that when hired, UOP told them that the job had tremendous financial potential and they could make a lot of money.' UOP promised to double or triple their salary in 3 to 6 months if they successfully perform their duties."

While the Corporate Director of Enrollment stressed the big dollars that come with high enrollments, he characterized the compensation plan for enrollment counselors as "smoke and mirrors" so that UOP can "fly under the radar" of the Department. All enrollment counselors indicated that they were not shown the matrix [system of required enrollments for promotions] until after they were hired. Recruiters who had not yet completed their first salary evaluation were unaware that their salary would be based on anything but numbers of recruiting activities. Many commented that the bottom line was: "If the enrollments are not there, don't expect a raise."

A number of enrollment counselors said UOP threatened them with loss of their jobs if they failed to meet the quota. Many expressed concern about losing their tuition benefits if they failed to meet enrollment numbers. At the online campus, even harsher methods were used to "punish" those who fell short. Some enrollment counselors were taken to the dreaded "Red Room," where they were allowed no breaks and were forced to make several calls to prospective students with the managers sitting there providing criticism at every turn.

Over 70% of enrollment counselors reported that they were unaware of any factor affecting their income other than enrollment numbers. Some reported that while they were aware that their evaluation form included some "qualitative, highly subjective" factors, managers always assured them that UOP included these factors simply to deceive the Department and that UOP actually based salary raises on the number of students an enrollment counselor enrolls.

The report says it was widely known that the evaluation forms kept in the personnel files were meaningless. Enrollment counselors cited their concern for student customers, for whom UOP was not a good educational option, such as customers who, because of their family or financial situation, could not reasonably expect to complete a degree program at UOP. But UOP managers chastise enrollment counselors who suggest community college or anything other than UOP. The recruiters are told they are to do whatever it takes to get the students to enroll.

Investigators were told how ECs were careful to follow students until they met the criteria that resulted in credit to the enrollment counselor's enrollment count. The student must attend three nights of the first five-week course of a bachelors' program or, for graduate students, attend two nights be scheduled to attend a second class. After the student has met these criteria, the managers do not want the enrollment counselors to spend time with a student. Enrollment counselors thought that this system of selling the student and then dropping them once the enrollment credit is earned underscored UOP's lack of integrity and concern for the students.

ECs at the online campus were aware of numerous improprieties involving Title IV funding and the enrollment process in order to receive credit for enrollments. Enrollment counselors also told prospective students that student loans would pay all costs and those students would have no out of pocket expenses. In fact, student loan funding does not cover all costs. UOP begins vigorous collection efforts as soon as a student withdraws or completes a program…one enrollment counselor went so far as to say that he hears enrollment counselors "lie to students every day." ECs all expressed concern that students recruited were being deceived.

"A number of recruiters at the online campus were aware of instances where other recruiters had forged or 'cut and pasted' student signatures electronically onto master promissory notes and other enrollment counselor documents in order to get the application or enrollment credit by announced deadlines. Employees recounted that one recruiter was so good at forging student signatures, that he was dubbed 'The Doctor.'"[19]

Enrollment counselors claimed to the regulators that managers coached them on what to say whenever "visitors" (government visitors, accreditation visitors) were expected. Typically, they testified, required enrollments and/or application numbers are visibly posted on the walls and on desks. When visitors are expected, however, these posters and desk "reminders" are removed until the visitors are gone.

After the announcement of a site visit to the San Francisco campus, UOP management told some enrollment counselors at the Northern California locations that they should take leave or attend some function away from the premises. When contacted by the Department after the

19   U.S. Dept. of Education. *2004 UOP Program Review Report*, Feb. 4, 2004 paragraph 5.3.3.

site visits, these enrollment counselors indicated that they were absent for interviews because they had reputations for being honest and frank.

* * * *

In mid-2004, the ED regional office in San Francisco was in the process levying a fine against Apollo for illegally obtaining federal funds, finding Apollo in violation of the ban on incentive compensation. In response, Apollo management circumvented Donna and went directly to Secretary of Education Rod Paige. APOL waited to announce the settlement until September 7, 2004. The stock was $84. The settlement amount was determined *not* by the regional office that had jurisdiction over the company, but from Washington. Paige announced his retirement from the ED on November 13, 2004. Shortly thereafter, he became a lobbyist for Apollo at the Chartwell Group.[20]

Paige's replacement, Margaret Spellings, wasn't much better. On May 10, 2007, Spellings testified before the House Education and Labor Committee in response to criticism from New York Attorney General Andrew Cuomo that the Education Department had been "asleep at the switch" in overseeing student loan programs, allowing corruption and conflicts of interest to spread. Spellings has further gone on record to say that she is disregarding the suggestion by the Inspector General to hold the loan companies accountable. Spellings was nominated to the Secretary of Education by Bush on November 17th, 2004. She served four more years and was later appointed to APOL's Board of Directors.[21]

* * * *

Here are some excerpts of the heated written exchanges: APOL to ED, March 1, 2004:

"Todd Nelson, CEO of Apollo Group Inc. said, "As set forth in this letter

---

20   "About Chartwell," *Chartwell Education,* http://www.chartwelleducation.com/pages/about-us.php, accessed July 8, 2014

21   "Form 8-K: Apollo Group, Inc.", *Securities and Exchange Commission,* http://www.sec.gov/Archives/edgar/data/929887/000119312512265951/d364792d8k.htm, June 8, 2012

and my previous letter to Secretary Paige, we strenuously disagree with several of the key findings, assertions and characterizations in the Report. Perhaps more significantly, we disagree with the Report's core premise—the criticism of our salaried compensation system for enrollment counselors. We are confident that our compensation system was (and continues to be) materially impacted by qualitative, subjective, non-enrollment factors."

"First, as previously noted our current compensation system for enrollment counselors—is not based 'solely' on enrollments. Second, we have not breached our fiduciary duty to the Department of Education or misled or deceived the ED in any way with regard to the manner by which we compensate our enrollment counselors. Third, the legal standard upon which the Report is based—that 'salary adjustments based on success in securing enrollment remain prohibited'—is simply incorrect and contrary to the new regulations, as well as the statute. True, schools could alter salaries semi-annually, but not beyond that, like firing someone or *reducing* one's salary, for not making quota."

Todd continues, "As I have indicated in all of my communications with the Department, the Report, if disclosed, will cause great (and we believe unjustified and unfair) *harm to many thousands of employees, students and shareholders* of Apollo and UOP and that harm only increases with time" (emphasis added).[22]

* * * *

On March 12, 2004, Donna Wittman fired back. "In your letter, you assert that the report is based on an improper legal standard with regard to salary adjustments. To the contrary, as stated in the report, salary adjustments are not prohibited where they fall within the following 'safe harbor.'" The letter goes on to say that UOP failed to provide information related salary history, bonus material, student status reports, and the identity of each student who was not withdrawn or graduated and who had no recorded attendance *for 180* days or more prior to the response, as well as the identity of each student who was not withdrawn or graduated and who had no recorded attendance for 60 days or more prior to your response. UOP

---

22   March 1, 2004 and February 9, 2004 letter emphasis part.

continued to fail to provide the requested documents, especially around salary history for employees, enrollment history, training material, etc. In a response on May 20, UOP claimed they have been responsive and forthcoming.

* * * *

On a March 12, 2004 in a conference call with Wall Street, Nelson suggested that Department of Education reviews "are a normal part of doing business," and that "over the years, we have had many of these kind of reviews." Then, in a June 24, 2004 conference call, he said the review "continues to go from our point of view very smoothly…they have requested some information back from us, we obviously have conducted the research and gathered the information and it looks great." Later, he added, "And, again, as you know, that's just, for us it's a normal course of business. Certainly nothing—nothing that we see, we feel that the data that we produced will create any problems for us."

Much later, I found a letter written by Todd Nelson on February 9, 2004, just five days after receiving the program review. In that letter, he assailed the report as "irresponsible and outrageous," claiming, "The report is devoid of any serious factual or legal analysis. Rather, it relies on gossip and innuendo. It uses inflammatory language to describe issues that, at most, are in contention between Apollo and the Department. It reads more like a John Grisham novel than a serious report by a federal agency."

Even worse, Todd says: "Especially in light of the Computer Learning Center ('CLC') debacle and the serious adverse consequences that ensued, we would have thought that the Department would have exhibited more careful supervision prior to letting its staff issue a report as inflammatory and outrageous as this one. As the Department learned, or should have learned, it is difficult, if not impossible to undo the damage done by the actions of lower level staff if reports are issued and publicly disclosed. The Department's conduct in the CLC matter and in this case, stands in stark and sad contrast to the manner in which the Department handled similar allegations involving ITT Education…Based on that analysis, that matter was settled by ITT's making a nominal payment to the Department and the Department essentially agreed there was no violation. I cannot understand why, in this instance, the Department is reverting back to the CLC model."

"In addition," Todd continued, "it is imperative that the Department take all appropriate actions to ensure that the report *not be publicly disclosed, whether by release, FOIA or leak. Release of the report would significantly, irreparably and unfairly damage UOP and its many thousands of employees, students and shareholders.* At this point, we remain willing to work with you, but if the report is released and the damage is done, we will have no choice but to vigorously defend ourselves."

Todd said he believed the Department should withdraw the report, *reassign personnel*, and direct them to conduct an independent and objective review of the allegations.

* * * *

This is from a lawsuit against APOL: "That on-site program review was conducted between August 18th and the 23rd of 2003. And on August 22nd of 2003, there was actually an interview, an interview which the evidence will show was an interview between representatives of Apollo and Donna Wittman, the team leader of that on-site program review team who notified them that, in fact, they had made some adverse findings, and that, in fact, a Program Review Report would be issued in approximately 60 days. And I want you to remember that, because that equates to approximately October 22nd of 2003."[23] Insiders sold stock in the fourth quarter of 2003. Donna told me she sought out the SEC about insider trading regarding this matter, but failed to persuade them to intervene.

"You also heard that, oh, but Mr. Nelson went and reported the existence of the Program Review Report to the largest shareholder, John Sperling. Mr. Nelson reported to him [John Sperling] on average two to three times a day, keeping him informed of what was going on in the company because he was his boss."[24] Nelson, John Sperling, and Peter Sperling

---

23   Case 2:04-cv-02147, Document 574, *Dept. of Education*, Aug. 25, 2008, p. 56.
24   Ibid., 127.

made timely sales in October of 2003, knowing the program review report would be coming soon.[25]

Apollo Group received the program review document on February 4, 2004. That document was kept hidden from the public for six months. Then-CEO Todd Nelson later claimed that the company failed to make the final program review document public because the company's management believed that it did not contain anything that would have been important to shareholders. In a later lawsuit, he admitted that he had lied to investors and analysts in conference calls and SEC filings throughout 2004.[26]

Nelson informed John Sperling, the founder of the company, in early February 2004 about the contents of the program review, but failed to disclose it publicly. On August 19, 2004, "The Department of Education is making it pretty clear if they were to fine the company for every single violation, every single improper payment to an enrollment counselor, the potential exposure could be in the *hundreds of millions of dollars.*"[27]

Much later, on January 16, 2008 Bloomberg reported that Apollo was fined $277 million for withholding the program review from the public. The jury allocated 60% of the amount to Apollo, 30% to Todd Nelson, and 10% to Kenda Gonzales. Both testified during the trial, with Gonzales admitting that the company withheld the U.S. Department of Education report because it didn't want media coverage of the contents.

On the August 25, 2004 conference call Nelson said, "And he says, 'The good news is from our point of view that we still feel very comfortable that the outcome,' he's talking about the program review, 'will end up not having any impact on our ability to grow on our students or employees or anything of that nature. But as with any regulatory issue, it's not over until it's over.'"[28]

I received a copy of the program review in October, and was shocked at the arrogance of the company. Investors had no clue about the severity

---

25   "Insider Trading Chart," *InsiderTrading.org,* http://insidertrading.org/insider-selling. php?sort_by=acceptance_datetime&asc=&symbol=apol&date_from=2003-08-27&date_ to=2005-03-26&submit=+GO+, accessed July 8, 2014.

26   Case 2:04-cv-02147, Document 490, *Dept. of Education,* Jan. 16, 2008, p. 6.

27   Case 2:04-cv-02147, Document 574, *Dept. of Education,* Aug. 25, 2008, p. 62.

28   Ibid., 64.

of the findings as evidenced by the ED's responses, but insiders did, hence the abnormally high insider selling in late 2003. The evidence was so damning I felt the ED could have suspended the company's access to Title IV funding for not fulfilling its fiduciary responsibility to handle federal funds appropriately.[29]

* * * *

Also in February 2004, ITT Education (ESI) was served with a search warrant and related subpoenas from the U.S. District Court in Texas. Federal agents combed through the company's corporate offices in Indianapolis and ten ITT Technical Institutes. The search warrant and subpoenas relate to information and documentation regarding placement rates, retention rates, graduation rates, attendance rates, recruitment and admissions materials, student grades, graduate salaries, and transferability of credits to other institutions. These campuses were shut down on Wednesday but were open for business again on Thursday. The company stated that it had not been informed of any specific allegations or charges and the U.S. Attorney's Office in Houston commented that "no conclusions should be drawn from today's activity." One of the brokerage firms covering the sector, CS First Boston, said, "We believe a key take away from the call was Rene Champagne's (CEO) comment that ESI is doing everything they can to assist the ED in its investigation. Through various channel checks, we have been able to confirm that the ED's Office of Inspector General (OIG) has been involved and likely turned the investigation over to the Department of Justice, suggesting some concern on the OIG's part..." ESI's stock went from $60 to $34 from February 13 to February 26 of 2004.[30]

* * * *

---

29   Under ED regulations, if they encounter egregious violations of federal laws they are authorized to issue an "emergency action," which effectively allows the government to shut down an errant school.

30   On April 1, 2004, Goodkind Labaton Rudoff & Sucharow LLP filed a class action lawsuit on March 31, 2004 in the United States District Court for the District of Columbia, on behalf of persons who purchased or otherwise acquired publicly traded securities of ITT Educational Services, Inc.

At the end of April 2004, Jefferies & Company, a brokerage firm, made the following comments: "We spoke with Sally Stroup, Assistant Secretary of the Department of Education, this week and came away with a general sense that the government had *not* stepped up its regulatory scrutiny. It seems unlikely that the ED is creating an environment for the proprietary schools that is more onerous from a compliance standpoint… We note the company received no restrictions from the Department of Education based on the recent raids conducted by the DOJ. We note that charges have still not been made as a result of this investigation and of the company. We find the lack of restrictions intriguing considering that a few years ago the company was restricted from Title IV funds at any new campuses while the government was investigating charges surrounding a whistleblower action that was eventually dismissed."

* * * *

On July 26, 2004, I obtained a copy of a very strongly worded, threatening letter written to the "senior management" from "all enrollment counselors" at APOL complaining about the horrific work environment. The letter was posted on one of the sites people used to complain about UOP. It attacked the school's policy of reducing salaries for people who miss quotas and the company's unwillingness to pay overtime wages. "You assume that we each fear losing our jobs, having our salaries reduced, having school benefits taken away, enough that it will keep us in line," the letter asserted. "You are overlooking one very important factor about using fear to motivate. You can only motivate with fear, as long as people are afraid. There is no more fear here, only hopelessness. Hopeless people are very dangerous, because they have nothing to lose. So you are about to have this blow up in your face if you continue down this path you are on." It was signed, "Sincerely, The Voice of UOP Enrollment."

* * * *

On September 14, 2004, the *Arizona Republic* published the following headline: "Student-recruitment tactics at University of Phoenix blasted by feds Univ. of Phoenix; audit leads to $9.8 million fine." The country's largest for-profit university was excoriated by a review that painted a picture of a school so hungry to enroll new students that it threatened and intimidated its recruitment staff in meetings and e-mail, pressured them to enroll unqualified students, and covered up its practices to deceive regulators. San Jose recruiters recalled being told heads would be on a chopping block if its enrollments didn't come up.[31]

* * * *

All this bad press may have started to take a toll on APOL's stock, which fell from $84 in early September to $72. Once the full contents of the program review were disclosed, Apollo's credibility came under fire. The truth contradicted what Nelson told shareholders about the severity of the findings. Due to the program review, by November, APOL was trading just over $60. Lawsuits were filed in October in connection with the late disclosure of the program review contents. The findings were very relevant, in fact, because they revealed the company's behavior was much worse than investors could've imagined.

* * * *

My first contact with Donna Wittman was in October 2004. At first, Donna was uncomfortable speaking me. However, after I explained what short sellers do, she softened her stance a bit. She was certainly apprehensive about talking specifics regarding Apollo, which was understandable. I didn't press the issue, but I did explain my role in Computer Learning Centers and that I had become an ally of her counterpart in another regional office of the ED that oversaw CLC. Half-joking, I even suggested she contact her for a "reference" and did a little name dropping to keep her attention.

---

31   Dawn Gilbertson, "Student-Recruitment Tactics at Univ. of Phoenix Blasted by Fed," *The Arizona Republic,* http://www.azcentral.com/families/education/articles/0914apol-lo14.html, Sept 14, 2004.

I never asked Donna if the Department was going to take action against Apollo before it was publicly announced. I submitted several FOIA requests for documents that went through her office. I and everyone else on Wall Street were asking for the same documents, which slowed the fulfillment of the requests. I was giving rather than getting information, outside of asking her for clarification on certain regulations.

In my early conversations with Donna, I sought to understand as much as possible the 2004 program review. Donna said she had made numerous PowerPoint presentations all the way up to the Secretary of Education's office regarding her findings at UOP. She was grilled extensively on her conclusions and methodology. Once the report was given to UOP, Donna claimed that for six months, pressure was placed on the ED to fire her or discredit her work. UOP allegedly tried to cover up the report and bury it. But who filed that first FOIA for a document that no one knew existed? The stock didn't fall to the $60s until Herb Greenberg's article came out in mid-October.

Donna told me the higher-ups at the ED protected the company by drawing narrow parameters around the program review. She was only allowed to ask for certain types of data from the company, so in fact the "comprehensive program review," as it was referred to, was actually a misnomer.

In 2004, a couple years after Computer Learning Centers, I started supplying her data on a routine basis regarding the bad behavior by the industry. Even after a decade of supplying information, nothing came of it. It seemed that senior people inside the ED were actively defending Apollo and the rest of the industry. At one point, I even asked Donna whether she might lose her job for speaking to Wall Street or the press. There was a stone wall being put up by the Department. And there shouldn't have been, unless they wanted to cover up their failures to regulate the industry properly. Many years later, Donna told me she had been pressed by higher-ups not to disclose information to outsiders, but she fired back that the taxpayer has a right to know what is going on in the government. And it was perfectly within her right to explain ED regulations to people, like me, outside the government. Going through public relations was a joke.

In one of my early conversations with Donna, I was looking for an explanation as to why Apollo was fined $9.8 million for incentive compensation violations when CLC had been charged $187 million. In theory, if the ED forced CLC to return the total amount of tuition earned from incentive compensation violations, then APOL should have to do the same thing. The violations were exactly the same, if not worse. Then I read the $9.8 million settlement was based on the 60 students interviewed for the program review, not the whole school. During the negotiations of the settlement the Department told UOP, "We're ignoring all of the analysis that you gave us and all of the statistical analysis and all of the system-wide analysis that you and we have done and we're going to rely solely and exclusively on the interviews that the review team conducted with those approximately 60 enrollment counselors…We could ask for a very large fine but what we want is $81 million."[32] Donna said the settlement came down from above. She found out about the settlement after the fact, in the newspaper, even though it was the responsibility of the regional office to levy the fine. By then, it was reduced to $9.8 million. She never spoke of it again after that. And UOP got away with not having to make any changes to its business practices.

* * * *

On a September 7 conference call with investors to discuss the settlement, Nelson said that "we felt positive about the progress of the review," in reference to an exit interview on August 22, 2003, when investigators finished their fieldwork. He added the company had been surprised earlier that year at the "negative tone" of the report. Just how he could've felt "positive" about the review's progress at the exit interview or surprised by the report's negative tone is anybody's guess.

On October 18, 2004, Herb Greenberg of CBS MarketWatch.com wrote, "On a subsequent conference call, an analyst asked, 'Now that we've got these agreements, is there anything else from a legal or regula-

---

32   Case 2:04-cv-02147 Document 574, *Dept. of Education*, Aug. 25, 2008, p. 111. The next day the fine was negotiated down to $15 million until finally reaching $9.8 million

tory perspective that we need to know about?"[33]

Todd Nelson responded that other than the kind of "little things" any company has, the settlement literally takes care of everything material.

"Feeling equally good about his own position," the article continues, "is attorney Dan Bartley of the Bartley Law Offices, who is leading the $3.3 *billion* false claims charge against Apollo. 'They're [APOL] trying to act that this is all over with,' he says, 'but it isn't.'"

Herb's article really drove it home here: In a March 12 letter to Apollo, the ED made explicit reference to a request made in the exit interview: that Apollo "must develop a corrective action plan" that included major changes to its compensation committee and provide at least 11 different pieces of information, such as an employee salary history and student status reports. Apollo began a somewhat testy exchange, responding that the request for a student status report and enrollment reports "would be an undue burden...." On April 29, the ED responded that the University of Phoenix had "failed to provide considerable required documentary evidence." The ED failed to press the issue further. But the settlement also avoided the corrective action plan Donna pushed for.

* * * *

I was having several intense conversations with clients about the "next step" in all of this. When I obtained my copy of the program review, I almost thought they sent me the wrong document. In my mind, thinking their problems were systematic and not isolated instances or human error, the NASD exchange could've or should've halted the stocks' trading entirely right then and there and not reopen it, pending an investigation. That was a little ambitious, to be sure, but I argued how much of the program review was "in the stock." Even though the media covered some of this, there had been no press release specifically for the program review. Everyone on Wall Street was getting the program review at different times based on when they filed the FOIA. When I received my copy, I thought I was at the front of the bus. No one had it. Even though I received it through FOIA,

---

33   Herb Greenberg, "Why Apollo Remains Risky" *Marketwatch.com*, Oct. 18, 2004 http://www.marketwatch.com/story/why-apollo-remains-risky-2004-10-18.

some of my clients weren't sure if I should have it and definitely not sure if they should trade based on its contents. Was this something that wasn't supposed to be released by FOIA? The findings were so material I assumed an investigation of some kind might prevent the public from obtaining the report via FOIA. The public can't file a FOIA for an OIG report. Over the next few days others received their copies as well, making my clients more comfortable about shorting the stock knowing it was widely distributed.

The stock was still at $74 through September. People were afraid to short it on the basis that surely management would've released such a document instead of being as stupid as to try to hide it. In hindsight, it was a lay-up, but at the time, my clients and I felt trepidation. It was like no one read the *Arizona Republic* article. In fact, I recall one client suggesting that he wanted to short the stock after it started to make a big move down, not before which was a no-brainer.

* * * *

On October 19, 2004, *The Arizona Republic* followed up: After receiving a blistering government report on recruiter pay practices at the University of Phoenix, the school's parent company president told regulators that disclosure of the report would cause "great harm" to the company's *employees, students and <u>shareholders</u>.*"[34]

The letter to the ED and the impact of the eventual release of the report on Apollo's stock raised questions among some experts about whether the company had disclosed the investigation to investors. The warning in the March 1st letter, according to experts, said the company considered the report to be a material event, meaning under securities law, it must be disclosed in a timely manner.

"Nelson and other executives never publicly mentioned the February 5th report until the matter was settled for a record $9.8 million in September, and then only in passing during a conference call. The company failed to admit any wrongdoing in the settlement."

"Given the CEO's statement to the Department of Education, investors

34   Dawn Gilbertson, "Apollo Told Feds: Inquiry News Would Cause Harm," *The Arizona Republic,* Oct. 19, 2004.

as well as the SEC should be alarmed as to why this information wasn't made available publicly on a timely basis," said Lynn Turner, former chief accountant for the SEC and former director of the Center for Corporate Financial Reporting at Colorado State University."

One analyst asked about the program review on a quarterly conference call earlier in the year, but Todd Nelson said the findings were not relevant, since the fine for the program review was not sizable enough to hurt the company's financial position. Any normal human would disagree given the content of the review. He had no idea how big the penalties could be, which could include full refunds for students as Dan Bartley was asking for, and rightly so, in my view.

The report, details of which were first reported in the media a week after the settlement, contained serious factual and legal flaws even though it was prepared by department staffers, meaning it was subject to review at the department's higher levels. "We believed then and still firmly hold that it would have been irresponsible to disclose the Education Department report prior to a full resolution of the issues it raised," APOL CEO Todd Nelson said. "Our shareholders could well have been subjected to an *unwarranted share-price drop* had we disclosed the report prematurely and with these issues unresolved."

Inadequate or misleading disclosure opens up a company to potential shareholder lawsuits and scrutiny by securities regulators. Scrutiny has intensified in the aftermath of high-profile corporate-fraud scandals. Apollo was hit with a shareholder lawsuit related to the disclosures in the report. Apollo's stock has since fallen further, along with the rest of the for-profit education industry, hitting $68, a low it hadn't seen since December.

The University of Phoenix, the nation's largest private university, with more than 200,000 students (later 470,000), had to make substantial changes to recruiters' and supervisors' salary compensation system, the Department said.

Some experts said that Apollo should have disclosed the report to investors, and that Nelson's acknowledgment of the potential harm it could have caused indicates the company considered it to be a material event. Russell Piccoli, a securities attorney and litigator with the Phoenix law firm Marsical, Weeks, McIntyre and Friedlander, said a company can't have it both ways, claiming something is immaterial while essentially insisting to regulators that it is material.

"'If they had a fear that release of the information would have a significant effect on the market price of their shares, then that in and of itself is evidence of the fact that it needs to be disclosed," he said… Adds Carolyn Brancato, director of the Conference Board's Global Corporate Governance Research Center in New York, 'If the company writes to someone else and says this is going to have a huge effect on it, then the company itself has determined that it is going to be material.'"

* * * *

In the fall of 2004, I heard from an enrollment counselor that APOL was making employees sign documents stating their income was not performance-based…retroactive to March 2004. They gave the enrollment counselor I spoke to a raise despite missing targets, supposedly, to make it look as though they are not performance based. People are still leaving because no one can make quota and if employees don't make numbers under the new matrix,[35] they get a 10% pay cut and no one was allowed to work overtime.

Next, the Apollo management wrote a letter to staff and faculty about the review settlement. Someone posted it on the Internet. The letter was signed by Laura Palmer Noone, President of University of Phoenix. "Two weeks ago, University of Phoenix issued a press release announcing that it had reached an agreement with the U.S. Department of Education (the "Department") on a review of recruitment practices. This announcement has generated some media coverage, much of which contains distorted and inaccurate information. The purpose of this letter is to provide you, our staff and faculty, with an accurate account of this issue and to reassure you that University of Phoenix has always and will always operate with the

---

35   UOP uses what it calls matrix. It's a table that shows the numbers of registrations enrollment counselors are required to make to move up to the next pay grade. The matrix was often changed to confuse regulators.

highest level of ethics and integrity and in a manner fully compliant with regulatory guidelines."[36]

The letter continued, "Much of the media coverage has centered on allegations which appeared in the Department's report that were subsequently proven to be misleading and inaccurate. It is important to note that the focus of the review was administrative in nature and did not criticize or question the content, caliber, or quality of education at the University. The review was conducted in response to allegations made by a small group of disgruntled current and former employees. The University is confident that the allegations in the Department's report are false and would have been proven so. However, the University agreed to a monetary settlement with the Department for one simple reason—to avoid lengthy administrative proceedings."

* * * *

On August 19, 2004 a lawsuit was filed against ITT Education (ESI). This complaint amends the initial lawsuit after the DOJ launched an investigation. According to the complaint, more than a dozen former ITT employees confirm that ITT used a host of tricks to satisfy student information, including inflating enrollment figures, counting students as "enrolled" who never attended ITT, double counting enrollees, changing and falsifying grades, and misrepresenting attendance and placement rates. These actions were allegedly done to inflate operating results and the share price, from which management and directors benefited through the sale of shares and inflated compensation packages. [37]

Here are a few quotes from the lawsuit:

"Multiple employees around the U.S. admitted that ITT fraudulently reported enrollment figures by counting as enrollees those students who merely expressed an interest in the school but either never showed up for class *or later dropped out*, double counting enrollees, and manipulating attendance and placement rates. Under this policy many students who

---

36   Laura Palmer Noone, Letter Sept. 22, 2004. Found on the Internet

37   1:04-cv-00380-DFH-TAB. An amended class action complaint was filed against ESI in the Southern District Court of Indiana.

were included as part of the institute's "gross enrollment" failed to show up for class. Nearly 70% to 80% of the prospects included in the gross enrollment never attended class."

"Defendants sold 826,166 shares, in aggregate, and reaped more than $27 million dollars in illegal insider trading proceeds. Significantly, all these trades occurred *after* Defendants learned of an investigation by the California Attorney General into ITT's California institutes, but *before* this probe was disclosed publicly to investors."

"Former employees also say that executives regularly manipulated the enrollment figures by extending the start date of the semester by a week or two after classes had actually started to increase enrollment figures. This policy was implemented companywide and came down from senior management."

"One former instructor claimed that attendance records were 'horrifically manipulated.' He complained to his superiors, including ITT's legal counsel. Former instructors not only recounted specific instances of attendance and grade falsifications, but also noted that certain incriminating documents showing the fraudulent conduct had been turned over to the Office of the Inspector General of the Department of Education. The former instructor stated that Defendants "knew in October 2002 about the fraud and that their employees were systemically changing attendance records and the information had been turned over to the feds." There was never any follow-up by ITT management with this former instructor on any of the issues raised at the October 2002 meeting.

Jefferies and Company Analyst Richard Close had this to say about ITT: "Two instances of destruction of documents were detailed in a legal complaint. Former employees said that they removed and destroyed financial aid documents and records related to attendance and grades. This was apparently completed prior to when auditors from the State of California were to arrive to review the school. In Memphis, Tennessee, a former employee described that the director of recruitment erased six weeks of recruitment data prior to the February 2004 raids and investigations that occurred at other ITT schools."[38]

---

38   Richard Close, "ITT Educational Services, Inc. (ESI) - $30.88" Jefferies & Company, Inc. (August 20, 2004)

* * * *

October 26, 2004: The California Attorney General's office launched an investigation into Sallie Mae, the student loan finance provider, focusing on its private loans to students at for-profit career-training schools. The probe also highlighted Sallie Mae's exposure to for-profit colleges, which have recorded explosive growth but have come under intense regulatory scrutiny. The New York Attorney General also went after SLM for making illegal inducements.[39]

The California Attorney General has separate probes into ITT Educational Services, Corinthian Colleges, and other for-profit education companies. Career Education—facing probes by a U.S. grand jury and the SEC—derived 24% of its $1.18 billion in 2003 revenues from students' private loans, which originate from Sallie Mae. Sallie Mae's private loans pay about 7% interest on average, but some have carried rates in excess of 25%—compared with less than 4% for average federal loans.

* * * *

On January 31, 2005, *60 Minutes* aired a piece on Career Education and for-profit universities in general, alleging that CEC had violated the law. Like the *WJLA* story, the evidence included hidden camera footage of an interview with an undercover *60 Minutes* reporter posing as a potential student. The admissions representatives were recorded guaranteeing a specific salary upon graduation, despite the illegality of such promises. Three former enrollment representatives attested to the hard sell tactics they were force to use on prospective students.

The show also interviewed three former students unable to gain employment in their field of study. The story raised other issues such as

---

39   ED-OIG/A09H0017. The OIG published a report saying Fifth Third Bancorp should be kicked out of the loan program and pay a fine of $315 million for illegal inducements. I talked to the attorney at the NYAG about it and gave him the report that went after SLM for illegal inducements. See also *SLM vs. Richard Riley* District of Columbia 98-3040. SLM is accused of providing "improper inducements to the school to steer students to SLM." They are paid "the incentive fee paid by the plaintiff to Scholl College for each loan portfolio it acquires..." They let SLM go because they said even though inducements are illegal, it's not clear what Congress's intent was for improper inducements.

the placement rates but that issue and others are less important than the salary guarantee. While *60 Minutes* was probably not the primary program of choice for the schools' prospective student demographic, it should turn the heat up on the regulators. *60 Minutes* thought about doing a follow-up piece, but it was rumored that they caved under the threat of legal action from the industry.

****

Members of the House of Representatives Education Committee on Monday evening called for an immediate hearing regarding issues raised by a *60 Minutes* report on the for-profit higher-education industry...In a letter to Rep. John A. Boehner, Reps. George Miller of California, and Dale E. Kildee of Michigan—said that it was "imperative" for the panel to "perform due diligence and convene oversight hearings" on the allegations to determine whether they were widespread throughout the industry.

Congress held a hearing in a large room somewhere on Capitol Hill, which was quickly packed, as half of Wall Street seemed to descend on Washington to see the fireworks in Congress. Four of us took the train down together.

I left with mixed feelings about the hearing. On the one hand, it was a total farce, with several Congressmen calling for more pressure and enforcement on the bad apples in the industry. Clearly, many Congressmen were clueless about the industry. Most of the questions were directed at the person from the Office of Inspector General (OIG) at the DOE. The IG was under pressure by one or two members for not having better enforcement in place, i.e. there were questions about the number of investigations at any given time, of which there are few. The hearing made the Republicans look bad, which could have some longer-term implications, but since the Republicans controlled the committee, the heat falls more squarely on them. Several Republican members of the committee later criticized *60 Minutes,* claiming the reporting was biased and unfair.

More importantly, after the hearing, three other short sellers and I met with a committee staffer. We expected high fives and "good job, guys" for bringing so much documentation to the attention of the committee about fraud in the industry. But it wasn't to be. To our total shock and dismay, the staffer said that while Boehner was willing to call the *60 Minutes* piece an outrage and demand an immediate hearing with the cameras on, he had no intention of doing anything beyond what we had seen that day on camera. As of this moment, the issue was going away and it would never see the light of day again. She didn't lie.

My heart sank under the weight of my own idealism. I had gone to college in Washington, DC, so I was well aware of the amount of cynicism required to work in that city. I guess I had forgotten just how sleazy the Congress could be. The four of us caught a train back to New York with our tails between our legs. What could we do to get a real regulator to do something about this? Under the Bush Administration, the answer was "nothing."

* * * *

Other journalists exposed the money behind the politics. Steve Burd, a journalist for *The Chronicle of Higher Education*, reported, "A *Chronicle* investigation reveals that over the last year and a half, officials with the loan industry and proprietary institutions have given, individually and through political-action committees, or PACs, almost $1-million in campaign contributions to the 49 members of the House Committee on Education and the Workforce, according to Federal Election Commission records through the end of May."

I obtained lists of campaign contributions. APOL had its own political action committee as well as others they funnel money to. "More than half of the money, about $540,000 has gone to Reps. John A. Boehner of Ohio, who heads the full committee, and Howard P. (Buck) McKeon, who leads the panel's subcommittee on higher education. Mr. Boehner received about $136,000 from lenders, and $102,000 from for-profit schools; and Mr. McKeon got about $175,000 from the loan industry, and $126,000 from proprietary institutions."

"Sallie Mae was the single largest donor by far, giving about $185,000. The Apollo Group, the parent company of the University of Phoenix, was the top-giving proprietary institution, donating nearly $70,000."

Steve followed up in a separate article, quoting John Boehner: "'We can't condemn an entire sector for the errors of a relatively small number of bad actors, but we can't turn a blind eye to those errors either,' Mr. Boehner said. 'This is the case in the for-profit education industry. It's also the case in the nonprofit education industry.'"

* * * *

On March 9, 2005, I received a call from Donna Wittman. It was still early in our relationship. She was very interested in the hearing. I had encouraged her to testify. It was a long shot to say the least, considering APOL tried to have her fired for writing that program review. She said that unfortunately in California, there were too many crooks in the business to catch them all, and budget cuts had gutted regulatory agencies' ability to monitor the industries they were tasked with overseeing. In fact, she just completed a program review on an unnamed company, which exhausted her remaining budget for the fiscal year until October. There would be no more school visits, anywhere, until then. She was often paying for gas and office supplies out of her own pocket.

The IG has a different budget so they are separate. She said with a half a penny in her budget she could save the taxpayers one million dollars, but she lacked that half-penny. She would like to see like to see the regional offices given a percentage of money that they save the government from fraud. It's probably not practical, but it speaks to her radical thinking. I read her some of the finer quotes from the COCO lawsuits and she said there was nothing she could do about it. COCO has over a dozen schools in California.

I had the feeling she wasn't telling me the whole story, naturally. I told her my frustrations over not having FOIAs filled and that I thought the Office of General Council (OGC—the ED lawyers) was holding them back, not wanting to tip their hands. She thought the schools themselves were responsible because they have a degree of influence over what was being released, under the auspices of "trade secrets." In reality, they don't want the documents to come out, just as APOL arranged to have the program review delayed by six months before getting into the papers. I could sense her frustration. Deep down, it seemed she would have wanted to have greater regulatory scope than what she was given.

* * * *

May 13, 2005: Apollo was rallying in the month of May, dipping at one point to $66 but rallying all the way back to $80, and taking my blood pressure up with it. On May 26, 2005, I sent clients an email suggesting they short it on the earnings.

I *never* know which of my ideas, if any, my clients act on, nor am I privy to how big their investments in my ideas are. I live in a vacuum because I never know if I am doing a good job or not. They only way I can tell is when they decide to renew their subscription. They want to protect their anonymity regarding their investments. In any case, this spares me a lot of stress.[40] It can drive you mad losing money in the markets especially for people you care about.

* * * *

November 7, 2005, email to clients: The ED filled a FOIA request for information regarding some of the CECO schools. I submitted my request for information on November 4th of 2004. It took a year to get the documents. I doubt many people, if any, outside of the ED have seen these documents. I believe no one on Wall Street has seen them. I have good news and I have bad news: The good news was that the school, Sanford-Brown, a division of CECO was found to have a 48.69% error rate in making timely refunds. In 1997, the refund error rate was 70% so I guess 48% was an improvement. The bad news was the dollar amounts were not that big.

---

40   Further, it is written into my contracts with clients that I am not allowed to trade stocks I recommend. I have not personally bought or sold a for-profit stock in roughly 10 years.

They were charged only the interest on the late refunds, not the actual amount that was supposed to have been refunded. This report was from January of 2002 when the company was under much less scrutiny than it was now. No wonder the schools were so frustrated. There seemed to be no consistent pattern for penalties related to violations.

Here was a good example of the change in enforcement. Under the CLC methodology the ED was asking for full refunds for illegally recruited student loan money. If there was a commission earned based on enrollment made then all of that money had to be returned. California was using the same methodology for CECO's schools that the ED used for CLC. State consumer protect laws are likely more cumbersome for the schools. However, this was where the "Hansen Memo" comes into play. The school was only paying interest on late refunds. So let's say a refund should've been $1,000 and it was 30 days late. Instead of being charged $1000 for a return of a late refund, the school only has to pay the interest on $1,000 for a couple of days, which was negligible. Therefore schools that are keeping money that was supposed to be returned are recognizing the full $1,000 as revenue and no one would be the wiser. No wonder earnings and revenue looked so good after the Hansen memo.

* * * *

In December 2005 and January 2008, the U.S. Department of Education's OIG issued two scathing reports to Todd Nelson, then CEO of Apollo Group. The December report alleged that UOP failed to use the correct number of days in a payment period for calculating student withdrawals. The school was marking down a higher number of days completed, systematically, to keep more tuition. UOP performed about 154,500 return calculations for students receiving about $759 million in Title IV funds during the corresponding payment period. However, UOP applied an inappropriate methodology to determine the "percentage of Title IV aid earned" for calculations performed from September 1, 2002 through December 7, 2004. They did not have a policy to review the accuracy of the payment period end dates for the purpose of calculating the return of Title IV aid.[41]

Paraphrasing: The ED looked at a pool of 25 student records out of 158 students for whom UOP performed Return of Title IV calculations in March 2004 who were at higher risk of having an incorrect Return of Title IV calculation. UOP had determined that each student had earned *all of the Title IV aid* disbursed for the payment period and that no Title IV funds needed to be returned to the Department or lenders For all 158 students, we determined that, based on our recalculations that, for 19 of the 25 calculations, 76%, $62,715 (47%) of the $133,289 of Title IV funds disbursed for the related payment periods *should have been returned to the Department* or lenders. Based on the sample results, we estimate that $419,761 of the $892,127 of Title IV aid disbursed to the 158 students should have been returned to the Department or lenders. With a 90% confidence level, the OIG determined that the actual amount that should have been returned for the 158 students is at least $335,555 or as much as $503,967. That's about as systematic as it can get. Why stop at 158? Should all of the refund calculations be examined? How much money are we talking about for 154,500 calculations?

"UOP has *continued* to disburse Title IV funds to students enrolled in its Associate of Arts in General Studies program, which is *not* an eligible program for purposes of Title IV. In our prior audit of UOP, we reported that, as a result of our work, Federal Student Aid (FSA) notified UOP that the Associate of Arts – General Studies was an ineligible program." *UOP's internal control procedures did not prevent the improper disbursements.*[42] On January 10, 2008, the ED wrote the following to APOL: "…UOP systematically monitored students' status and progress, readjusting the beginning and ending dates of payment periods to accommodate leaves of absence, 'no shows', failed courses or repeated courses. Referring to this process as 'remapping', UOP readjusted

---

41   "University of Phoenix's Processing of Return of Federal Student Aid for the Higher Education Act (HEA), Title IV Programs," *U.S. Department of,* ED-OIG/A09F0008. December 22, 2005

42   In a letter to UOP, dated February 26, 1999, FSA advised UOP that the Department had determined that the Associates of Arts – General Studies program did not prepare students for gainful employment in a recognized occupation as defined in 34 C.F.R. 668.8(d)(2)(iii). In the letter, FSA informed UOP that "[a]ny disbursements of Title IV student financial assistance funds made after February 25, 1999 will be considered liabilities." August 24, 2005 Control Number ED-OIG/A09E0015.

payment period end dates and re-scheduled second disbursements to assure that students actually completed their first payment period and were eligible for a second disbursement." This readjustment often changed the student's attendance to 60% of the classes, at which point UOP was allowed to keep 100% of the money for the cost of the class. Students were not aware that they were being charged for the whole class, or that UOP was rounding up their attendance to fit their refund policy.[43]

The big question is: what percentage of students drop prior to the 60% mark? Here is how APOL understates it default rates. In instances where the student drops, the school becomes the bank before Title IV ever enters the picture; hence, the high accounts receivables balance. I did a spot check of the complaints against APOL on ConsumerReports.com and RipoffReport.com, resulting in 715 complaints against UOP. [44, 45]

* * * *

My revenue recognition fraud thesis implied that the late refunds, incorrect refunds, or no refunds at all were benefiting the company's revenue—on purpose. What if the error rates found were systematic and widespread? That could mean the company owed one giant refund and the government just hadn't come looking for it—yet. It wouldn't occur to the ED to care because they don't think in terms of revenue recognition fraud. And the SEC deferred responsibility to ED. I wasn't betting on the SEC saving my bacon, however; I was counting on fundamental changes in the business to irreparably harm Apollo Group as new enrollments slowed. My Ponzi scheme thesis started to shape up.

---

43   FADL ED-OIG/A09-F0008 January 10th, 2008. In its report, the OIG concluded that UOP's determination of the number of days in the payment period for R2T4 IV purposes prior to December 8, 2004, both before and after DCL GEN-04-03, was improper and in violation of HEA § 484B(a)(3)(B). The OIG noted that during the entire period from September 1, 2002 through December 7, 2004, UOP recognized that its initially scheduled payment period dates were inaccurate in many cases, requiring it to "remap" those dates… As to the period after the February 2004 DCL, the OIG found that UOP's ten-month delay in implementation of DCL GEN-04-03 to be untimely.

44   See http://ittakestime.org/post1341.html#p1341; this one happens to be ITT instead of APOL, but the complaints online all read similarly.

45   "Univ. of Phoenix LIARS and SCAMMERS," http://ripoffreport.com/reports/0/429/RipOff0429308.htm, Feb. 28, 2009.

* * * *

I pulled a few of the more important findings from this 104-page report I received from a FOIA request regarding WIU (a small division of APOL), which encompassed several years worth of letters between the company and ED. In a letter dated March 22, 2006, it was stated that, "WIU has a serious finding of non-compliance with its Return to Title IV (refunds)... The institution is advised that a repeat findings in the future audits or failure to satisfactorily resolve the findings of this audit may lead to an adverse administrative action."[46]

In an August 11, 2005 letter, the ED wrote, "From a sample of 75 students, the auditor noted 11 students that had refunds. From these the auditor noted that seven instances in which the Title IV refund was not returned timely. This is a 64% materially significant error rate."[47] The ED concluded that the last date of attendance for students who quit was incorrect. ED required the company conduct a file review of the entire universe of students that withdrew.

ED also found that *37% of refunds were not made within 30 days*, one out of eight refunds was inaccurate, and one out eight was unpaid and 2 of 8 were incorrect calculations. While these numbers seem small, one would think ED might continue their investigation. It used to be that error rates over 10% triggered mandatory audits by the OIG, but not these days. Due to late refunds, the school had to post a letter of credit. The document states that refunds must be paid within 30 days of the last date of attendance. Of the 30 or so late refunds, only six were less than 100 days late. The rest were 500+ all the way up to *816 days*, nearly three years. The refund amounts averaged around $1,500 each.

* * * *

At an analyst conference in 2006, the senior executives from the major for-profit companies gathered together to talk to investors about the

---

46   OPE-ID-02171500 Dated July 22, 2008.
47   UOP's own auditor found a 24% error rate in the refund calculations (WIU Compliance Audit, 2008, p .22).

industry. This was a Stifel-Nicolaus sponsored conference. I was invited by one of my clients. He and I took the train to Washington, DC, where I used the time to explain the industry. Before dinner and after the presentations there was a happy hour. During the happy hour I met one of the largest shareholders of Career Education, who held just shy of 10% of the shares. He was extremely arrogant, young, and full of himself, but he didn't have a long-term understanding of the sector. I felt like a spy because little did he know that I was recommending CECO as short. The stock was in the low $30s. I didn't let on that I knew more than he did because I didn't want to tip my hand. I asked him one question only, to which didn't know the answer. In past days, I tracked certain money management firms that were long for my short ideas to see what else they might own that I might be able to short, but rarely did I come face to face with them.

At dinner, they put one executive at each table of about seven people. Everyone had a nametag naming their firm. Mine had my client's company name, not my real company name (his idea). At my table were several young analysts from Fidelity Investments and other large mutual fund complexes that owned stocks in the space, and a few private equity analysts.

At my table was Omer Waddles, the former President of ITT Education (ESI). He was president when ESI was raided by the FBI at ten schools across the country simultaneously in 2004, and now was working for a private equity firm. I was sitting across from him. The young analysts were looking up to him, like a God, peppering him with questions. It was making me sick. As the conversation went on, I couldn't help myself, so I asked Omer Waddles what he thought about Computer Learning Centers. He groaned and opined that the government's actions were unnecessary. I asked then why the company was caught shredding documents the night before the ED arrived. Clearly, they were afraid of something. The eyeballs started rolling toward my end of the table.

But then he shocked me and said, ITT and the other for-profit education companies *recruited the CLC employees* around the country. I guess they wanted to learn how to commit fraud. CLC had about 18 schools scattered across the country. So I said, "How did it feel when the DOJ came?" I said, again having impulse control issues.

He looked me in the eye and said, "Like an enema. Who are you, again?"

I told him I was just some freelance analyst who followed the space for a long time. Several of the mutual fund analysts started passing me their business cards. The next day I stood just a few feet from Todd Nelson. I hated him and everything he stood for. He came off very above-board, corporate and professional, but in my mind, under all that was a calm, cool, and collected criminal who should be in jail for embezzling billions of dollars from the taxpayer, turning himself into a billionaire in the process.

* * * *

December 19, 2006: On this date a shareholder class action suit was filed against Apollo Group.[48] The suit asserted that starting on February 27, 2004; management had the obligation to disclose the contents of the program review, but failed to do so. That date represented the first official comments since the receipt of the report on the 4th. It characterizes APOL's behavior as "active concealment of the truth." Plus, the positive earnings report for the second and third quarters were "false, deceptive, and misleading statements," causing APOL's stock to rise to $98.

As part of the lawsuit, the attorney interviewed several employees with interesting allegations. Confidential Source 7 "confirmed that UOP officers encouraged lying or misleading potential students as 'part of their practice'...for example, by lying to students about the transferability of credits of other institutions."

"According to Confidential Source 10, who was employed by UOP in Phoenix, Arizona as a Financial Aid Compliance Auditor from July 2001 to May 2004, beginning in 2002, [an] internal investigation...discovered that many financial aid forms *had been fraudulently filled out* and signed by that [enrollment] counselor. As a consequence, the investigation was then extended to other counselors at that campus and eventually across all of UOP's campuses throughout the country as *widespread instances of fraud relating to financial aid applications was discovered.*"

"According to Confidential Source 10, *approximately 30% of the files that were reviewed had been fraudulently completed by enrollment coun-*

---

48   Case 1:06-mc-00558-CKK District Court of Arizona.

selors… Indeed, by early 2003, *upper management was aware* of the fraudulent completion and signing of applications by enrollment counselors and that it was widespread and should have been reported to the DOE. Approximately at that time, a conference call was conducted by the Vice President of Financial Aid, with all directors of financial aid managers to discuss problems uncovered during the national internal investigation, which was continuing when Source 10 left UOP's employment in May 2004."

Then the court asked if Todd Nelson knowingly engaged in misrepresentations or omissions. He answered "yes" to those questions and stated that, yes, those statements caused the plaintiff harm—*and* he was found to have violated the securities laws. Todd Nelson sold shares of stock in October and November of 2003, *after* the meeting with Donna regarding her preliminary findings but before the release of the review on February 4.[49] I pressed the SEC on this one in 2009, but I was told the statute of limitations on insider trading had expired by that time.

Later, while wading through a series of documents filed in the *Hendow* case, I found a deposition of John Sperling filed on May 20, 2009. John Sperling was founder and Chairman of the Board of Directors of APOL. I found a few quotes that offer a look into Sperling's sick psyche: "I would say there is an endemic hostility toward for-profit education on the part of many of the—many members of the bureaucracy of the U.S. Department of Education."[50]

Sperling continued, "In all of the time I've been with the company it has been absolutely necessary to have an effective and omnipresent political action program. For example, today I think we have some 36 political lobbyists at the state level, we have 6 at the national level and there's a rule or I call it 'Sperling's law' that no innovation, educational innovation can exist beyond the political power to protect it. So I saw my job to protect the company, and I told people… Don't worry about being

---

49   On January 16, 2008, Apollo was fined $277 million for withholding the program review from the public. The jury allocated 60% of the amount to Apollo, 30% to Nelson and 10% to Gonzales. Both testified during the trial, with Gonzales admitting that the company withheld the U.S. Department of Education report because it didn't want media coverage of the contents.

50   2:03-cv-00457-GEB-DAD document 301-0, May 20, 2009.

called a diploma mill. Don't worry about all the negative things being said or done. I will take responsibility for that. I'm the outside person. My job is to protect you." It wouldn't take long for me to realize this was the real source of the corrupt behavior by the company.

If the company received a negative program review report, the ED could limit or suspend access to Title IV money, effectively putting that company out of business. Sperling referred to the program review's importance because of this, further proving the materiality of the document.

* * * *

There was a lawsuit filed against COCO. Notice the similarity between this suit and the APOL suit above. It can also be compared with the *Taubenfeld* suit against CECO too.

"CW [Confidential Witness] 19 described how the school's Registrar collected attendance records from teachers every day along with their call sheet showing that the teachers had called the absentees. The records documented the student's name, the date, whether they were present or not. However, 'the Registrar would enter the students as present when they were missing from class,' CW 19 said."[51]

"After having rightfully failed students, I became aware that the school routinely changed the grades to reflect that the students had passed these classes when, in fact, I had failed them." She goes on to say they threatened her with her job and tried to force her to sign a contract saying that she wouldn't fail students. She continued, "It was common knowledge of staff members that enrollment numbers were manipulated in order to maintain Federal funding."

"A former Controller in COCO's headquarters, CW 27, stated to investigators that Corinthian engaged in accounting fraud, including improper revenue recognition, during the Class Period, at least, Q3 03 and Q4 03 (periods that were covered by Corinthian's 2003 Form 10-K."

"Numerous former COCO employees, at different schools throughout

---

51   *Conway Investments vs. Corinthian Colleges* U.S. District Court of California Western Division Case#: CV-04-5025. See also *Alan Alvarez vs. Rhodes College Inc, Corinthian College,* filed March 2 in Florida.

the country, admitted that Corinthian fraudulently inflated enrollment figures in at least the following ways: counting as enrollees those students who merely expressed an interest in the school, but either never showed up for class or quickly dropped out; counting as enrollees students who started without proper or complete processing (known as 'false starts'), including those who failed to meet the minimum criteria; double counting enrollees; and falsifying attendance records."

COCO allegedly inflated enrollments by manipulating the "start" dates for each quarter so that students were constantly being enrolled. According to CW 36, COCO *manipulated the start dates* for programs so that there were as many as five different start dates a month, with one almost always falling on the last day of the month when the books were closing. This allowed COCO to count a student who "started" on the last day of the month in that month's enrollment numbers, without the risk of having that "start" reversed in the same month.

A former director of admissions at another Bryman campus, CW 29, reported that students were given incentives for *lying on their financial aid forms* to get more money from the government. Specifically, CW 29 said students were told to misrepresent their ages and lie about where they were living to make it appear they were living on their own when they weren't.

* * * *

From 2003 to 2008, the OIG issued many reports criticizing the Department for its lax enforcement. Unfortunately, the damage being done went unchecked over many years. Several government reports from the OIG and even the GAO started to show cracks in the industry, such as low graduation rates, rising default rates, poor oversight of accreditors and private collections agencies—all these were highlighted by the OIG as being rampant in the for-profit education industry. The OIG excoriated the ED for the way it measures default rates.[52] Students who ask for deferments are dropped out of the default calculation. The number of people asking for deferments has doubled from 10.1% in 1996 to 21.7% in 1999. The OIG was also critical of

---

52   ED-OIG/A03-C0017, *Dept. of Education*, Dec. 2003.

a change in the calculation of default rate formula: that it understates the true number of students who are defaulting on their loans. The OIG said, "schools may continue to participate in the Title IV programs, even though a significant percentage of their students may default. Defaulted student loans cost taxpayers money." The for-profit sector has disproportionately higher dropouts and deferments than other types of schools such as private colleges, community colleges, and state universities.

* * * *

Later, Senator Tom Harkin held a series of hearings in July 2012 to uncover the true magnitude of the fraud being perpetuated by the industry. Slightly more than one in five students who attended a for-profit college (22%) defaulted on a student loan. In contrast, one student in 11 at public and non-profit schools defaulted within the same period. Students who attended for-profit schools default at nearly three times the rate of students who attend other types of institutions. The consequence of this higher rate was that *almost half of all student loan defaults* nationwide are held by students who attended for-profit colleges. The three-year default rate across all 30 companies examined increased each fiscal year between 2005 and 2008, from 17.1% to 22.6%, a 32.6% increase over four years. Apollo's default rate has similarly increased, growing from 12% for students entering repayment in 2005 to 20.9% in 2008.

The GAO conducted an undercover investigation, finding massive fraud across the for-profit sector. It was discovered that the industry was manipulating a regulatory loophole in the two-year loan default calculation, so the Department and Harkin sought a so-called "third year" default rate calculation. It was found that many for-profit schools had dropout rates in excess of 50%, default rates in excess of 50% in the third year, and repayment rates less than 50%. Most of the schools received more than 85% of their revenue from the student loan program and more money from the GI Bill. Student loans are not dischargeable in bankruptcy. Thus, countless students are now saddled with debt owed to the government, which they may never overcome.

* * * *

By late 2008, Sallie Mae declared they would no longer provide loans to "sub-prime" borrowers at for-profit schools, a term that carried a lot of meaning at that time. They specifically mentioned the high default rates from Corinthian College, although all of the large public for-profits were largely blind-sided, as SLM had been active in providing funding to their students; however, the defaults caused SLM to write-off a disproportionate number of bad loans from the for-profit industry. In the absence of SLM, the schools started to make loans to students directly, effectively becoming a bank to their students, lending to generate their own revenue stream. That kind of conflict of interest is always a bad idea, but who would care? Of course that led to meaningful write-offs of bad debt in the months and years that followed. The industry then lobbied for and received an increase in the maximum amount of Title IV loans that can be borrowed by students, while raising tuition 5% per year every year. SLM was in plenty of trouble all by themselves. In a lawsuit filed against them in January 2006, it was alleged they were falsifying loan records and phone records to lower their default rates.[53]

The massive growth of the industry and its predatory recruiting has caused a wave of student loan defaults that the taxpayer must ultimately shoulder. For example, in 2008-09 the University of Phoenix received $657 million in Pell grants. By 2010, that number was $1.2 billion. At $5,000 per Pell grant per student, roughly 50% of Apollo's 400,000+ students were receiving Pell grants. The graduation rates at for-profit schools are half the average for post-secondary education, around 25% compared to 55% depending on whose numbers you look at or believe.[54]

There were legitimate concerns about quality of education, too. On February 2, 2007 *The Chronicle of Higher Education* published an article entitled, "Intel Cuts 100 Colleges From Its Tuition-Reimbursement Program for Employees":

"In an unusual move late last year, the Intel Corporation restricted

53   *Zahara vs. SLM Corporation* 1:06-cv-00088-SEB-JMS filed 1/19/2006.
54   "Subprime Opportunity," *The Education Trust,* http://www.edtrust.org/sites/edtrust. org/files/publications/files/Subprime_report.pdf, 2010.

the number of colleges its employees could attend if they wanted to get their tuition reimbursed...As a result, about 100 colleges and universities, including several for-profit institutions like the University of Phoenix, no longer qualify to participate in the company's reimbursement program . . . An Intel spokeswoman, Gail Dundas, said the company decided last year to examine the effectiveness of the education program because of its $25-million annual price tag. She said Intel instituted the new policy after finding that employees were attending institutions, 'that were not of the highest value to the company,' and that many employees left the company after completing their educations because their new degrees did not improve their prospects at Intel."

"The Apollo Group, which owns the University of Phoenix, said in a written statement that it had traditionally had a good relationship with Intel, educating hundreds of its employees. Apollo said that Intel was not concerned about the quality of Phoenix's programs, but that 'Intel would prefer that their employees earn degrees in areas that are more suited to the work they perform, such as engineering.'"

CHAPTER 3

2009: The Hunt

January 2009

The for-profit education regulatory landscape changed in January 2009 when President Obama was elected. The Obama Administration immediately appointed Bob Shireman as deputy undersecretary at the DOE; Shireman had formerly been at the White House under President Clinton. I was hopeful that a new administration would be more aggressive in cleaning up the corruption in the sector. Colleges and student groups loved to see Bob return to Washington. Several names were being talked about regarding the key posts that would need to be filled under the secretary of education, who was responsible for overseeing all policies, programs, and activities related to postsecondary education, and assistant secretary for postsecondary education. Bob was probably the strongest candidate.[1]

In his early weeks, Shireman immediately set into motion the negotiated-rulemaking (NegReg) process. That's a process the ED goes through every few years to make small changes to the ED regulations. The first issue on Shireman's list to be addressed was to revoke the Safe Harbors, which would effectively render incentive compensation illegal—again.

1   Kelly Field, "Obama Faces Wide Pool of Picks for Post-Secondary Post,"*Chronicle of Higher Education,* http://chronicle.com/daily/2009/01/8938n.htm?utm_source=at&utm_medium=en, Jan. 5, 2009. (Other names include: William Kirwan, Juliet Garcia, Linda Darling-Hammond, Michael Dannenberg, Jane Oates, James Kvaal, Sharon Robinson.)

The repeal of the Safe Harbors has since had a devastating effect on the industry.

In the first week of January I wrote to Bob to voice my skepticism of the for-profit education sector. I had spoken to him in my research travels in prior years. I emphasized my strong belief that their systemic, pervasive fraud had sullied the entire sector and wished to send him my documentation to prove it. I also admitted that I am a paid research consultant recommending the shares of the sector be sold short. Despite that, I noted, my experience spans more than a decade. I am knowledgeable about the industry and how public companies especially are walking a fine line between legal and illegal behavior.

The Apollo marketing machine was scooping up the lowest of the low, offering dreams of riches that would never appear, leaving students saddled with loan debt they were unable to repay. Stop this injustice. The executives of these companies needed to be held accountable and he could make that happen if he was up to the task. I pointed out to Bob that he needed to talk to Donna Wittman in San Francisco. She was the key to for-profit education fraud. He should also speak to Nancy Krop, the attorney handling the *Hendow* suit against the company.

* * * *

January 6, 2009: With APOL at $78, I wrote my first report of the year, entitled "The next Ponzi scheme." One theory I had about potential decline in stocks focused on the issue of marketing expenses. It seemed that Apollo was showing exceptionally strong revenue and enrollment growth in earlier years due, in part, to the large sums of (in essence) taxpayer money used for marketing. If the regulatory environment became more difficult, the company and industry would presumably have to spend increasing amounts of money on advertising to maintain their enrollments. That would slow earnings and beat down the stock. That's a lot of advertising and you, the taxpayer, are paying for it. I had started to suspect there were a lot of students dropping out. I thought if there was a Ponzi scheme then it would collapse when advertising could no longer generate positive growth in new enrollments to replace the old enrollment, which is what happened in 2011.

In fiscal year 2009, for-profit schools spent $4.2 billion or 22.7% of all revenue on marketing, advertising, recruiting, and admissions staffing. Has the demand for education really increased that much? I hardly think so. Rather, for-profits have been crowding out legitimate attempts by the poor to elevate their socio-economic status through the Pell program as it was designed.

* * * *

One issue that continued to plague the industry was the high incidence of default. In December 2008, plaintiffs filed another class action suit (*Russ vs. UOP*) on behalf of students. In the suit, it was alleged, even though each student withdrew from UOP within weeks of enrolling, they attended long enough to incur charges. UOP was in possession of each student's federal loan money, however, rather than returning the amount owed for tuition, without the knowledge or consent of the students and without the legal right to do so. By returning the students' federal loan money, even after the students incurred a charge, UOP effectively prevents such students from ever being considered in the cohort default analysis.

The suit alleged that by returning a student's loan money to the lender, UOP was paying off that student's loan and eliminating the student's contract with their lender. UOP then seeks to collect directly from the student the amount owed for tuition that it should have satisfied with federal loan money. UOP also does not have the right to seek a payment directly from a student who has chosen, with UOP's assistance, to pay for his/her education by using federal loans. Unsuspecting students are routinely bombarded with calls, letters, and e-mails from UOP to collect tuition along with threats that refusal to pay will result in referral to collection agencies and negative credit reports.

After attending classes for approximately three weeks, one student decided to withdraw from UOP, but according to federal guidelines and UOP policy, UOP was entitled to a part of the tuition corresponding to the amount of time the plaintiff attended the school. Such a sum was to be deducted from her federal loan monies that had been paid to UOP on behalf of the student. Instead of accepting this prorated payment and properly crediting the federal loan money toward tuition, UOP, without the student's knowledge or consent, gave this portion of her federal loan back to the bank and now sought to collect the tuition directly from her. It was an illegal attempt to convert a Title IV loan owed to a third-party lender into a new and different debt owed directly to the school.

* * * *

Education Management (EDMC) and the re-emergence of Todd Nelson, former APOL CEO: Competition was one factor that supported my short thesis. I was banking on a slowdown of tuition revenue and enrollment growth as more competitors entered the market. APOL was clearly the leader and for its size, it was able to maintain a strong growth rate for an extended period of time. However, they were now facing competition from LOPE and BPI. EDMC was taken private in 2006, but took steps to become public again in an IPO. The company had approximately 96,000 students as of October 2008 vs. 80,300 in 2007—revenues for fiscal 2008 were $1.684 billion. In 2008, they employed approximately 2300 admissions representatives representing a *148.6%* increase since June 2006. In 2006, revenue was $1.095 billion, increasing 60% to $1.6 billion in 2008. EDMC went public, again, in October of 2009 right after a sizable merger, which would explain the abnormal growth rate. EDMC was getting 75% of its money from the Title IV program. Private loans in 2008 were $341.5 million. EDMC has 89 total schools, most of which were accredited by the ACICS.

* * * *

The Department of Education stipulates that schools are not allowed to get more than 90% of their revenue from the Student Financial Aid program (Title IV). Most of the publicly traded for-profits received over

80% of revenue from the student loan programs.[2] Students who are recruited under the Department of Defense's GI Bill are exempt from the calculation. Once schools figured that out, the rest followed suit, causing harm to veterans coming back from overseas deployment. The companies were merciless in their exploitation of our troops. It was so bad that Senator Dick Durbin and veterans groups came forward to insulate the GIs from deceptive marketing practices.[3] In April of 2012 President Obama issued an executive order that required "Principles of Excellence" forcing schools to provide GI's with proper disclosures around cost of attendance, and the amount of costs covered by the GI Bill, better clarity for marketing practices, and standards for refunds.

* * * *

Grand Canyon (LOPE) was another for-profit school that was allegedly violating the ban on incentive compensation. Prior to becoming a public company, Grand Canyon was established as a Baptist-affiliated institution with a strong emphasis on religious studies. The school initially focused on offering bachelor's degree programs in education. APOL's CEO Brian Mueller resigned on July 1, departing to become CEO of rival Grand Canyon University.[4] Brian Mueller's reputation, I heard from several former employees, was long on greed and short on character at both UOP and Grand Canyon. I heard several stories from enrollment counselors I interviewed about his ruthless behavior, forcing employees to be more and

---

2   "Report: Ad Spending in U.S. Down 1.7% Through September," *Multichannel News,* http://www.smartbrief.com/news/iab/storyDetails.jsp?issueid=B149B9DD-EAFA-42BB-BC8C-D7EC42A50730&copyid=83E9806C-2A0B-4E87-A72F-653EB4FBBA2C&brief=iab&sb_code=rss&&campaign=rss, Dec. 11, 2008.

3   On September 22, 2011, Sen. Tom Carper, the Chairman of the Senate Homeland Security and Government Affairs Subcommittee, held a hearing on "Improving Educational Outcomes for Our Military and Veterans," focusing on the quality of education for the military...On January 22, 2012, Sen. Richard Durbin of Illinois introduced a bill that would change the 90/10 Rule.

4   Mr. Mueller previously served as the chief operating officer of Apollo Group from December 2005 to January 2006, as chief executive officer of the University of Phoenix Online, a unit of the University of Phoenix, from March 2002 to November 2005, and as chief operating officer and senior vice president of the University of Phoenix Online from May 1997 to March 2002.

more aggressive in their recruiting practices, having to engage in hard sell tactics from the scripted interviews before being hired. He simply moved over to Grand Canyon, bringing his bad behavior with him. I followed him, eager to short Grand Canyon, too.

I was surprised to read about the legal trouble Grand Canyon was having prior to going public. It was rare because the investment bankers could be putting themselves at risk; even though the company disclosed its legal problems they can still be sued.

There was also already a whistleblower filed against them.[5] Here are a few excerpts: "The pressure to achieve enrollment numbers is so great that Plaintiff is informed and believes, and therefore alleges, that some enrollment counselors have submitted applications containing fictitious names and social security numbers and other(s) have committed forgery on admissions documents, including but not limited to scholarship forms, fee waivers and other memoranda of understanding required for an enrollment number to count for the counselor."

GCU lured the plaintiff away from the University of Phoenix with the promise of much better money and the assurance that it was a "Christian" institution with strong ethical and moral character. Nevertheless, the COO told the plaintiff: "If you don't get the number of enrollments we tell you to get, I don't care how great you are at doing other things for the school you will be fired...this job is about bringing money into the school, period."

And here are some excerpts from the prospectus filed with the SEC: On August 14, 2008, the Office of the Inspector General of the ED served a subpoena on Grand Canyon University requiring them to provide certain records and information related to salary adjustments from January 1, 2004 to the present.

"During the preparation of our financial statements for 2005, 2006, and 2007, and for the six-month period ended June 30, 2008, our management identified material weaknesses in our internal control over financial reporting, as defined in the standards established by the AICPA,

---

5   First amended complaint in *U.S. ex rel Irwin v. Grand Canyon Education, Inc., et al.* D. Ariz. (2007). Document 11 in Case No. 2:07-cv-01771-DGC. Filed under seal 09/14/2007. Unsealed, deemed by court as filed Aug. 11, 2008. (Order to be unsealed entered Sept. 5, 2008.) This is a *whistleblower* action under 31 U.S.C. § 3729, *et seq.* of the False Claims Act filed by Relator/Plaintiff Ronald D. Irwin, in the name of the United States Government and himself.

that affected our financial statements…We are currently in the process of remediating these material weaknesses, but have not yet been able to complete our remediation efforts."[6] Not exactly something that should give investors confidence.

"The Attorney General of the State of Arizona requested extensive documentation and information from us and other institutions in Arizona concerning student loan practices, and we provided testimony in response to a subpoena from the Attorney General of the State of Arizona about such practices." In one of its SEC filings prior to coming public, in late 2008, the company noted it had received a whistleblower suit against them.[7]

* * * *

On January 9, 2009, I wrote: "Apollo Group (APOL) -- $87.10. Sell Short into Strength." Apollo's upbeat earnings report made me very unpopular, and the stock ran from $75 to $87. Telling clients to sell short into strength is rarely received well, even though my conviction could not have been stronger. Portfolio managers respect that as long as you have confidence and can back it up, which I could. I would be right over a longer time-frame. APOL reported an upside earnings surprise of $1.12 compared to a $0.98 estimate. A brokerage firm raised their APOL target to $104 from $78 following the results. Earnings were above expectations at $1.12 vs. $0.83 driven by much better than expected revenue and higher gross margins and lower selling and promotion expenses.

One analyst on the conference call asked, "Ok, can you give me the number of credits that the average associate usually starts with, or is that something you are not providing?"

Management answered, "No. We don't provide that either, *but it could be as low as zero.*" Wow. Did he really just say that? It's easy to have high enrollments when students are not taking classes. How many are taking zero? No one asked.

---

6   From a regulatory standpoint a disclosure like that should stop an IPO in its tracks.
7   *Irwin vs. Grand Canyon University* 2:07-cv-01771-DGC, District of Arizona.

* * * *

January 13, 2009. APOL went from $86 to $78, round-tripping the spike from the earnings report, due to an Internet investment site called Citron. It was nice to see Apollo take a hit following Citron's "reporting" regarding a lawsuit in the 10-Q. It was old news already but the market hit the stock hard anyway. A report from BMO Capital Markets: "Stock Falling on Allegations Regarding Lawsuit *Flash:* APOL stock is down roughly 5% this morning following a report by Citron Research alleging the company may be 'manipulating numbers' following the disclosure of a lawsuit in its recent 10-Q. The lawsuit, filed in December in the U.S. District Court for the Eastern District of Arkansas (*Russ*) by three former UOP students, alleges the UOP improperly returned the entire amount of the students' federal loan funds to the lender after these students dropped from their courses shortly after enrolling." The Citron report cites a number of potential reasons for this alleged action, the most serious, in my view, were the understating of its default rates (these students would be excluded from the calculation). While these allegations, if true, are concerning, as is typical in this space, the damage done to the company's market cap by these negative headlines tends to be more than the potential financial obligations.

* * * *

According to UOP's own website, applicants must be employed. Is recruiting the unemployed a new business plan? I can see how unemployment might reduce the number of leads. I can't see how unemployment would cause such a dramatic drop in Internet leads. UOP's admission requirements stipulate: "To enter an associate or bachelor degree program, you must be currently employed. If you are not employed, you must have access to an organizational environment that allows you to apply the concepts you learn in our courses. Selected undergraduate programs require applicants entering with less than 24 transferable credits to have current employment or access to an organizational environment and one year of full-time work experience."[8]

---

8   "Admissions Requirements," *University of Phoenix,* http://www.phoenix.edu/admissions/admission_requirements.aspx?sidenav=1, accessed July 8, 2014.

* * * *

January 15, 2009: I exchanged emails with a UOP enrollment counselor, who indicated that Internet lead flow was slowing down. Another email from a different enrollment counselor read, "We enroll lots of unemployed students. For UOP they need to have work experience or access to work environment via family, friends or spouse if never employed. For Axia, they only need access to work environment as well." That last one was loosely interpreted. They could utilize a family member or friend's work environment by asking questions or going there to observe.

* * * *

Another competitor of Apollo was starting the process to enter the public markets. Bridgepoint Education (BPI) filed a registration with the SEC of their intent to go public. Touting its achievements, the company declared, "In March 2005, we acquired the assets of The Franciscan University of the Prairies, located in Clinton, Iowa, and renamed it Ashford University. As of September 30, 2008, we offered over 760 courses and 41 degree programs with 37 specializations and 21 concentrations. We had 30,547 students enrolled in our institutions, 98% of whom were attending classes exclusively online. At December 31, 2007 and September 30, 2008, our enrollment was 12,623 and 30,547, respectively, an increase of 1*82.3% and 140.2%, respectively.*" Doesn't that growth rate seem a little odd? In 2007, Ashford University derived 83.9% from Title IV programs (calculated on a cash basis in accordance with applicable Department of Education regulations).[9]

* * * *

DV's next earnings report contained an interesting revelation: "Management indicated they are helping students to secure co-borrowers [aka parents] and realize the benefits of taking a heavier course load. The

---

9   The schools made these weird acquisitions because they didn't have to reapply for accreditation which would've been cumbersome. Instead, why not buy a company that already had accreditation, which often lasted up to 10 years. It was a backdoor way of avoiding the accreditation process.

students' access to funding from parent co-signing student loans is severely limited. Due to general economic conditions, weakness in the credit market, such as lower access to home equity lines of credit etc. the pool of co-borrowers and the amount of money a co-borrower has access to, declined sharply in recent months, leaving students without access to co-borrower help. The decline in subprime lending could have a negative effect on college enrollments."[10]

Management of DV continued, "Now one impact that they have seen is on average course loads…So, a student who, for example, may have previously taken four courses—I'm just making up an example—maybe now they're taking three courses. It's not all students. It's not across the board, but we're seeing a little bit more of that as one and probably the main impact of the economy that we've seen. [They are] just taking a little bit lighter academic load at DeVry University, undergraduate in particular. And so we're active on that, we're counseling students on the benefits of taking a heavier course load in order to graduate sooner."

*   *   *   *

January 21, 2009: Steve Burd of the New America Foundation published an article that read: "Soon after Arne Duncan is officially sworn in as the new Secretary of Education, he should break with the past by opening an investigation into allegations that the University of Phoenix (UOP), the country's largest chain of for-profit colleges, has deliberately and improperly attempted to manipulate its cohort default rate and, by doing so, put students in harm's way."[11]

The allegations came to light in December when the details of a federal class action lawsuit brought in December by three former UOP students became public. According to allegations, the university had been paying

10   Basically, there was a link between the housing market bubble and the college tuition bubble. Parents, short on cash, were using their access to home equity lines of credit to pay college tuition for their children. When the real estate market collapse and people could no longer refinance at low rates or use HELOCs, many of which were cancelled by the banks, subsequently pressured the students' ability to pay for college.

11   Steve Burd, "Memo to Duncan: Investigate the University of Phoenix," *http://www. newamerica.net/blog/higher-ed-watch/2009/memo-secretary-duncan-investigate-university-phoenix-9601, 2009.*

off the federal loans of students who drop out soon after enrolling without their 'knowledge or consent.' The institution then allegedly turned around and demanded immediate repayment from these former students.

* * * *

A January 22, 2009 report from BMO Capital Markets read, "…the case against Apollo Group (APOL) concerning return of Title IV funds filed a voluntary dismissal, closing the case. The class-action suit filed December 8, 2008 in the U.S. District Court for the Eastern District of Arkansas alleged APOL violated the Higher Education Act by manipulating Default Rates by returning 100% of students' Title IV funds after the students dropped from their courses shortly after enrolling—essentially paying off these loans. The case alleged APOL would then pursue repayment of the loans directly from the students, subjecting the students to more onerous repayment terms than under Title IV."

This news boosted APOL's stock from $85 to $90 in what seemed like ten minutes, which wrecked my day. When investors figured out that the case wasn't settled but was merely being re-filed in another state, it took a hit and then went right back down again. Confusion over the jurisdiction in which the lawsuit was filed was puzzling some investors.

* * * *

A January 23, 2009 Credit Suisse report called APOL a buying opportunity despite the legal wrangling and expected short-term volatility. "APOL shares rallied yesterday in reaction, we believe, to news of the dismissal of the lawsuit filed December in Arkansas alleging that Apollo wrongfully returned Title IV funds to the ED to manipulate down default rates; we think some investors had believed that the dismissal meant that the issue had been put to bed. Although we expect news of a re-filing to weigh on APOL shares short term and potentially increase volatility in coming weeks…"

January 30, 2009: Interview with former Apollo financial aid counselor (MB): In November of 2007, UOP consolidated the financial aid counselor ("FA") function from the regional schools to a centralized location. There was a purposeful calculus to centralizing the FA function. Under the auspices of trying to make their business more efficient, the company figured out that they could benefit if students have a difficult time quitting school. Students who try to drop out often cannot, as they are unable to reach the financial aid office. When the regional schools had the financial aid staff physically located at the school, the ratio of FAs to students was 1:300. When the company consolidated the financial aid function, they more than doubled the ratio to 1:600-700, making it twice as hard for students to drop out. Students were encouraged to continue to attend class and not drop out. If the student logged into the online class or signed into the on-ground class, the school was permitted to continue to count them as having attended. So there was no way to quit.

The goal was to get the student to the 60% threshold, which is when the school gets to keep all of the money for length of the course. Good business practice or illegal? From the spirit and tone of the ED regulations, it is reasonable to infer that a recurring error in the company's favor constitutes further investigation.

February 2009

Then, an uptick in APOL insider selling occurred. From January 15 to 27, John and Peter Sperling, along with other senior executives, unloaded shares of Apollo. CEO Joe D'Amico sold 166,000 shares on January 15. Through most of January and the first half of February, the stock was above $80.[12]

February 4, 2009: (APOL) -- $85.54 Sell Short: In a recent hearing in California, several of APOL's internal documents were entered into the public record. The question was whether or not they have changed their behavior. I suspect not, based upon the FOIA documents received in the *Chad McKinney* case, which was similar to the *Hendow* case. I have

---

12   "Insider Trading Chart," *InsiderTrading.org*, http://insidertrading.org/insider-selling. php?sort_by=acceptance_datetime&asc=&symbol=apol&date_from=2009-01-01&date_ to=2009-06-01&submit=+GO+, accessed July 8, 2014.

excerpts from public internal emails regarding the use of quotas. I am not counting on the whistleblower to make the short. However, it was helping to direct the research and ask smarter questions of sources as they come up. I am counting on the economics of student recruitment to make the short profitable.

Here is an example of an internal email conversation between two UOP managers: "I have a copy of Tony Williams' promotion to EC [enrollment counselor] II. The first page of the evaluation really needs a little more information. "hit EC I's numbers" *would get us into trouble* with the Department of Education when they audit the personnel files. Could you redo another first page, email it to me and I'll hold it for the original paperwork. Thanks, Ron."

The response was as follows: "Ron, I just received Linda's PAF and evaluation. *We can't mention starts or enrollments or any conversion* to starts in an evaluation. Would you please redo the first page and send it to me? If you give me your fax number, I'll send you some examples of how this needs to be filled out."

The following correspondence read: "Brian, I just received a copy of Susan's salary review. On the first page of the evaluation, you refer to starts. *That's a no-no*. You'll need to redo the first page. If you no longer have it, then go into My Management Toolbox, and fill out the first page of an evaluation and email it to me. Then I'll hold it until the original arrives." Clearly, they were trying to prevent a paper trail showing their incentive compensation practices.

* * * *

The *Chad McKinney* suit filed in San Diego on January 9, 2009 posed a meaningful threat to UOP. The whistleblower at the heart of the suit alleged the company failed to implement substantive changes to the incentive compensation environment regardless of any written policy changes following the 2004 program review settlement. The case was chock full of email quotes from enrollment managers explicitly threatening people with termination for failing to make quota. The *Hendow* case addressed allegations prior to the program review, while the *McKinney* case made similar allegations after the settlement. One telling email submitted as evidence with the court was titled: "RE: IF YOU DON'T BLITZ AT 11:30 MICHELLE SAYS YOU'RE FIRED."[13]

* * * *

On February 9, 2009, I interviewed the former Apollo Vice President. The following interview notes were shared with Bob Shireman and several other enforcement personnel in multiple federal and state agencies:

"Source left company in 2003 because of a 'philosophical difference with Brian Mueller.'" He believes schools should be measured based on number of students that graduate, not the number that are enrolled. They have too much focus on enrollments. "We as a society should not be lending to students that don't graduate." Source was not surprised when I asked him if 40% of students drop out within the first three classes. Many UOP students have dropped out of other schools already so the quality of students was low. Whenever a student dropped out in a short period of time the student was automatically put into collection and considered a "cash payment."

I told source that I heard Internet lead flow was down 25-30%+. Source is an enrollment manager at another school. That level of decline didn't surprise him. He said, "I am constantly interviewing UOP enrollment counselors. They are giving me similar numbers." The industry has realized across the board that the Internet lead flow generates a lot of low quality leads so the industry was making a more concerted effort to cut the number of leads given to the ECs that have little or no chance of being enrolled.

When pressed about whether or not there was fraud at UOP, source said they are pushing the envelope of ED regulations and they are taking advantage of students who don't know any better. I had the feeling from the conversation that even if the source knew about fraud, he was certain-

---

13   *McKinney vs. Apollo* 3:07-cv-02373-WQH document 119-8 January 12. 2009. Blitzing refers to a set time during the day when ECs must make an attempt to secure enrollments by making a higher than usual volume of calls.

ly thinking of saving his own skin and did not want to share it with me. I felt he held back a considerable amount of information.

* * * *

February 12, 2009: Apollo Former Enrollment Counselor Interview: KM was an employee with AppleOne, a temp agency, and was contracted to work at UOP as an enrollment counselor. As an enrollment counselor, KM was responsible for tracking her students' attendance until the second meeting of the second class. Each class was approximately four weeks long, so KM would track about six weeks of attendance for each student. Once that time frame had passed, the student would count as an enrollment for quota. Attendance was kept by student services. KM would receive a flag on her computer if one of her students did not sign in for a class or turn in an assignment. Enrollment counselors did not have access to the actual attendance records and could not change them.

KM would call the student to "motivate them" to attend class and complete their assignments. When KM first started, the quota was four new students for each of the first three months. The quota changed to three for the first month, four for the second month, and five for the third month. After that, six to seven new students a month were required to keep your job. Employees were very open about salaries, including raises and reductions. If numbers were not met, salaries were reduced. KM knew many employees who had their salary cut. *Half the enrollment counselors she worked with had their salary cut two and three times.* KM said it was not unusual at all to have your salary reduced at one review, and then six months later, after the standards weighted percentages had all been changed, to receive a raise. Some of the leads that were given were eight and nine years old. A lead management team was in place and would take a lead away if the lead was not being pursued.

According to a separate source, nearly 100% of APOL enrollment counselors are also students. Many other jobs are also filled by students. According to a whistleblower, using a back of the envelope method, UOP had 6271 enrollment counselors alone. Assuming $22,000 of annual tuition, UOP could be generating revenue by $137 million.

* * * *

In February 2010, I revealed some evidence I found in a lawsuit against Kaplan University. The lawsuit reads, "The most blatant case of fraud by Kaplan in this 90/10 scheme may have been Miss xxxx Social Security number is xxx-xx-1969 was given the "Gift of Knowledge" in 2005 to pursue an MBA with Kaplan. Ms. xxxxxxxx never paid a dime of her own money to Kaplan. All of her tuition was paid though the Gift of Knowledge fund and Kaplan reported her to the government and the (HLC) Higher Learning Commission as a cash paying student, thus *helping the 90/10 compliance out."*

That's interesting because this is essentially a loophole around the 90/10 regulations. In the case of ESI they had a $300 million program to help students. COCO, DV, and CECO all developed their own programs as well, which could have been tools to manipulate the 90/10 ratio lower. They spent approximately $100-$150 million each making such loans. Call it a scholarship or whatever; I suspect the schools used that money to maintain their compliance with the 90/10 rule.

* * * *

February 17, 2009: Report to clients: APOL was at $80.96. Apollo filed its 10-Q on January 8, 2009. "In the course of other discussions with the DOE, we were informed that we likely will be the subject of an ordinary course, focused program review during fiscal year 2009." The company received notification on February 18, 2009. Donna said they knew earlier than that. There seems to be enough smoke surrounding the stocks now, driven by the lawsuits and macroeconomic issues. There are enough possible negative outcomes, for example, a rapid rise in student loan defaults that could weigh on the shares. More lawsuits and bad press could come from anywhere. These are some of the synergies in motion.

Further, in mid-February, the schools started to report the new default rate data released by the government. ESI filed their 10-K with the SEC after the close on February 18. I was stunned by the impact on ESI's stock, which tumbled $20. Most of the schools received their data on February 9, but several schools waited for the revised numbers.

February 19, 2009: Steve Burd of the New America Foundation again ventured into the fray with his intrepid reporting. Steve was one of my many contacts in the industry. I have a unique relationship with members of the press. Because I am not a direct competitor of theirs, they are more likely to develop a professional relationship with me. I was willing to share information with them and they, in turn, shared information with me. My activities mimicked those of an investigative journalist, though my audience was strictly confined to my hedge fund clients. Therefore, it was advantageous to cultivate multiple relationships with journalists across the country. Some were friendlier than others, but most were willing to share information for the greater good. I always wished to share information about the for-profit sector.

February 23, 2009: The preliminary ("draft") default rates for FY07 were sent out to schools on February 9, 2009. *They were not released to the public.* Official defaults for FY07 will be released in September 2009.[14] ESI filed their 10-K after the close of the market on February 18 with preliminary cohort default rates for FY07. The very next day, it dropped from $126 to $103, taking APOL down with it, from $84 to $75. Many schools released the preliminary numbers available to investors, but not UOP, which failed to make their preliminary numbers public. It was also interesting that APOL executives were selling stock on February 4, just five days before the draft CDRs were given the to the schools by the DOE. Perhaps they knew that the numbers would be soft.

Then, on February 24, 2009, according to the ED, APOL reported its defaults under two ID numbers: one for UOP and one for WIU. WIU had a default rate of 27% in 2006 and 11% in 2005. The stock slid from $80 to $74 when those numbers came out, despite assurances by management that that number would decline.

---

14   Sybil Phillips, ""FY 2007 Draft Cohort Default Rates", *Dept. of Education,* http://www.ifap.ed.gov/eannouncements/020909DraftCDRFY2007DistributedFeb9.html, Feb. 9, 2009.

* * * *

By this time, my immediate goal had become figuring out when the program review document would be made public, as it could cause a rapid decline in the stock prices of APOL and the rest of the group. Trying to time the release of information from the ED was hazardous business. The ED grants extensive and ample opportunity for management to explain any findings in a program review. Should program reviewers find larger, systematic issues, and not just minor mismanagement, an OIG audit would likely follow, which could extend well into 2010. This doesn't make for a very good short thesis—a worst-case scenario from my timing standpoint. According to the regulations, the ED was on-site for approximately one week, unless it finds more grave issues. In this case, the ED could be on-site for several weeks, and extend the process even further, given APOL's size.[15] Unfortunately, I think the purview of the program review team was limited to only certain things, which prevented the ED from finding more egregious violations.

* * * *

Meanwhile, the student suit filed in LA remained active. One student complained, "I recently received a notice informing me that funds had been returned to my lender as I had a 90 day break in attendance. I then received notice that I owed the university the amount returned. What I came to learn is that I was been charged for class that was removed from my schedule because I had a balance due. UOP does not allow you to move on to the next class if you have financial obligation due. I can understand, but what is frustrating is the lack of communication from my academic counselor and that it takes weeks for my financial counselor to call me back, unless I owe them something. Can someone explain to me why I am paying for a class I wasn't scheduled for?"[16]

---

15   "On-Site Review Procedures," *Dept. of Education*, http://www.ifap.ed.gov/iposguid-ance/doc0020_bodyoftext.htm, March 3, 1994

16   Jason, "University of Phoenix," *ComplaintsBoard.com*, http://www.complaintsboard.com/complaints/university-of-phoenix-c160082.html, accessed July 8, 2014

* * * *

I found several hundred complaints, if not thousands, about for-profit schools on www.complaintsboard.com and on www.ripoffreport.com, but they rarely had names or email addresses. I often tried to cross-reference using myspace.com, which at the time was more popular than facebook.com, and made ample use of LinkedIn to find sources. The various former enrollment counselors provided a wealth of insight into the industry's shady business practices. Usually, for a short seller, research like this is impossible, because there just aren't that many people who are disavowed, but UOP's arrogance and greed created an abundance of disgruntled employees that made my work easy. If people are unhappy with their job, they quit or get fired and that's the end of it. I had never seen a situation where so many employees of a company were so angry. As I uncovered systemic patterns of abuse stretching across huge swaths of the U.S., my anger grew at the company's high-pressure tactics and routine deception of unsuspecting low-income students.

One complaintsboard.com post stated the following[17]: "Let me start by saying that I was an enrollment advisor for University of Phoenix Online, and AXIA/WIU Online under Apollo Group for 3 years. I recently quit from my position as one of their highest paid advisors. I would like to address the organizations misuse of funds. They have been for many years now, embezzling monies from their employees and Title IV funding. Now, if there is a decrease in enrollments as compared to prior years, but the CEO is still claiming huge growth in years to come, how does the company make up for that? By *counting scheduled students as enrollments for their report without every actually having those students start*. So how does UOP make up the money difference in the accounting department? 2 ways: First, it decreases the pay of its employee workforce and (for years) violated AZ and Federal Overtime law by making overtime mandatory but refusing to pay employees overtime wages."

"The money is in the hands of UOP a week or two after you attend

17   Parker, "University of Phoenix," *ComplaintsBoard.com,* http://www.complaintsboard.com/complaints/university-of-phoenix-c109429.html, accessed July 8, 2014

your first day of class. Why do they take so long to distribute the funding? Two reasons. One is to keep their official default rate down. *Considering they lose about 30% of enrollments after the first class*, it would look very bad for them if all these students started defaulting on loans they don't think they need to pay back because they didn't take a full class."

* * * *

Eventually, my persistence paid off and I managed to make contact with individuals who had left complaints on the site. Here are my notes from another former enrollment counselor interview on February 12, 2009:

CT worked at APOL for 3 years: UOP routinely held meetings on the various ways to lie to students. She said they were told routinely to lie about Pell grants, the amount of financial aid students would receive, and when they would have to pay loans back. They were told routinely to lie about the transferability of credits. Financial aid reps routinely refused to take calls from students, and referred them to the ECs, and the ECs told students to continue to sign in, or else they would be put into collections.

"As an employee, enrollment counselors were allowed to attend classes for free. If you failed to make your quota the company would take away lead flow or good leads, making it harder and harder to make quota. When you are a student and fail to make quota, the school pulls your tuition reimbursement and sends you a bill for several months of classes already taken and paid for by the school. They were put into collections immediately."

* * * *

Another APOL enrollment counselor I interviewed, herein called BB, was referred by CT. BB stated: "Some enrollment managers, whose salaries are also based on enrollment, choose to look the other way on purpose when students wanted to quit and were being prevented from doing so. This source also indicated that when an EC quits or is fired, the EC only has to pay for classes in which they are presently enrolled. Source indicated that it is very hard to get fired as an EC. When an EC fails to make quota, that person's salary is guaranteed to be reduced by 10% every six months. Over time, there is not enough salary to stay."

BB explained that he worked as an enrollment counselor at UOP from 2006 until December 2008. He previously worked at AIU (CECO). At first he thought UOP was better than CECO, until he was told to "enroll everyone you talk to." No one got promoted except those that made quota and many of the managers were poorly trained. He recounted several ugly stories. For example, 80% of ECs weren't making quota, but stayed until free tuition ran out. As a penalty for not making quota, they suspended his free tuition for six months. He received a 1% performance raise in December 2007. But in January 2008, they changed his review and suspended his tuition *and* his wife's free tuition in retribution for questioning management.

BB was told never to use the phrase "free tuition" with prospective students, though he found out later from students in one of his classes that they were promised more than free tuition: allegedly, they were promised that *UOP could arrange for them to get excess money from Title IV to spend however they wanted.* He said the students would, for example, apply for a Pell grant of $4,000 and be informed they were eligible for the full amount while the paperwork was being processed by the ED. However, it was often the case that the student was eligible for only $2,000 of grants, at which point, the student was then pressured into coming up with the additional $2,000. Once BB figured this out, he resigned. It was a culture of public humiliation and verbal abuse.

* * * *

Over time, my interviews with former employees expanded beyond the enrollment counselors to personnel in academic affairs, operations, and financial aid, which gave me a more comprehensive picture of UOP's overall crappy behavior. UOP was becoming the roach motel: You can get in but you can't get out. As I dug deeper and deeper into UOP, it occurred to me that should the federal government ever choose to really enforce the regulations, they might have ample evidence for cutting off the institution's access to federal funds. Yet, it seemed that considering UOP's clout and sheer size (400,000 students at this point), the agency had adopted a "too big to fail" mentality with respect to reining in the private education behemoth. CLC put a lot of real students out on the street virtually overnight. While a sizable chunk of the 400,000+ students may not actually be attending classes, the ED would have to find a home for those students as well. So from a political standpoint, finding fraud and doing nothing about it seemed more politically correct than ever.

Through my work contacting students who were enrollment counselors, I understood the complexity of the Apollo short should not be dismissed. It's a bizarre company to analyze, as the company's product was being consumed by its employees. The greater the number of employees financed with government funds, the greater the revenue. Consumers grow as more employees are hired and consume services, but are rarely fired and continue to consume, creating revenue greater than the salary they earn. What if the business slows down? The revenue will go down, too, at an accelerated rate. Is this not a Ponzi scheme defined?

CHAPTER 4

Kroll Comes Knocking

In February 2009, I received a strange call from Kroll & Associates, a well-known private investigation firm. Over my 20 years of short selling, I have experienced numerous occasions in which shady companies have gone to great lengths to find out who is recommending their stock short. Narcissistic/egomaniacal management always wants to find out who is not willing to drink their flavor of Kool-Aid. And short sellers take a particularly vindictive pride in exposing nefarious activities, especially after being harassed by a private investigator. I never knew how much Apollo knew about my activities; probably very little until they started reading the book. So they hire firms like Kroll to find out. Most serious hedge funds know it's much better to just keep quiet about short ideas rather than pound the table on CNBC or some other venue.

One day around 5:30, I received a cryptic call from someone asking to speak to my research assistant, who works from home. When I asked why, he said he heard that my assistant had been calling enrollment counselors at UOP. The private investigator then said, rather euphemistically, "Well, management of Apollo heard that he was asking questions and we have been hired to help people answer questions about the company. Can you tell me what his questions pertained to? Maybe we can help him by going to management and asking them for you."

I said, "I have no reason whatsoever to give you any information about what we are doing. I don't need your help and I don't need to ask management any questions."

He shot back rather forcefully, "Well, if we just knew the questions we could find you the answers."

"I am sure UOP would love to know the questions I am asking of its former employees," I retorted, "but it's none of your business. I am doing research on the company and that's all I have to say." And the call went around and around like that for 15 minutes.

I called my assistant to ask him what happened and got the old, "oh, I meant to tell you" excuse. Evidently, every short seller on the planet had started doing what we were doing to find information about UOP: calling Apollo's 800 numbers in an effort to get enrollment counselors on the telephone, either by posing as students or stating outright their desire for information. This happened so quickly and on such a large scale that the UOP call center of enrollment counselors was getting inundated by Wall Street, long guys and shorts calling for information. I heard from an enrollment counselor that management told all the enrollment counselors that they would be fired if they were caught talking to anyone from Wall Street.

The feeding frenzy really cranked up as hedge fund analysts were calling APOL enrollment counselors. Information around accreditation and transferability of credits was of great interest to short sellers. Several of the enrollment counselors were asked if their credits would transfer to Columbia Business School or Harvard, and in almost every case the enrollment counselor said, "hold on," only to come back five seconds later to say the classes taken at UOP would transfer, which was clearly not the case. Some short sellers were making tape recordings of these interviews, which were rumored to be circulating around the investment community, although none ever reached my desk.

I berated my assistant half-heartedly, but his explanation was interesting. He had gone to myspace.com and found hundreds of UOP students. He contacted them, asking them to share their experience attending UOP. What he did not know, so I can't fault him, was that many of the so-called students were also enrollment counselors.

* * * *

During the course of my research, I started to routinely email several state attorneys general. It was my experience from Computer Learning Centers that they could wield significant influence over for-profit companies operating in their states. In the case of Computer Learning Centers, back in 1998, the Illinois Attorney General demanded that CLC return funds to student or provide debt forgiveness to students recruited by incentive compensation. In the case of CECO, it was the California Attorney General that pursued them so aggressively, not the ED. Perhaps state AGs could even band together, like in the major suits against the tobacco industry.

I started with the New York Attorney General's Office, which had a suit against Sallie Mae several years prior, so I knew they were aware of fraudulent behavior in the student loan business.[1] I branched out to several state AGs over the next year. It took me awhile, but several of them (Maryland, Florida, Massachusetts, and Wisconsin, for example) eventually sought to pressure the for-profit education industry. In all, I think I mailed evidence to at least 25 state attorneys general.

To Shireman I wrote: "Bob, I have a copy of the transcripts of interviews with University of Phoenix enrollment counselors making comments that could be illegal. Since I only have one hard copy I am going to mail it to the Office of General Counsel. It would be humorous if it wasn't so sad to listen to the enrollment counselors say that UOP classes can be transferred to Harvard etc. A more efficient way to incentivize enrollment counselors would be to pay them based on graduation rates or some longer period of time. It would cut down on the misrepresentation."

March 2009

March 4, 2009: APOL stock price started to get spanked, falling from $74 to $66 intra-day. Sometimes it is hard to know why a stock falls when there's no news on the tape. At times, my email or phones will light up, but in this

---

1   There were really nasty lawsuits and testimony about SLM and corruption in the lending business, specifically *Zahara vs. SLM Corporation* 1:06-cv-00088-SEB and testimony in Congress by Andrew Cuomo on June 6, 2007.

particular case, it was coming from an online investment research web page.[2] There are several of these rumor-oriented online services, originating with The Motley Fool on AOL in the '90s. Most of the time, they are not coming up with proprietary data; however, this particular day they did get some good data to crush Apollo. I will take what I can get.

Citron wrote an article about the exact salary enrollment counselors would receive based on a certain number of enrollments. I had been following the *Hendow* and *McKinney* cases closely, but had not seen this document. Tens of thousands of pages were being made public from these suits. As documented in the suit, earlier in the decade, Apollo embarked on a path of becoming more of a marketing company than an educational institution. Since the year 2000, Apollo has seen their enrollment increase in size by 200%, the faculty increased 100%, during which time the ranks of its enrollment counselors swelled by a staggering 1000%. Expressed another way, the student to faculty ratio went up from 9:1 to 15:1. Again, Citron had come up with something that was already out there; they were just a little louder and armed with a bigger distribution list than I had.

* * * *

Early in March, I was reaching out to Bob Shireman again to ask him if he would be interested in meeting with me regarding my research findings in the sector. He agreed to meet over the next couple of weeks. I said something to the effect of—depending on what kind of discussion you would like to have, you may want to invite a lawyer in the Office of General Counsel. I have also bcc'd the OIG's office on many of the emails I send your way.

The Department published a very interesting document suggesting graduation rates for four-year for-profit students fell from 25% to 18% and from 32% to 24% for students in school for six years versus a national average of 57% for six-year students and 36% for four-year plan students. If that many students are failing to graduate and the for-profit sector reports 1.4 million students and Apollo has almost 400,000 students, this

---

2   "Citron Exposes Apollo's Big Dirty Secret," *Citron Research,* http://www.citronresearch. com/2009/03/04/, March 4, 2009.

would imply a large number of students never graduate. And ED numbers don't track transfer students, do they? This was an early indicator the numbers were awry, I just didn't it yet.

* * * *

One issue that I put on the radar was that of increased competition, which was why I kept an eye on advertising. I was banking on a slowdown in sales and enrollment growth across the sector as more competitors entered the market. APOL was clearly the leader and for its size it was able to maintain a strong growth rate for an extended period of time. On the short side, I am always looking for "the iron law of larger numbers" that says as companies grow larger, growth becomes harder to maintain and eventually slows. Think of a bell curve. I was looking to catch the back half of the curve, only having to pick the decline in a stock price once the company's growth rate slows from double digits to single digits or lower. In the case of for-profit education, using federal student loan money for advertising, the industry could spend themselves out of trouble through increased advertising. I thought competition would cause that advertising to lose traction. Unfortunately, there was a nearly unlimited pool of poor people for the schools to prey upon. Still, when the Apollo children were coming public and throwing vast sums at advertising similar to Apollo, the potential risk to their business and stock price increased substantially.

* * * *

I sent a quick message to clients: APOL shares have come under pressure in recent weeks due, in part, to the overall market weakness, but also due to the rising default data and other macro comments that can be extrapolated from the industry conference calls, etc. They are reporting earnings on March 31st. The estimate for the quarter was $0.66 vs. $0.41. This one could be hard to make, as it implies 60% growth. I would look for negative comments on the call regarding fundamentals going forward instead of an outright earnings miss. High advertising expense, lower returns, increased regulation, etc. are possible negative outcomes and I have several more potential outcomes. Shares have retreated from nearly $90 to $63 in the last two months and back to $70 in the last week. I recommend using any strength to press the position. In other words, short more.

* * * *

Meanwhile, as LOPE, EDMC, and Bridgepoint (BPI) came public, they were able to raise almost limitless sums of cash quickly, which went right into sales and marketing expenses. From FY09 to FY11, EDMC's revenue increased from $1.6 billion to $2.8 billion. So they were giving UOP substantial competition as well. I didn't make a big deal about it, but as a taxpayer I was certainly irritated by the amount of money these companies were getting from the loan program that went toward advertising. It would be nice if the companies had to come up with their own money to pay for advertising, but how to separate that out would be impossible. Later, when Senator Harkin began having hearings, Congress sought similar solutions, wanting to come up with a way for the taxpayer to not foot the bill for advertising. Even when enrollments fell there was still a steady flow of funds coming in to attract new students.

"The University of Phoenix's marketing budget is huge; in 2007 it spent $222 million on domestic measured media," according to TNS Media Intelligence, "with the largest chunk devoted to online marketing."[3] When it comes to big spenders of online display ads, forget Procter & Gamble or General Motors: the biggest buyer is the University of Phoenix, a for-profit institution that devotes an average of *$20 million monthly to online ads, mostly for display.*[4]

Brian Mueller, the president of APOL, left to go to Grand Canyon University (LOPE), and Bridgepoint had other Apollo people as well. One of my sources told me that when Brian Mueller left to go to Grand Canyon, he took many of UOP's best executives and enrollment counselors with

3   Rupal Parekh, "University of Phoenix Seeks Ideas for its $200M Account," *Ad Age,* http://adage.com/agencynews/article?article_id=127638, June 9, 2008

4   David Kaplan, "Display's Big Spender," *Gigaom.com,* http://www.paidcontent.org/entry/419-displays-big-spender-university-of-phoenix-category-continues-to-wait-f,   June 18, 2008

him. He did this by offering free classes which they did not need to attend. I believed my source because she was a former enrollment counselor at UOP, so she knew a lot of the UOP enrollment counselors were recruited to Grand Canyon. She had been at UOP for many years. But my source also taught at Grand Canyon as an adjunct professor. She taught classes that were supposed to be full with 20 people; however, the attendance was low, and only a couple of students showed up. When she looked on the list she recognized that all of the names of students not in attendance were former Apollo enrollment counselors. There was a brain drain and it didn't take long for Brian Mueller to turn a quiet little religious college into the same machine he ran at Apollo.

CHAPTER 5

The Rat

March 19, 2009: I wrote the incoming SEC Chairwoman a letter about UOP. The basic premise of the letter was similar to the letter to Arne Duncan. Here, though, I referenced revenue recognition fraud instead of student loan program fraud. The companies have had and continue to have on-going legal and regulatory battles. Under the Bush Administration, the voices of investigators and lawyers in the Department who have fought to expose this fraud have been suppressed. The DOJ simultaneously raided multiple ITT schools several years back, only to let them go with a nominal fine. The University of Phoenix has many lawsuits against them that allege fraud, including a whistleblower action that was filed a few years ago. Under the Bush Administration, the DOJ was lackadaisical in pursuing the suit, despite depositions from former employees verifying UOP's deception practices.

Shortly thereafter, I was contacted by a senior enforcement attorney with the SEC. She said they would be interested in looking at more of the information I had accumulated on the industry over the years. I sent several of my research reports and interviews from former UOP employees along the way. During the next three years I included her on a small list of regulators to whom I sent my growing repository of evidence. I called Donna Wittman to let her know I had spoken to the SEC and told her that I wanted to tell the SEC my theory about a high percentage of students coming in and out of the school, leaving room to overstate enrollments.

Donna said, "UOP would much rather overstate their enrollments by paying back the loan and putting the kids into collection than worry about the late refund issue, because the amount would be so large."

I said, "So if 50 percent of the students are dropping out, they're overstating their enrollments by 50 percent?" Later, a lot of this came out in the GAO report and Senator Harkin's investigation.

She said, "Yes." I tried to convince her go tell the SEC that, because it means that 50% of the 420,000 students and a fairly hefty chunk of the revenue are false. It would be better heard if she said it to them. Even if they are not generating revenue from them, the enrollment numbers are too high. Wall Street was using those numbers for earnings modeling.

My worst fear in all this would be Donna losing her job for speaking to me. Donna wouldn't tell me how much pressure she was under from the higher-ups to not talk to Wall Street or the press. She simply responded, "Don't worry about me. I am a big girl." If I had to guess, they were used to Donna being a maverick.

Expressing my concern, I said, what are you telling the higher-ups? She said that the taxpayers had a right to know how the student loan program was being administered and regulated. Of course, I had to assume she was talking to lawyers, my competitors and customers. She never shared that information with me, either.

Donna had said to me in passing, regarding the SEC, "It would be much better if I go and talk to them, because there are a lot of things that I can't tell you." It was kind of a thorny topic, because I just didn't want to cross the line and be too close to this thing. I was uncomfortable being a middleman. I was never told whether they spoke to each other directly. Again, my relationship with Donna was usually me bringing information to her, not the other way around, and me using her as a resource to explain federal regulations governing the industry.

* * * *

March 25th, 2009: I received another rather annoying call from Kroll asking me all kinds of probing questions. This time they started with, "We have been retained by APOL's general counsel for several months so we understand the company and we understand you have been contacting our employees and wanted to know if we could help you by answering questions, if we knew the nature of the questions."

I was already in a foul mood that day, so I said, "You have just met the rattlesnake in the corner, go away!"

March 30, 2009: With APOL at $78.43, the stock ran all the way back into the high $70s before the earnings report. This is such a painful part of short selling and it happens all the time. I guess the only consolation was that the bulls have to go through the same process when it goes down, but it always feels like the shorts are the ones getting hurt the most when it comes to earnings reports. Earnings reports are very binary. You make or lose a lot and it's a 50/50 shot no matter what the numbers look like. You can't know how the market will react.

The stock was nearing its 52-week high, which meant that if the company reported an upside earnings surprise, as they always seemed to do, it could run up really fast and break out to a new high, causing my clients to lose money. Investors, particularly momentum-oriented aggressive growth funds, like buying stocks that break out to new highs. If they missed numbers, the stock would sell off and my clients would win. As with any shady management, they cheat so they can almost always report an upside surprise, doing almost anything to make the numbers.

And not only does the company have to make or beat earnings per share, but earnings have to be of a certain quality. Sometimes the bulls that own the stock will tolerate certain earnings shenanigans but other times they won't tolerate it at all, selling off an upside surprise. Typically, if a company buys back a lot of stock during the quarter, or suddenly has a lower than expected tax rate, or even cuts the growth rate of marketing expenses, the company can beat estimates.[1] These gimmicks lower the quality of earnings.

Other times, the earnings press release reveals a big, negative disclo-

---

1   APOL bought back nearly $500 million of stock for several years in a row to offset the declining growth. Your tax dollars at work.

sure. It's like, "Hey, we beat estimate by 25%, but we are being investigated, ok?" Earnings take on less importance if that happens. Emotionally, it just plain sucks to do a lot of work and have it come down to a big swing in the stock caused by earnings. It's easy to sit here as the consultant pounding the table and telling clients to get short, but quite another for them to actually do it. I just try to at least get the research portion right and let them worry about trading.

Heading into APOL's second quarter, I reviewed my interviews with former enrollment counselors and others to allay my fears. I wrote seven reports since the first quarter conference call, and remained confident that APOL was facing an accelerating wave of factors that doomed their business to long-term decline: economic recession, new competitors, regulatory headwinds, enrollment mix, rising default rates, low graduation rates—there are almost too many to count.

APOL stated in its conference call, "[W]e don't expect to maintain this level of new enrollment growth over the long-term as we believe some of this growth is attributable to current economic conditions." That's not counter-cyclical like it was supposed to be. I expect new enrollment growth to continue to emanate from the associate's degree programs. While it may make a good headline for total enrollments, I would prefer this to be the case because of the associate's programs' lower average selling prices and higher dropout rates.

* * * *

Sometimes companies can "pull forward" revenue by offering discounts. This was a sort of "take from Peter to pay Paul" strategy, but it does allow companies to report stronger numbers over the short-term. The following advertisement appeared on the APOL web page: "Start in April. Save up to $197! This offer is only available to new degree-seeking students beginning new degree programs at University of Phoenix. Application deadlines for students attending online vary through April 23, 2009 and students must start their first course between April 7, 2009 and April 28, 2009."

How was it possible for students to start class before they are accepted? Students are starting classes under the assumption that Title IV financing was already in place? However, in some instances, this turns out not to be the case, and often, the student was unable come up with the difference and subsequently drops out.

If enrollment counselors lie about the true cost of admission, fail to provide any detailed information about interest rates, total debt, payments, and other documentation, then enrollment could be very strong. One enrollment counselor was told by APOL to automatically tell students that they were entitled to $4,000 of Pell grants when in reality, in was never more than $2,000. When these students were unexpectedly billed for the other $2,000, they dropped out. Falsely encouraged by enrollment counselors, students assume their acceptance or that credits from other schools will transfer, and therefore start classes. Subsequently, the student was not accepted, but is still liable to APOL for the portion of classes that they took. Because classes are truncated to five weeks, these accruals could be substantial. Students routinely cannot get final loan documentation for 60 days after the time of the first class.[2]

As one former employee put it to me, "[APOL] teaches you to lie to students." This source talked in detail about seminars the company organized to teach enrollment counselors how to inform students that they will get a high amount of student aid and not have to pay it back. Further, enrollment supervisors look the other way when counting questionable enrollments because their bonus, too, is based on the number of enrollments. Many of these mid-level managers were former enrollment representatives with low to no professionalism. The *Chad McKinney* (page 11) suit and my own interviews indicate that the threat of revoking free tuition was a normal tool employed by mid-level management.[3] One post by an enrollment counselor bragged about getting free tuition while also taking out student loans to pay personal expenses.[4]

2　　I kept a list of several hundred names of enrollment counselors at the time in case I need to further verify these questionable business practices.

3　　I have an additional post made by an enrollment counselor claiming even though enrollment counselors were given free tuition, they borrow $10,000 from Title for personal expenses. www.uopsucks.com, Nov. 22, 2004.

4　　www.uopsucks.com (from a post that we saved before the site became defunct.)

* * * *

On March 31, 2009 APOL reported earnings rallying the stock from $78 to $81. With the upside surprise it continued to trade up *after the close of the market but before the earnings conference call*—before anyone had a chance to find out about a program review not mentioned in the press release. I was thinking, "Oh, man this is going to hurt." APOL reported a fairly healthy upside surprise. Of course, the hair on my neck went up as I had visions of the stock going from $81 to $91 as it had done in the past.

But then, the conference call changed during the Q&A session from excitement about the upside earnings surprise and 26% revenue growth to pointed questions targeted at the program review. On the call, management said, "Finally, we have been told informally that because of our size, we along with other large universities will likely be subject to annual focused program reviews." Immediately, the stock started to sell off hard. This was a major oversight shift by the department, clearly indicating their concerns about stories of impropriety in the press. Several of my clients were aggressive options traders, so this really made their day.

I started frantically exchanging emails during the call to encourage clients to sell short the stock after the market closed, which they could do. They knew about the program review on February 18. I had the letter from Donna. She was asking for the works: attendance, recruiter compensation, returns of Title IV data, withdrawals, etc. Why didn't they tell shareholders earlier? I guessed they didn't consider it to be material. But John and Peter Sperling sold a lot of stock in January and February.

Kelly Flynn, one of the best analysts on the Street, asked for more details regarding the program review. "What does a focused program review mean? I mean you said it is normal course, but then it also says focused. What does that mean, what is the focus?"

Joe D'Amico (co-CEO) responded: "The auditors asked for certain files from us, certain student files, and then they looked at all elements of Title

IV related to those files rather than coming in and doing a complete re-view that would go well beyond the student files…I will say that nothing has come to our attention that causes us to believe that this is anything but ordinary course of business."

* * * *

In February 2009, the ED performed an ordinary, focused program review of UOP's policies involving Title IV programs. Though the company had not received the program review report resulting from the visit, they still could have had access to the preliminary findings, as it was customary for an exit interview to be conducted by ED officials following the weeklong site visit. The findings were severely negative and most likely would have caused the stock to go down, especially if there were repeat violations from the 2004 review. The Sperlings would've, should've, or could've known the findings of the program review *before* it went public, given its importance.

As I spoke to clients after UOP reported, we joyously realized the bulls were burned badly by this number despite management's ability to cre-ate an upside surprise. Our issue was not with the stock behavior per se, but when exactly the company became aware of the program review. There were a lot of insiders selling in January 2009; the stock was in the $80s *before* the price dropped off to the low $60s *after* the review was disclosed. Doesn't it seem plausible that the Sperlings, as board members, were made aware of the review in that time-frame? There was a substan-tial uptick in insider sales on October 30 and 31. [5] Buried in the October 28 10-K they disclosed that the company would be the subject of a pro-gram review in 2009. But clearly not many people saw it, including me, as the stock was trading up at the beginning of the call. However, as soon as management uttered the phrase "program review," everyone started thinking back to the 2004 program review.

The department publishes a program review guide titled, "Program Re-view Guide for Institutions 2009" which is basically a calendar. I pulled some

5　　"Insider Trading Chart for APOL," *InsiderTrading.org,* http://insidertrading.org/insid-er-selling.php?sort_by=acceptance_datetime&asc=&symbol=apol&date_from=2008-09-01&date_to=2009-06-01&submit=+GO+, accessed July 8, 2014.

numbers from the text talking about timing of when the review might be complete. Because the schools can ask for extensions and the department leaves open a 30 to 90-day window it was even harder, if not impossible, to guess with any accuracy when a review might be forthcoming and when and what management knew. If I overlaid the insider trading, I estimated that senior management was well aware of the preliminary negative findings in the 2009 review, many of which were repeat offenses from the 2003 review.

My clients, of course, wanted to guessimate when the program review would be made public and increase the size of their short investment in anticipation of a negative review. Unfortunately, the review guidelines were a little loose. The ED guidelines suggested the visiting regulators stay on-site for one week, followed by an initial program review report up to 75 days later. The review was conducted for a week, perhaps two, and adding 75 days, management would have been in possession of the preliminary program review in mid-May, followed by a 30 to 90-day time-frame to respond to the program review findings, followed by an extension of up to 60 days, and then followed by a Final Determination Letter 30 to 90 days later.

Based on the program review guide, it stood to reason that management of APOL already had seen the preliminary documents and findings. This raised questions about the timing of some of the sales. The Sperlings sold stock in late July while the company was in possession of material non-public information. Coincidence?

April 2009

April 1, 2009: The following day, before the market opened, APOL was $73. The stock dropped to a low of $63.44, not exactly what investors would expect given the upside surprise. It seems reasonable to assume the discussion of the program review was the real driver that caused the stock to decline. Management also disclosed that the Department would be conducting reviews annually versus the prior administration that left six years between reviews. I am sure the Street felt betrayed by management. They should have disclosed the program review sooner during the quarter rather than wait until the earnings call in late March. During the quarter, management appeared at an analyst conference on February 24, 2009. They could have disclosed it then.

UBS came out that morning suggesting that student starts and retention were strong. And expenses appeared to be under control. Rather half-heartedly they raised estimates to $5.12 in FY10, from $5.00, versus consensus of $4.60. But I am sure Kelly Flynn felt like she was thrown under the veritable bus by management.

BMO Capital Markets analyst Jeff Silber said, "FY2Q09 Big 'Upside Surprise', Solid Enrollments; Raising Estimates: Last night, APOL reported FY2Q09 EPS of $0.77 versus $0.41, well above our $0.60 estimate and the consensus $0.65. New degreed enrollment and total degreed enrollment grew 23.1% and 20.4%, respectively, compared to our 24.6% and 19.1% estimates, respectively. While APOL 'missed' our starts estimate, we believe our estimate was fairly aggressive and likely among the highest on the Street."

The whole group was affected going down 5-10%.

Advertising expense was quietly up only 4.4% for the quarter. I suspect that number was down largely to the collapsing of advertising prices on the Internet. APOL management stated during the conference call: "First of all, *we did postpone* some of the investments or at least haven't made all the investments that we intend to make on the advertising front…We know that our normal growth [ph] on the new enrollments was obviously, as we talked about last quarter, *was slightly below last* quarter's, but you also have to look at the advertising dollars behind that as well…Yeah, they were *down* somewhat like, somewhere in the 200 basis points year-over-year as a percent of earnings." That means expenses will be higher next quarter, lowering earnings. The low advertising number indicated that this was a low quality earnings report.

The conference call was negative despite the numbers. Bad debt was higher and will probably stay higher. Management said: "Bad debt is principally triggered when a student drops or leaves school, and then it either forces us into a situation where we need to collect them …I think, generally in the economy that profile student, that individual is having a harder time paying their bills…we are seeing that in lower collection rates."

That was very interesting, since they were increasingly recruiting low-income, high-risk students to expand access to greater amounts of grant and loan money. The by-product of that aggressive strategy would be high bad debt and high receivable, not the economy.

The last program review was performed in 2003 and released in 2004. February 2009 will be the most current review, which means UOP had a six-year window with no serious scrutiny from the government. Now, they are telling investors reviews will be done with much greater frequency because of their size? Who changed that policy and why? An annual review could force major changes of corporate practices and even draw regulatory scrutiny. This should slow enrollment growth further, causing the stock to fall over the course of this year and beyond. With the ED looking over their shoulder in 2009 they might have quit whatever it was they are saying to potential students. That alone would slow their revenue and enrollment for the rest of the year and possibly beyond.

Unfortunately, after the last program review, the industry lobbied the Department to keep the program review reports hidden from the public until the very end. That meant the industry could delay the public's view of dirt found by the ED. The Bush Administration sought to reign in the Freedom of Information Act to help companies like the for-profits hide their activities. Even if the ED found systemic impropriety, the investment community would have no knowledge of it for several months after the release of the final program review when the final determination letter could be obtained, which could be years later, not months or weeks. That also meant if the ED found fraud, the company would know about it many months, possibly even a year, before the public, including investors.

Management attempted to downplay the review. "We just happen to be so large that it takes them a lot of time [to complete a program review] and they have a lot of other schools in exactly the same position." The call participants seemed a little confused, and the latter half of the Q/A seemed to deteriorate further as management was pressed about the program review. Management: "I mean the revenue, as you know; we changed our refund policy in March of last year. So just over a year ago, we are lapping that now. So there is clearly various things that impact the revenue per student. *One of them is the number of refunds and in particular*... Some of the price increases come through net of the change in that refund policy and that's going forward we would expect to see similar kinds of numbers."

* * * *

April 7, 2009: Around this time, several *Hendow* documents were made public.[6] Documents showed that enrollment counselors were given bonuses of all-expense-paid trips based on their enrollment quotas. Separate from the salary versus incentive compensation dichotomy, these awards constituted an illegal "bonus."[7] UOP attempted to spin these bonuses as "business" development, but—as many witnesses would testify—these trips were no work, and all play. There was a precise quota of enrollments an EC must meet to receive the Sperling bonus.

One of the documents filed by the Plaintiff from *Hendow* stated: "To further mask its illegal compensation scheme, UOP maintains separate review files on its enrollment counselors (one file contains legitimate review criteria produced to the federal government and the other secret file containing the actual, illegal quantitative enrollment review criteria). UOP also developed a glossary of 'code words' used in documents."[8]

---

6   Joint Statement Re: Discovery -- Civ. S-03-0457 GEB DAD.

7   20 U.S.C. §1094(a)(20).

8   Disclosure statement: Mary Hendow and Julie Albertson Relators. This is a 50-page document chock full of detailed allegations of fraud perpetuated by UOP. Exhibit H page 16, March 7, 2003.

The performance reviews allegedly rate counselors based on qualitative factors, such as "job related skills," "working relationships," "customer service," and "supervisory skills." "UOP, however, does not rate enrollment counselor performance or determine compensation based upon those fake performance reviews." The local campuses have reviews UOP uses to rate performance and determine enrollment counselors' compensation, based on the enrollment activities. Some of the forms also contain some qualitative factors, but the qualitative factors play no role in determining compensation and are not part of the performance evaluation process.

* * * *

April 8, 2009: I went to Washington, DC to meet with several government officials interested in for-profit education fraud, and delivered a mountain of evidence to the SEC in particular. But they were very clear this was going to be a one-way street only and they would not be communicating with me routinely by phone. They simply asked that I continue to send relevant information.

My second meeting was at the Department of Justice with Jay Majors who was a trial attorney in the consumer protection office. He was a point man for all False Claims Act cases against for-profit schools. That meeting was supposed to last just a few minutes but went almost an hour and a half. I explained why the revenue recognition was flawed based on students who drop out within the first three classes. No services are rendered and no expenses are incurred if 35-50% of the students drop out within three classes. I explained how and why the enrollment counselors intentionally prevented students from dropping out of class until the 60% mark, when the company can keep 100% of tuition from Title IV. The government had the option to take control of the case and prosecute it, but they never did, except once against Westwood. DOJ refused to intervene in *Hendow*. It continued as a whistleblower without the government's participation. I just couldn't understand it. I explained how I was told by a financial aid rep that the company made it difficult for students to drop out by firing 50% of the financial aid staff a year and a half ago. I don't care if they changed their policy for rounding up. I explained the issue regarding transferability of credit, showing examples of prospective students being told credits will transfer to cream of the crop private universities.

I then discussed how I interviewed an enrollment counselor who recommended borrowing $20,000 when tuition costs only $15,000, stating that the company would write a check for $5,000 so the student could pay off other personal debt and have "walking around money." I explained my theory, based on interviews with enrollment representatives, that free tuition to enrollment reps and their families should be counted in the incentive compensation. The enrollment counselors are not fired because the company wants to keep them as students to give them free tuition, thereby jacking up revenue without having their salary cut as a negative form of incentive compensation.

I went through the history of CLC and brought CDs with all of my files on the industry from the last decade: student suits, shareholder suits, government documents—every kind of suit and news article imaginable that contributedto the mosaic. I was disappointed that the DOJ had not read or seen any of these suits. I brought a dozen of miscellaneous documents to support my data points. I provided copies of several of my own research reports. I walked him through the default rate manipulation. I brought up the issue of insider trading by APOL by management in and around the last program review in 2003. I recommended tracking insider trading in and around the current program review. I stressed to him that this was a major problem that needed to be addressed immediately, especially given that Apollo was approaching $4 billion of revenue and 400,000 students, of which potentially 200,000+ per annum were being left in collections for services not rendered.

Jay asked only a few questions, making notes of the important points. He asked if I minded if he shared my documents with high superiors and the general counsel at the ED. I didn't tell him that I had been supplying documents to the Office of General Counsel and Inspector General's office continually for many years. I closed the meeting with very strong words that this was a problem that the DOJ and SEC needed to address; that it was likely beyond the ED's capability to handle alone. After I told Jay that

I had a meeting with Bob Shireman at the ED, to my surprise, he asked if he could come along.

The meeting with Shireman was expected to last 15 minutes, for the purpose of "putting a face to a name." However, it lasted 90 minutes. I repeated the same presentation to the ED, gearing it more toward Title IV and less toward the accounting, talking more about the student suit in LA. Bob brought a woman to the meeting who he failed to identify herself. And she offered no business card. She used to work in the IG's office. Her first response was that she thought they closed all of these [fraudulent for-profits] down back in the '90s. I told her this was not true, that, in fact, the former CEO of ITT told me two years ago that the rest of the for-profits recruited the employees of CLC on purpose.

Aside from the meeting, I never spoke directly to Bob Shireman again until months *after* he resigned. Like the SEC, his rule was that our relationship was a one-way street. Like the others, he asked that I send him information, but told me not to expect any conversations.

I made my way up to Capitol Hill. I felt like a traveling salesman going door to door. There I met with a legislative assistant for Congressman Tim Bishop from New York. He was interested in the rumors around Capitol Hill regarding the for-profit sector. Eventually, his legislative assistant moved over to Senator Dick Durbin's office, which was even more vocal about pursuing the sector. We talked about how much lobbying the industry had been doing on Capitol Hill. They were clearly trying to buy influence from members on the House Post-Secondary Education Committee and the Senate HELP Committee. They were sophisticated and convincing salesmen, a force to be reckoned with. I provided one aid with many documents regarding misbehavior in the for-profit sector and later taped interviews with former employees to be shared with others on the Hill.

* * * *

April 17, 2009: Much to my surprise, Deutsche Bank's Paul Ginocchio initiated Apollo with a buy and a price target of $80, with the stock at $65. It was a valuation call more than anything. Nevertheless, with the stock falling from the high $80s to the low $60s in less than four months, I was feeling confident in my recommendation. I contacted clients suggesting they short into any rallies. Ginocchio also started ITT Education as a Buy.

Also on April 21, Credit Suisse wrote a 46-page report on the education sector, downgrading it due to "Washington worries." Kelly Flynn wrote, "We are downgrading Apollo, ITT and Lincoln to Neutral from Outperform mostly due to rising concerns that a more challenging legal/regulatory environment could hinder longer-term growth and hold back valuation multiples near-term."

"We have little conviction on how the sector will react to earnings season. Further, although we expect enrollment growth to remain strong for the next few quarters...The ED announced last night the appointment of Bob Shireman as deputy undersecretary. He will 'advise the Department on college financial issues and other higher education initiatives' according to the ED's announcement. Shireman, who had been consulting the Obama administration on education issues, is the founder of the Institute for College Access and Success, a non-profit focused on, among other things, the negative implications of increased debt levels by college students."

(Paraphrasing) We worry proposals could seek to tighten restrictions on incentive compensation/ marketing practices, *make it easier for students to withdraw* from school quickly when they want to. ED could also require colleges to disclose more "quality related" metrics, such as life-time student loan default rates. Although we can't predict how such proposals will progress, we do think their mere existence would contract the sector's valuation.

The Shireman appointment made me think that "more Washington oversight" has become a "best case scenario" for shorting the sector. Congress or the ED could contemplate legal or regulatory changes that could adversely impact for-profit education sector growth more significantly.

* * * *

On April 21, 2009 a Bizjournal.com article reported, "Westwood Legal Precedent Alta Colleges Inc. of Denver"[9]—parent of Westwood College—had agreed to pay the U.S. government $7 million to settle a lawsuit alleging that it submitted false claims for federal student aid funds at its Texas schools, according to news reports. The for-profit college chain's Texas campuses were also accused in the suit of encouraging students to cheat on placement exams and of lying about whether students would be certified to work in some fields. I contacted both the regional DOJ office and the Washington, DC office to determine how the $7 million settlement was determined. Unfortunately, both offices refused to answer the question.

"This settlement demonstrates the government's commitment to enforcing the compliance standards required of colleges participating in the federal student aid program," Michael Hertz, acting assistant attorney general of the Civil Division of the Department of Justice, said in a statement Monday. "…its Texas campuses had engaged in practices 'designed to mislead prospective students and to misrepresent material facts to them.' The government found that the school recruiters had lied to prospective students about their job placement rates, saying that they were more than 90 percent when they were actually just over 50 percent, and about their ability to transfer credits to other schools. No other accredited colleges in Texas would accept Westwood's credits."[10, 11]

* * * *

One issue that I should mention is the issue of transfer of credits. It has been a scam among the for-profit schools, as they would often tell students their credits from other schools could be transferred and then later were told they could not. Often students had been to several for-profit schools,

9   "Reports: Alta Colleges, Parent of Westwood, Settles Suit for $7M," *The Business Journals,* http://www.bizjournals.com/denver/stories/2009/04/20/daily21.html, April 21, 2009.

10   Stephen Burd, "Rewriting the Rules on Trade Schools to Better Safeguard Students," *New America Foundation,* http://www.newamerica.net/blog/higher-ed-watch/2009/re-writing-rules-trade-schools-safeguard-students-12111, May 28, 2009.

11   "Reports: Alta Colleges, Parent of Westwood, Settles Suit for $7M," *The Business Journals,* http://www.bizjournals.com/denver/stories/2009/04/20/daily21.html, April 21, 2009.

getting churned up in the machine. The accreditors were responsible for ensuring the transfer of credits. The Higher Learning Commission (HLC) was the accreditor for several for-profit schools.[12] In another OIG audit in July of 2003, the IG sharply criticized the department's lack of oversight over the accrediting agencies. The department relies on the accrediting agencies for quality of education.

The Higher Learning Commission, whose Policy Handbook (June 2008, Section 3.8, page 51) states: "Each institution *shall determine its own policies* and procedures for accepting transfer credits, including credits from accredited and non-accredited institutions, from foreign institutions, and from institutions which grant credit for experimental learning and for non-traditional adult learner programs."

This was a situation of the fox guarding the hen house. The accrediting agencies themselves are made up of for-profit education company executives. "Quality of education" is vague and subjective and therefore hard to enforce. If you call a handful of UOP enrollment counselors and ask if you can transfer your credits to Berkeley, the odds are greater than 50% they say yes; they certainly have no incentive to say otherwise. Later, the OIG would send several threatening reports to the HLC criticizing their lenience toward for-profit schools and said they should have their charter revoked. Add that to the list of things the IG failed to enforce.

* * * *

I added this in my email to Bob. This grievance was posted by a student to ripoffreport.com: "I am a recent graduate of Axia College of University of Phoenix, receiving my A.A. last year. I transferred to the school with 23 credits from another institution, where I had maintained a 4.0 GPA. When I signed the paperwork for admission to Axia, I was told that I would have approximately 9 months until graduation with the amount of credits that I was transferring in; however, I was deceived. They had only told me this to get me to sign the paperwork, and then passed me off to another individual who had no idea what that person had told me and didn't care. After reading back through the contracts, I learned

---

12   *Higher Learning Commission,* http://www.ncahlc.org/

that what they SAID didn't matter as long as I signed the papers. After I signed the papers, they evaluated my credits from the previous institution, where I had finished every course with a grade of A, and told me that those courses were equivalent to the courses that MUST be completed at Axia or UoP and cannot be transferred in. I wound up having to repeat all of the courses that I had already successfully completed, delaying my graduation by a year and 3 months even though I maintained a 3.9 GPA during my program."[13]

* * * *

April 22, 2009: ESI was at $105 before they reported. I sent a report to clients suggesting they sell short aggressively into strength. It should blow up like APOL did following comments regarding increased level of scrutiny. ESI hit $95 yesterday but was now $106. The Street was going to be much tougher on them regarding the higher default rates and other issues. My biggest issue with ESI was the egregious and unexplained operating margin expansion.

After ESI reported on April 23, the stock climbed to $110, ten points above the close the previous day! I had a mild coronary for breakfast that day. I suggested clients "press" the rally *before* the conference call at 11 a.m. Generally, big funds tend not to be focused on short-term movements; however, it's nice to have clients either making money or breaking even in the short-run, not getting killed the first day or two of a new recommendation. So while I was not obsessed with the stock price that day, I remained cognizant of the pain I could cause them if the stock goes 10% or more against me.

ESI's sales were up 22.6%, but accounts receivables (money owed to them) increased to $51.5 million, up from $29.7 million sequentially and $15 million year over year. On the accounts receivable issue, certain schools, I began to notice, such as ESI, DV, and COCO, which were the most egregious offenders, started loaning money to students. Let's say

---

13   Bri, "AXIA College Of University Of Phoenix University of Phoenix, Apollo Group Delayed graduation scam, forced to repeat courses finished with an A Phoenix, Arizona," *RipoffReport.com,* http://www.ripoffreport.com/colleges-and-universities/axia-college-of-univ/axia-college-of-university-of-9a2f4.htm, March 25, 2010.

a student could borrow only $10,000 from federal loan programs, but the tuition was $15,000. The schools, evidenced by their high accounts receivables, started making risky loans to students themselves. If you can generate $15,000 of revenue at cost of $5,000 of bad loans, you are still $10,000 ahead. That's how the schools looked at it.

I brought this up with the SEC as well because it meant the companies could create their own revenue by making loans to risky students. The schools wanted revenue and earnings more than anything else, and even financially insolvent or dropped-out students represent a source of profit, as long as they kept making new loans to outpace the old ones. And as long as the government guarantees them, the loans grants in particular are pure profit. So during this period accounts receivables started to double and triple year over year as the schools created this artificial appearance of revenue growth. The bad debt expense from those receivables grew, but it was more of a footnote in relation to sales.

Much later Uncle Sam set up the Consumer Financial Protection Bureau. They contacted me about this issue, although they were mostly interested in the interest rates being charged to the students, not the fraud by the schools, which was misguided, and I told them so. ESI established a $300 million "PEAKS" program that was set up to help students with financing their college education. To say the least, it raised all kinds of conflict of interest issues, which explains why the CPFB went after them the hardest in 2014.

* * * *

April 24, 2009: Interview with former UOP financial aid representative: "SH" was a UOP financial aid representative two years ago. It was a very high turnover job. It became difficult to handle the volume of unhappy students. Many were dropping out. Yet she was the only financial aid person at the campus, and no one filled her job for several months after she left. The ECs had to pick up the slack in the absence of an FA. But they didn't have the training to handle financial aid issues.

The source corroborated that the dropout rate was upwards of 50%.

Source, "I have heard FAs told students they had to stay in class until their financial aid came through otherwise they would be put into collections… Yes, that's the way it worked. It was part of the strategy."

"The enrollment counselors were all students in their twenties. They would say just about anything to get students. I had to deal with a lot of very unqualified students being admitted that were illiterate. The ECs helped potential students take test for core competency. Employees were offered free tuition. The policy was that if you didn't finish your degree you had to pay back all of the free tuition, retroactively. They hooked you like that."

When asked about how much money a student could borrow, source said, "A lot of students went to school for the extra money to pay off other forms of debt. 'It is a strategy [used by the school].'"

Tellingly, SH's degree was in psychology, and she didn't realize until she was working there that their psychology program wasn't accredited. That's one reason she left.

May 2009

May 1, 2009: The education stocks were under a lot of pressure primarily because of Kaplan University, which is owned by the Washington Post (WPO). WPO was down $52 from $365. Their Kaplan division had revenue of $593 million versus $543 million. ESI was down 7% to $93, and Apollo broke $60 down 5% to $58.50. Management expected enrollments to slow to the mid-teens. I tried to recommend WPO as a short at one point, but I was yelled at a little because investors thought there was a break-up value if the company was sold in pieces, so I stayed away.

Strayer (STRA) also reported earnings, stating, "We're operating in what's perceived to be a public good, and governmental authorities and educational authorities have an opinion as to how that should work, and particularly given the fact that the government is heavily involved in terms of supporting education through the Title IV program. So I don't see the regulatory environment getting any worse or any more severe or rigorous than it has been for the eight years that Mark and I have been at the helm…anyone who has focused on Strayer's enterprise from a regulatory standpoint, is really asking the basic question of, is the enterprise an educational institution, or will it let the educational value suffer in order to generate shorter term financial gain?"

Based on these comments from management, I wasn't sold on STRA as a short. Not to say Strayer was squeaky clean, but the behavior didn't seem as egregious as the competition's. I mean, the others in the group made you want to take a shower after listening to the conference calls. One client in particular shorted a lot of Strayer well over $200 and stayed short for at least two years. By the end of 2012 the stock was under $50.

* * * *

May 4, 2009: CECO was set to report earnings in a few days. With the stock at $21, I recommend selling shares short based on the increasing uncertainty in the space. Thus far, despite upside EPS reports, almost across the board the stocks in the space have sold off thereafter. CECO total student starts were essentially flat year over year, as of December 2008. In FY08, 71% of starts emanated from the Internet. Again, while it is well-known that advertising rates are down significantly, returns are diminishing faster. CECO spent $449 million versus $487 million on "advertising and admissions expenses." On a percent of sales it's roughly the same as APOL.

May 6, 2009: CECO revenue was off 3.2%; online was up 7%. CECO grimly acknowledged that allegations of wrongdoing had resulted in reviews or investigations by federal and state regulatory agencies, as well as, their accreditors. "Further, allegations against the postsecondary education sectors may impact public perceptions of educational institutions, including us, in a negative manner. Adverse media coverage regarding other educational institutions could damage our reputation. The environment around access to student loans remains in a state of flux, with additional legislation and regulatory changes being actively considered at the federal and state levels. The uncertainty surrounding these issues could reduce student demand for CECO programs and could adversely impact revenues and operating profit." I am not sure anyone was drinking that Kool-Aid.

* * * *

May 7, 2009: APOL was strangely weak; CECO missed estimates. I interviewed a former UOP student today. MK was a former UOP student I found on one of the many Internet complaint message boards. Source started taking classes in August 2006 and withdrew in May of 2007. Source claims the company continued to charge her for classes *after* she withdrew. Source claims to have her drop date well documented, including correspondence from the company. Source indicated the company used a "waiver request form" on multiple occasions to draw down Title IV funds without her knowledge. Source spoke to an attorney who claimed to have several similar complaints. Source also claims to have been charged room and board expense while being only an on-line student.

She has 33 student complaints from www.complaints.com and 157 complaints sent to her from the Better Business Bureau in her state. The complaints don't have the students' names. Source has withdrawal papers from the date she withdrew. UOP kept asking her for more and more money, telling her to borrow more financial aid. She also found out they were not accredited for the classes she was taking. But when she switched to the local school and tried to get the transcript, she was refused and told she owed $2500 more to UOP. She insisted to UOP that she already withdrew. She had to pay an attorney to get transcripts.

Source was told later by a UOP counselor that UOP received one grant and one loan. The financial aid waiver form she signed when she first registered was used by UOP to draw down funds. They basically forged the signature with that form. She wrote an article in the local paper. Sounds similar to what was found in the 2003 program review in Arizona.

* * * *

On May 14, 2009, I wrote about changes at Apollo and wondered if they were going to clean up their act. "Whether it is driven by the whistleblower, the recent program review or some other force, UOP is actively seeking to change its aggressive recruiting posture. Management is increasingly critical of enrollment representatives promising anything to get the students to sign. At the same time, management is trying to increase retention. This represents a fundamental shift for APOL, which I see as an opportunity on the short side. The efforts to create higher retention are designed as an offset to the high turnover students. However, given its pattern of failure to provide a quality education, I don't believe that retention will go up even with increased access to Pell grants, et al, which pushed up stocks in the group earlier in the week."

Turnover of enrollment representatives and financial aid counselors was accelerating, causing instability for APOL, as an increasing number of less qualified employees attempt to handle higher workloads. Only 10% of a student's grade was contingent on attendance so students can still get a passing grade if they don't show up.

* * * *

May 26, 2009: "Education Department to Consider Changes in Student-Aid Rules."[14]

"The ED announced Negotiated Rulemaking 'NegReg,' which was a set of hearings designed to bring ED regulations up to speed with the current trends in the industry.[15] The rules could also: Require for-profit and technical institutions to provide more evidence that they are preparing their students for the work force. Tighter restrictions on incentive compensation are likely to be part of new rules. Negotiated Rulemaking panels will meet three times this summer."

* * * *

---

14   Kelly Field, "Education Department to Consider Changes in Student Aid Rules," *Chronicle of Higher Education*, http://chronicle.com/news/article/6533/education-department-to-consider-changes-in-student-aid-rules, May 26, 2009.

15   "[Federal Register Volume 74, Number 99 (Tuesday, May 26, 2009)]

May 27, 2009: "Career Education a candidate to go private, analyst says:"[16] "Career Education Corp., its shares lagging despite turnaround efforts by new management, is the leading candidate among publicly traded education firms to go private, according to an industry analyst. Career Education's stock market valuation remains well below market multiples paid by private-equity investors in 2006 for another publicly traded education company, said analyst Trace Urdan of Signal Hill Capital Group in San Francisco. He said private-equity firms have called him about industry prospects, but not about Career Education specifically. At the moment, education companies are buying each other, rather than selling to private-equity firms, in part because of credit conditions."

As a short seller, one must always attempt to evaluate the threat of a takeover of a public company. Generally, one would try to find an industry benchmark or a comparable measure for valuation, and use that as a guide for the types of valuation an acquiring company might be willing to pay. In the case of the for-profit education companies, one would have to weigh the potential legal liability against the value of the company. Takeover speculation can rally the whole sector, not just the target company.

At this point, CECO's stock was $23, so there was still plenty of meat on the bones to stay short. I was working from the premise that the Department of Education could at any time ask for sizable refunds or restrict the flow of funds due to misbehavior. In my mind, the value of CECO was zero, just like APOL. Even so, an acquiring private equity firm may not know it, and they might be stupid enough to buy it anyway. However, as the negative news started pouring out of every corner of government, those investors quickly realized they could not bet against a possible legislative change that would destroy the business model. Thankfully, they figured it out in time. It's not often, but there have been times where I've suggested clients sell short a stock rallying on speculation of a takeover.

* * * *

---

16 Steven R. Strahler, *Crain's* http://www.chicagobusiness.com/cgi-bin/news.pl?id=34189&seenIt=1, May 27, 2009.

May 28, 2009: – *Hendow* filings from 5/20[17]: This person worked at UOP from October 2003 to December 2007. First he was an enrollment counselor, then the Director of Enrollment at the online campus:

"As an enrollment manager, I provided performance evaluations every six months to Enrollment counselors based just on their enrollments. Although there other criteria on which they were to be evaluated, they were meaningless or irrelevant because when I became a manager, my supervisor told me that the review is really just all about the enrollment numbers, and 'that was just the way it is.'"

"As a director of enrollment, approximately once a month, I attended director-level meetings. At one of these meetings, at least one Vice President said that UOP was changing the matrix so 'no one will ever prove it's based on regs.' Vice President xxxxxx xxxxxxxx told me that the matrix is 'all just smoke and mirrors,' and 'we're flying under the radar.'"

The deposition was dated August 8, 2008 but didn't see the light of day until May 20, 2009, when many documents were filed en masse. One could argue the company shareholders were being hurt by the lack of access to these documents, almost one year prior.

This exchange was from a deposition:

"Q: Now, what do you recall at the Department of Education investigation, if anything?"[18]

"A: I recall that everybody obviously was nervous. We all were individually interviewed. The conversation started with the fact that we were aware that it was a federal offense to lie to a government agent. There were boards that had been up—they consistently posted our numbers as to who was the top recruiter, who had the most applications, who had the most starts. They were consistently having contests, and all of that stuff that day came down. We were looking like all these posters were being pulled down. . ."

"Q: What do you mean 'pulled down?'"

"A: Off the displays. There was an area where things would be on display. As I said, our daily numbers, or this is the local contest, whether it's to win a cup of coffee or, you know, a free lunch or, you know, you're way

---

17   Tom Corbett, *Hendow* deposition document 301-4, filed May 20, 2009.

18   *Hendow vs. UOP* Document 301-29 filed May 20, 2009. Deposition of Charlotte Gould.

up on top, Mary, because you are great, but you are way down here on the bottom of the—of the—you know, competing against each other."

"Q: Okay. Now, when you say these things were taken down, were they taken down the—the same day that the Department of Education investigation began at San Jose?"

"A: Yes. Immediately."

I found a deposition from the *Hendow* case. Jennifer Kahn, a recruiter who left Phoenix in 2006, complained to her boss about a prospect who couldn't handle college. In the deposition she said, "I had a student, let's refer to him as dumb as a doornail," Kahn said. "And my manager told me, 'Enroll him. It's not our call to say who has a right to an education.' As a consequence, he started, he went to the first night, he knew he was in deep doo-doo, and dropped. He never should have been there."

Tom Corbett, a former director of online enrollment at Phoenix who provided an affidavit in the [*Hendow*] lawsuit, said in an interview that the school's recruiters were like brokers peddling subprime mortgages. "The University of Phoenix's management culture is fueled by greed, the same as the housing scenario," Corbett said. "There was no emphasis on the student's actual values, goals, background, experiences."

CHAPTER 6

ED Induced Volatility

It was abundantly clear, at least to me, that Bob Shireman was going right after the for-profit education sector as soon as he came into his ED job. He was anxious to remove the Safe Harbors and had good intentions with the Gainful Employment legislation. On several occasions, Bob made unexpected public commentary that moved the entire group up or down a full 5% or more in one day. When dealing with public officials or the management of a company, everyone was supposed to get the same information at the same time to prevent anyone from having an advantage. This was not always the case with Shireman's office. In one instance, his assistant caused a huge move in the sector all by herself, talking one on one with a Street analyst. I don't fault him or his staff, and I viewed the rallies as shorting opportunities; however, we, bulls included, had to learn quickly to handicap off-the-cuff comments by him or his staff. My phone would light up in an instant from clients asking for an interpretation on something I hadn't heard about yet. It made me a regular Rolaids customer, for sure. And once people started thinking they might get lucky and talk to him directly, I am sure his phone lit up more than mine.

May 28, 2009: The ED announced this week that it planned to re-write its federal student aid rules, and was considering barring colleges from paying recruiters on the basis of how many students they enroll. Congress put this consumer protection in place in 1992 to prevent unscrupulous trade schools from taking advantage of financially needy students.

May 29, 2009: Shireman held a call with foundations and consumer advocate type organizations about the NegReg changes, followed by another call with the management of several for-profit schools. Then there was a call with investment analysts. Wall Street analysts generally do not like being a spoiler by asking hard questions. They like their investment banking business and there is still a level of bias against exposing negative information about any company or industry.

June 2009

June 2, 2009: Shireman held a conference call talking about the changes that might be made to the student financial aid program. It sounded as though he might be interested in revisiting the way the Safe Harbors were being enforced. I saw it as a big negative for the industry but the Street interpreted it as a positive. Beauty is in the eye of the beholder. They also talked about having some open hearings in Philadelphia, Denver, and Arkansas. My clients suggested that I go to Philadelphia and provide some sort of expert testimony on the industry, saying it would be an opportunity to bring some of the true issues to light.

June 4, 2009: The entire education space inexplicably fell by 5%, and rumors were circulating that there were two separate conference calls held by Bob Shireman. One was with the industry, during which, people told me, Bob had made some more disparaging comments regarding the for-profit education sector. There were comments about the issue of incentive compensation and the "Safe Harbor" provisions. Shireman said ED would enforce the ban on incentive compensation.

Deutsche Bank published a note stating, "We confirmed with the ED that there was a call with Bob Shireman and some traditional colleges on Thursday via two different sources we concluded that this call had a negative tone toward the for-profit education providers versus the more innocuous non-profits. We believe the Under Secretary was looking for stories that highlight any maltreatment of for-profit students and wants to portray them as victims. The call concerns us but the negotiated rule-making process is open. June kicks off public hearings related to negotiated rule-making process."

On June 11, Deutsche commented again: "We met with three education companies that we don't cover. We discussed long-term strategies and regulatory issues. We continue to believe that any legislative changes are *likely to be incremental and not material* to the public, for for-profit providers. The smaller private for-profits seem more at risk. If any share price weakness is created by the upcoming public discussions (starting Monday in Denver), we would use that opportunity to build positions… Compensation for enrollment counselors is the most often talked about potential change. Even if rules are tightened completely, we believe this *change is immaterial* to our investment thesis."

June 15, 2009: Mark Marostica at Piper wasn't any better, expressing similar optimism, citing historically low stock prices among industry players and stating, "We do not expect the public hearings will uncover any significant topics of interest incremental to the seven topics already outlined by the ED in the Federal Register on May 26, 2009."

* * * *

June 17, 2009. On days like this quitting seems like a good idea. Harris Miller, president and CEO of the Career College Association, said in an interview that some investors had sought to sow fear that the Obama administration would deliberately target profit-making education firms. "Some folks don't understand how Washington works, and others were just making things up," he said. Him, I wasn't worried about.

In any case, the market swirled with rumors and speculation over what Bob Shireman intended to do to reign in the for-profit sector. He was unaccustomed to dealing with Wall Street, as evidenced by several analysts and journalists taking his comments out of context and causing a misinterpretation of his thoughts. His apparent capriciousness gave my clients and me gray hair. I am sure it was no better for the bulls. If one analyst reached him, then everyone would want direct access, including me.

* * * *

June 17, 2009: A painful day for the short sellers. Dow Jones wrote: "Education Shares Up On Broad Market Weakness, Federal Overtures. Shares of major education companies rose two days after federal officials sought to reassure the for-profit education industry amid speculation of a regulatory crackdown. Apollo Group Inc. (APOL), was up more than 4%, DeVry Inc. (DV) was up over 5%, Strayer Education Inc. (STRA) was nearly 4%, Career Education Corp. (CECO) was up over 4%, Corinthian Colleges Inc. (COCO) rose nearly 6% .... But investors were also reassured when a federal official told an audience at the Career Colleges Association's annual conference Monday that the department is 'agnostic' about for-profit or nonprofit management structures when it designs federal rules, Urdan said."

* * * *

June 19, 2009. With APOL at $67.34, I published an APOL research report. Bob Shireman made this comment: "When low-income students are saddled with debt and have a low probability of completion, they end up worse off than if they hadn't attended college at all. You end up in a very difficult situation to get out of—ever."[1] I wrote to clients, the Career College Association conference and the Street analysts attending the hearings are using their voodoo public relations machines at full throttle, selling investors on the concept that it is business as usual at the Department. That is far from the truth.

Shireman seemed to already know what he wanted to do and was not relying on the negotiated rule-making process to provide insight. A cynic might claim the entire process was just for show. The for-profits (represented by Elaine Neely of Kaplan) were on defense throughout, continually using dramatic language such as "appalled," "shocked," and "flabbergasted" in response to the Department's proposals, especially going after incentive compensation. It was clear the Department was making more than just "shot across the bow" effort to regulate the for-profits. Several

---

1   "Robert Shireman Quotes," *ThinkExist.com,* http://thinkexist.com/quotes/robert_shireman/, accessed July 8, 2014.

heated exchanges erupted between Elaine Neely of Kaplan and Margaret Reiter (formerly at the California AG's office). Reiter cited an example of a crippled person being admitted to a for-profit massage therapy curriculum that required standing. Elaine quickly commented, "A school like that should be shut down." *Make a mental note of that comment.* I thought about putting a file full of documents on Neely's desk at the hearing, but held back. In my view, with the exception of the Department officials and one or two others at the table, few if any were aware of the potential fraud occurring at the publicly traded for-profit companies. The states, the Department of Education, and the accrediting bodies, in theory, provide enough overlapping regulatory hoops for schools to jump through that abuse of Title IV is stymied. Unfortunately, that is not the case. An astute and unscrupulous institution can and does find holes in the overlapping circles of protections.

* * * *

I was having second thoughts about sharing data at one of the ED's upcoming hearings. Shireman was giving the public an opportunity to make suggestions on how to improve Title IV programs. One of my clients was saying, "hey, we've have to raise the noise level as much as possible." My client wasn't willing to stick his neck out, but was more than willing to put mine on the chopping block. Meanwhile, a source in the ED kept telling me that UOP still has people in the organization, in the ED, that plays favorites with them. Maybe I could create a counter-balance to that corruption.

Not much news of any consequence came from the first two hearings. The third would be held in Philadelphia (just a couple hours from New York), and everyone would get ten minutes in front of the microphone to share their perspective on how the Higher Education Act regulations should be modified. The ED wasn't prepared for the onslaught of documents from all angles. There were around 300 submissions from everyone from former students, former employees, to lawyers suing the industry, to short sellers.

June 22, 2009: Giving the speech was one of most nerve-racking things I have ever done. The audience was full of people from the industry. APOL had several senior people in the audience, as did the other major for-profit schools. In total there were about 150-200 people in attendance. I almost lost my nerve, but I felt so strongly about what I had to say, and I wasn't going to keep it inside. And there was a shortage of naysayers up at the microphone.

Here are some excerpts from my speech, some of which came from FOIA documents that few, if any, had seen: "With a former APOL lobbyist at the helm of Post-Secondary Education, enforcement was lax despite numerous inspector general reports urging better enforcement. This disservice to tax payers has enriched the managements of the for-profit industry and left in its wake thousands of students who bought into the hopes of a finer future only to be overrun with student debt."

"I personally have no investments in the industry. I am here before you today to bring to your attention an issue which has received some press but has yet to be properly addressed by the Department; that is the corruption and chronic misbehavior of the for-profit education industry. Apollo Group, parent company of University of Phoenix, is largest school in the country. In 1998 the company had 71,000 students. That number grew to 157,000 in 2002 and is presently 397,000."

"In FY08 the company spent $322 million on advertising, most of which was on the Internet. At the present rate of growth advertising will likely reach over $400 million in 2009. Through heavy industry lobbying efforts and a friendly administration, the so called 'Safe Harbor' provisions were established that effectively nullified the ban on incentive compensation for enrollment counselors."

"This loophole has allowed the industry to bypass the regulation and claim ECs are paid based on factors other than quotas, which testimony from former employees in the *qui tam* has proven is false. I am including depositions from the whistleblower. Hiding behind the word 'solely' in the Safe Harbors violates the spirit of the original law. This loophole has created a wave of defaulted debt and the taxpayer bears the burden."

"UOP did not have a policy to review the accuracy of payment period end dates for the purpose of calculating Title IV aid…UOP systematically monitored students' status and progress, readjusting the beginning and ending dates of payment period to accommodate leaves of absence, 'no shows,' failed courses, or repeat courses. Referring to this process as 'remapping,' UOP readjusted payment period end dates and rescheduled second disbursement dates," said the IG, who wrote another report on January 10, 2008.

"The Department found at APOL's WIU division that 37.5% of refunds were not made within the 30-day legal limitation. They found inaccurate refunds and refunds not paid at all. WIU incorrectly calculated refunds 25% of the time. Many late funds cite were up to 800 days late. Is this abiding by the spirit of the administrative capability statutes? I think not."

"The Department is ill-prepared through no fault of its own to deal with such ruthless sophistication and contempt for the law. Current regulations that are obsolete or have been softened by industry lobbying over years need to be improved. Nobody wants to talk about these issues. I've dedicated the last 12 years of my life examining this industry and I see very similar parallels between this and Countrywide Credit and predatory marketing practices that have occurred in the mortgage industry."[2]

* * * *

Later, several of my journalist friends texted and emailed me with congratulations for delivering a strong speech so well. From my standpoint I thought I stuttered through the whole thing. I didn't know someone could talk for ten minutes without taking a breath.

After the speech, I was emotionally shaken almost to a point of nausea. Chasing after me was a young attorney named Jillian Estes, from a Florida law firm that had filed a whistleblower lawsuit against Westwood College. Jillian made a presentation similar to my own, with a little extra legalese.

---

2   "Brown Sues Countrywide For Mortgage Deception," *California Dept. of Justice,* http://ag.ca.gov/newsalerts/release.php?id=1582&, June 25, 2008. (I hastily referenced a comparison of the for-profit education sector and Countrywide Credit. "The company sold ever-increasing numbers of complex and risky home loans, as quickly as possible. Countrywide was, in essence, a mass-production loan factory, producing ever-increasing streams of debt without regard for borrowers. Today's lawsuit seeks relief for Californians who were ripped off by Countrywide's deceptive scheme.")

We chatted for several minutes in the hallway. She was intrigued with my work, but I was so short of breath, my mind and body was coursing with adrenaline. I was having trouble putting my thoughts together. There was also a man who had followed her out into the lobby and seemed to be circling us during the conversation. Jillian and I developed a good working relationship over the following year or two after our introduction, though I can barely recall our first discussion.

As for our mysterious shadow in the hall, it turned out to be an executive from Westwood College, Jillian told me. Somehow I knew his name. It's a rare name. Then it dawned on me that he was a manager at Computer Learning Centers. I had obtained an employee list and I knew that Westwood, as well as Lincoln Education, was full of former CLC employees.

After Jillian left, he approached me to ask if he could talk me, which I flatly refused and kept walking. But he followed me anyway for about 40 or 50 feet toward the door. His intentions were unclear and I could tell he was very agitated. At the door, he encroached on my space. There was no one else around. I turned and cocked my fist and said, "One step closer and I am going to knock you out." He backed off from there, but only barely. Given my adrenaline rush I could've knocked out Superman at that point.

* * * *

Officials from Westwood and UOP used the hearing as an opportunity to defend their institutions against allegations of impropriety. A regional vice president of Westwood College said he was deeply offended by Ms. Estes's "frivolous" claims and vowed to disprove them "in the appropriate forum."

Robert Collins, vice president for student financial aid for the Apollo Group, accused short-sale investors of spreading misinformation about his company to deflate the value of its stock. "It's unfortunate that many short-sellers make their living by shorting Apollo stock," he said, before addressing issues raised in a 2004 Education Department program review and an inspector general's report.[3]

---

3   Kelly Field, "For-Profit Colleges and Consumer Advocates Weigh In on Potential Rule Changes," *Chronicle of Higher Education*, http://chronicle.com/daily/2009/06/20510n.htm?utm_source=at&utm_medium=en, June 23, 2009.

Collins also made a more important comment in his short few minutes at the Philadelphia hearing. I think he was the last to speak. Regarding the 2003 program review of UOP, Collins said, "We did settle with the Department as we had no desire to enter into a protracted dispute with our primary regulator. HOWEVER, the settlement did not require that we change policies or practices because we were, in fact, abiding by the law." So after all this time and evidence they were still willing to hold fast to that view. I won't spoil the story here, but the ED took issue with that comment later.

* * * *

June 23, 2009: William Blair published a report on the hearing, writing little that was new, although there were more negative comments directed at the for-profits than in previous reports. Most of the comments related to poor student outcomes, aggressive marketing tactics and spending. He wrote, "We remain of the opinion that schools will have to provide students with more disclosures upfront to ensure students aren't being 'duped' into attending school, will have much tighter rules around incentive compensation for enrollment counselors and will have to report more outcomes related data (graduate placement rates, etc.), but we do not expect any game-changing actions such as limiting marketing spending or profit margins…I believe tighter regulations in some areas will raise the barriers to entry for new participants and put poorly-run schools out of business, trends that are good for well-run schools."

His report made disparaging comments about my credibility, specifically, my comments about the graduation rates. I pulled the numbers from the ED site and suggested he refute my numbers. The ED web site reported that WIU had a 27% default rate in 2006, up from 11.4% in 2005. The graduation rates were still abysmal reported at 27% for associates, 38% for bachelor, and 60% for masters from the period September 1, 2005 to August 31, 2006. I never heard back. Online graduation rates were in the 9% range.

* * * *

June 23, 2009: Yesterday, documents were filed in the *Hendow* case in which employees discussed increased salaries based on increased recruitment and how that should not be mentioned in writing.[4]

Here are UOP employees emailing each other: "From Beverly Young to Heidi Hall. November 14, 2002: 'I have redacted performance review and am having to *white out any mention to enrollments on the evaluation. Be sure there is never any reference to starts on an evaluation.* You're recommending a new salary of $40,000 a 42.9% increase. No can do. Apollo guidelines cap at 10% for someone in the lower third of the salary range.'"

Despite APOL's attempts to keep these documents under seal, the court refused.

* * * *

June 24, 2009: the ED started posting transcripts of the first two hearings. That became a wealth of knowledge. One presenter was Henry Harrison: "I'm greatly concerned about students over-borrowing. We seem to be in a vise between the extremes of the Department of Education insisting that a student should be able to borrow monies up to the absolute limit and our concern about students borrowing for the wrong purposes, being able to repay it, you know, causing default rates and costing the government more money. It seems to be, you know, a rebirth of the perfect storm we had in the housing market where, you know, people are pushing money at borrowers. It becomes a real problem and I don't think we're doing the students, I don't think we're doing the country a service by just, you know, marching on these orders from the Department of Education to give them every cent to which they're entitled."[5]

I was in constant contact with the ED, seeking incriminating documents from the other speakers, but the ED was completely overrun with documents, and was struggling to upload them on the site promptly, as some information had to be redacted. They said if I came to the ED, in

---

4   Case 2:03-cv-00457-GEB-DAD Document 328-3, June 22, 2009.

5   http://www.harrison.edu/ CEO of a for-profit college.

Washington, I could have access to the documents *prior* to their publication online. The documents could be highly incriminating and could cause the stock prices across the industry to decline. Unexpectedly, one of my more passionate and slightly impulsive clients immediately left New York and went to the ED office in Washington. One attorney, Scott Levy, wrote a 26-page scathing recount of fraud in the for-profit sector, so it wasn't just me, by any means, bringing information about the fraud in the sector to the ED. He singled out ESI in particular, which I think was/is his passionate archenemy he fought for years. He hates the industry as much as I do.

June 25, 2009: I exchanged emails with attorneys and several journalists in the following week or two as we sifted through the ED submitted documents. One document said that Westwood was charging students 18% interest to borrow money, from the school, to attend classes—in effect, not just inflating their revenue stream but also becoming a subprime lender in the process. It then occurred to me that if the industry was making refunds late, they were likely also collecting interest on that money and counting it as income while possibly owing the money plus interest and penalties back to Title IV.

COCO and ESI were hammered the most last year when Sallie Mae came out saying they would no longer subsidize private lending to subprime borrows—I guess the default rate was too high and collections were unsuccessful. Both companies said they would expect to lend about $75-$100 million to students...

* * * *

June 25, 2009: A colleague sent me an email that put a smile on my face: "I was sitting in front of the Apollo folks and their Blackberries were going a mile a minute when you were speaking. Did you get to hear their response at all at the end? You looked and sounded passionate about the subject. While I wouldn't put anything past the industry, I certainly hope they don't harass you. If they do, you should let a reporter know because then it becomes a story. I would love to have seen the look on their faces."

July 2009

July 9, 2009: APOL was doing pretty well, sitting at $64.00. Nevertheless, rumors were afoot about the California legislature taking action against the for-profit sector. I was skeptical because I knew the industry maintained an army of lobbyists there; approximately 16% of APOL schools are based in California.

* * * *

July 15, 2009: The stocks in the group were weak on the announcement that the California legislature was reinstating the consumer protection against fraudulent for-profit college activities.[6] The California legislature held a hearing regarding AB 48; one provision appears to ban incentive compensation. The new legislation would prohibit institutions from making untrue or misleading statements, willfully falsifying or destroying documents, improperly implying approval or licensure or failing to completely disclose what approval or licensure means, compensating an employee by bonus or commission for recruitment, and requiring personal contact information to access program information via the institution's website.

* * * *

Meanwhile, at the federal level, the ED was in the process of assembling and posting to their site all of the documents submitted by speakers at the June 22 hearing. One document from the hearing, however, grabbed me: "I am a former employee at Ashford University [that's Bridgepoint's (BPI) dba]. There was no regard whether a student really belongs in school, the goal is to enroll as many as possible. They also go after GI Bill money and currently have separate teams set up to specifically target military students. While it is illegal to pay commissions for student enrollment

---

6   Avi Salzman, "In California Budget Deal, Bad News for Colleges in 2010," *Barron's*, http://online.barrons.com/article/SB124769987540548303.html?mod=googlenews_barrons, July 16, 2009.

Ashford does salary adjustments…As long as [students] finish their first class we get full credit, and after that they are no longer our problem. Also, they don't even have to pass the class to get credit. We just need to make sure they log in 2 separate days a week, 4 out of the 5 weeks of class. Whether they do any work doesn't matter, they just need to log in then out again to get attendance credit and we get credit for them attending class. The first class is purposely designed to be super easy, too."

The letter continued, "It's almost impossible to know the atrocities that take place at Ashford unless you are on the inside, or a former student victim. During the 2 weeks new employee training, we are told to always consider the best interest of the student and how to go through a qualifying process. But once you get on the sales floor the way they actually conduct business is quite opposite and many people quit because of this as well. This has a striking resemblance to the mortgage crises? Many employers are also quickly starting to figure out that online degrees are for the most part useless and don't compare in any way to a real degree."

* * * *

July 29, 2009: After I spoke in Philadelphia, several UOP current and former students and employees started contacting me, each with different horror stories. As this picked up speed, it filled in the mosaic of the entire company nicely.

A UOP student wrote to me: "Last time I checked the BBB, they had over 200 complaints on the UOP. I did not go to my Attorney General and here in Illinois we do not have any UOP schools only available through online courses. The enrollment counselor also said it was their policy that you have to finish 3 out of 4 classes in a block to have them all paid for. I was told that if I took 1 more class through the UOP that all my classes would be paid for and I would owe nothing. I was told that I could start teaching with my associates, but this is not the case…I have to have a 4-year degree before I can even apply for my license to teach which they did not tell me this. So I thought the whole time I was enrolled until the very end that I could start teaching after I got done with my associates."

Another said, "Now, whenever I went to withdraw from UOP altogether they tried to pressure me into 'taking a break' but I told them that due to financial hardships I could not keep my Internet. Which is not true but if I told them anything else I had read they would hound me constantly. I do not think that they paid off my student loans, but Josie told me that whenever I withdrew I would owe for my last 2 classes although in an earlier phone call she told me all of my classes were paid for and I owed nothing. I am assuming if they had paid them off I would have gotten a bill for the 7k. They did say that they was sending all of my funds back to the lender and my Pell back."

* * * *

Barron's wrote that July also brought an uptick in insider selling by senior management.[7] During the month, the Sperlings made some exceptionally sizable sales of stock, similar to February. Then, the news reported, "After a six month lull, two of the top insiders at Apollo Group (ticker: APOL) sold a combined $54 million in shares this week. John Sperling continues to own about 18 million or about 12% of the company. Peter Sperling owns about 9 million or about 6% of the company."

"John and Peter Sperling trade regularly in order to fund their philanthropic and other interests, notably in the environmental arena," an Apollo spokeswoman wrote in an e-mail.

"The Sperlings made some timely sales in January, cashing in about $71 million at average prices north of $88 per class A share. Apollo's shares had a nice run late last year into January, as newly unemployed people decided to go back to school. The shares hit a 52-week high of $90 on Jan. 22. But the stock has languished somewhat since then. Short sellers have latched on and some investors worry that the Obama administration will impose new regulations that hinder for-profit educators."

---

7   "Insider Trading Chart: APOL," *InsiderTrading.org*, http://insidertrading.org/insider-selling.php?sort_by=acceptance_datetime&asc=&symbol=apol&date_from=2009-06-01&date_to=2009-10-01&submit=+GO+, accessed July 8, 2014. http://online.barrons.com/article/SB124769987540548303.html?mod=googlenews_barrons.

These were for the most part the only sales of stock by insiders since January. Good timing. The SEC started an investigation, but closed it a year later without consequence. You judge.

This statement appeared in the Final Program Review much later in 2010: *"During the July 7th, 2009 exit conference with UOP officials, UOP indicated that it had taken action to address the concerns of the Department as stated in the March 2008 meeting… UOP stated that it revised its withdrawal process in June 2008 and August 2008 to provide 'more clarity to staff about processing of withdrawals and actions that must be taken by the staff.' On July 14, 2009, UOP provided the program reviewers with copies of documents reflecting the 2008 revisions and described training and directions given to staff to address the problem of failing to treat students' attempts to withdraw as withdrawal notification."* The Sperlings could have been selling stock based on information from the July 7 "exit conference." Given the importance of the review, which, if bad enough could prompt the government to suspend the company on the spot, it follows that a negative review would be reported to the board members on a very timely basis.

The ED found, "Review of the student files in the program review process revealed however, that throughout 2008, UOP *continued to fail to timely withdraw students who expressed a desire to withdraw*, resulting in

UOP's untimely return of Title IV funds. Further, the documents reflecting UOP's 2008 revisions and directions to staff were inconsistent and conflicted with existing UOP policies regarding determination of a student's withdrawal."[8] That wouldn't sound auspicious in the public version of the program review; no wonder they wanted to sell.

I made sure Donna knew they made such large stock sales with new information about the review in hand. I knew that would get her goat a little bit because she told me she called the SEC six years ago during the 2003 review and told them that the Sperlings and others were possibly engaging in insider trading based on the contents of the program review.

August 2009

August 3, 2009: RBC Capital Markets: ITT Educational Services, Inc. (NYSE: ESI – $97.35) "Double Down" on ESI: Defusing the Bad Debt. RBC writes: "We think market concerns about ESI's bad debt reflect a limited understanding and create a compelling opportunity to increase exposure. Investment Opinion Bad Debt Concerns are exaggerated: We believe that many investors currently avoid owning ESI due to concerns about the company's accounting for on-balance sheet student loans. Our analysis of ESI's accounts receivable suggests that these fears reflect a widespread misunderstanding of the terms under which ESI extends credit. Facts speak for themselves: In our view, the combination of ample loan reserves, high marginal profitability on a per student basis and an increasing probability of monetizing its on-balance sheet student loans lead us to believe that bad debt concerns are overblown. We are revising our 12-month price target to $131 from $114."

But this guy was just wrong on so many levels. Where to start? ESI had one of the highest levels of loan volume coming from private lenders. SLM and others exited the market because their losses were high, so ESI, and COCO, too, started making loans directly to students. That creates a risk of default. Like APOL, both schools recruited under-qualified students who had no ability or willingness to repay loans, especially if many of them dropped out. There was no point in

---

8   OPE ID 02098800 PRCN 200920926841, *University of Phoenix*, p. 20.

making students pay while they were in school, though I am sure they tried. This began an ugly pattern of rapidly rising accounts receivables on the balance sheets of the sector: COCO and DV jumped into the act, too. Receivables eventually grew at a rate near double the rate of sales growth, which became unsustainable over time, leading to more problems. Sure, revenue would look good when you are buying your own revenue stream. But if those students were likely to default, causing the company to write-down the bad loans, the earnings would not exactly look so good. In fact, so many loans may go bad that there are no earnings left over.

* * * *

A new whistleblower lawsuit surfaced regarding CECO[9]: "Plaintiff filed the complaint individually and as a putative class action and purports to allege causes of action for fraud; constructive fraud; negligent misrepresentation; and violations of the Georgia Deceptive and Unfair Trade Practices Act. Plaintiff contends that American InterContinental University, Inc., ('AIU') made a variety of oral and written misrepresentations to her during the admissions process. The alleged misrepresentations relate generally to the school's reputation, the value of the education, the competitiveness of the admissions process, the students' employment prospects upon graduation from AIU and AIU's ability to arrange beneficial student loans."

The Atlanta Journal-Constitution wrote: "American InterContinental University, a for-profit college with campuses in Atlanta, has defrauded federal grant and loan programs and the agency that approved its accreditation, a whistleblower lawsuit contends. The lawsuit alleges that AIU enrolled students who couldn't read and some who had no high school diploma. The college also rewarded its recruiters with bonuses based solely on the numbers of students they enrolled, a violation of the Higher Education Act, the suit said."

---

9   *Diallo v. American InterContinental University, Inc. and Career Education Corporation.* On March 19, 2008, the same counsel in the Amador and Adams actions filed a complaint in Atlanta, Georgia in the Superior Court of the State of Georgia of Fulton County on behalf of Tajuansar Diallo.

"We have evidence that AIU fraudulently attained its accreditation, meaning it sold a substandard education to its students," said Atlanta attorney Joseph Wargo, who represents the former employees who brought the suit. "This resulted in the government not getting what it bargained for." Wargo estimated that the alleged fraud amounts to more than *$100 million in grant money*, plus a sizable amount of federal college loans. AIU was acquired in 2001 by Career Education Corp.

* * * *

August 3, 2009: A UOP enrollment counselor who found me through my Philadelphia speech contacted me under the cryptic alias "Cheddar Boy." He described himself as a good-looking African-American man. He worked, he said, at a medium-sized campus, and laid out for me very detailed information about UOP recruiting practices at his school. He said he goes into the ghetto to recruit as many students as possible regardless of their ability to read or write.

He said students often sign up and don't understand or care that they are on the hook for student loans. He claimed the entire southeast U.S. has only two financial aid reps. It used to be part of the regulations that schools had to show they are able to handle federal funds under the administrative capability statutes, but, he stated, the enrollment counselors are performing the financial aid function and doing a very bad job at it. I had heard from a prior financial aid counselor that the ratio was one financial aid rep for every 800 students. Source laughed, saying they have 800 just in xxxx alone, and the same amount in Florida and another state. Source didn't know the total amount but believed each financial rep has a minimum of 2,000 students to handle—an impossible task. UOP was the roach model: Getting into UOP can take as little as a week or less, but getting out can easily take several months.

Enrollment counselors know how to sweet-talk poor students into believing they are entitled to free money. He bluntly stated (and I'm paraphrasing), "We have a lot of poor kids 'from the hood' and in places where factories have laid off a lot people. I recruit Tyrone from the hood who can't read or write.[10] That's the way it works!" Source indicated only four students out of every 100 are still enrolled after the first year.

I asked him if he was some kind of lone wolf, the only enrollment counselor doing such things. No way, he said, everyone recruits that way! Management was happy just as long as they have plausible deniability.

Source became very useful later on acting as a reality check compared to the PR the company started pumping out.

* * * *

One thing I started hearing about in August was a funny phrase called "Pell Runner" and "walking around money." "Walking around money" refers to the practice of taking out more loans and grant money than a student needs to attend UOP. For example, a student could get $5,000 from the Pell grant program plus another $7,500 or $8,500 depending on what year the student was attending. But the initial round of classes only cost $8,800. The Pell grant money went to the student and the loan went to the school. The student was supposed to turn the grant money around to pay the tuition. But that's not how it worked. What happened was the students figured out that they could get this walking around money and just keep it and spend it and never attend classes.

Then the enrollment counselors figured out that if they could make people look poor on paper, they could recruit students on purpose who they knew would "over-borrow" and become Pell Runners. And that's what was happening. The enrollment counselors would pitch students on getting free grant money and not having to pay it back. In many cases they signed up for loans and didn't realize they had to pay those loans back. The UOP enrollment counselors weren't necessarily telling them they were taking out loans. The enrollment counselor gets the students to count toward his quota. The "Pell Runners" received their "walking around money," disappeared, and the school recognized the revenue, reported it to Wall Street, generating huge returns, and no one was the wiser or cared.

---

10   Source's words, not my own.

I pressed Cheddar Boy about recruiting practices such as giving loans to students in dire financial straits with no educational background prior to enrollment, and no true ability to pay back loans. He said, "Dude, I do that daily," referencing the disbursement of Pell grant money that ends up being used for personal expenses, with no intention of attending.

I asked, "How do you know someone is going to abscond with the money?"

"I know because they can't read. It happens all the time. Those students quit almost immediately and keep the money until they learn later they are on the hook for a couple thousand dollars of loans," he said.

* * * *

An Associated Press analysis showed a major influx of both low-income students and the recently boosted government money that follows them into for-profit schools, from local career colleges to giant publicly traded chains such as the UOP, Kaplan, and DeVry. In the previous year, the five institutions that received the most federal Pell grant dollars were all for-profit colleges, collecting over $1 billion among them. That was two and a half times what those schools hauled in just two years prior. This year, the trend is accelerating. In the first quarter after the maximum Pell grant was increased last July 1, Washington paid out 45% more through the program than during the same period a year ago, the AP found. But the amount of dollars heading to for-profit, or "proprietary," schools is up even more—about 67%.[11]

Associated Press reports: "For-profit colleges boost enrollment by lending to students with shaky credit. Some of the nation's biggest for-profit universities and vocational schools are boosting enrollment in tough times by increasing loans directly to cash-strapped students, knowing full well many of them won't be able to repay what they borrowed. The schools still make money because the practice boosts their enrollment and brings in extra tuition dollars subsidized by the government. But some of these students could end up saddled with high interest

---

11   Justin Pope, "For-profit colleges boost enrollment by lending to students with shaky credit," *Associated Press:* Raleigh, North Carolina.

rates and loan payments they can't handle, a burden that could damage their credit for years to come."

Almost every time Congress raised the amount of money students can borrow, schools raise their tuition by the same amount, thus pushing tuition up and capturing Congress's freebie instead of helping the students. The for-profit schools typically raised tuition by 5% per year, right through the recession.

* * * *

August 12, 2009: I published a report with APOL at $66 outlining my conversations with Cheddar Boy. I had already been talking to the SEC for months sending copies of my notes and research reports. I called the SEC and talked to them about this source and whether they wanted his contact information for their investigation. I really wanted to drive home the implications of what Cheddar Boy was saying. They took the information but never called him. I offered to bring him to Washington at my own expense and they still weren't interested.

September 2009

September 17, 2009: BMO Capital Markets said of a Bridgepoint audit recently made public: "Management provided additional color on the recent disclosure of its Office of Inspector General (OIG) audit. While most of the issues in the exit interview were discussed previously during the course of the audit (e.g., academic engagement), the focus on enrollment counselor incentive compensation caught the company a bit 'off guard.' The OIG apparently disagrees with the company's policy, which had been vetted with outside counsel, and did not necessarily accuse BPI of violating the incentive compensation regulations. A draft report is expected by the end of September, after which the company has 30 days to respond. A final report will be released thereafter, after which the company and the Department of Education can 'work through the findings and proceed.'"

* * * *

September 17, 2009: At an analyst conference, APOL discussed at length their graduation rates, suggesting they were working hard and had issued a mandate to grow the programs in the UOP. Regarding graduation rates, the company stated, "I believe the numbers were 27% for our associate degree students was it 43—sorry, 38% for our bachelors programs, and 60% for our graduate programs…I've seen the area that we have the most opportunity for improvement that is in the bachelor area in terms of getting that higher and we're focused on doing that. We've seen retention improvements the last of couple of years now."

To not confuse the reader I won't complicate the issue too much; however, it's very hard to know which numbers are actually being quoted. For example, they may be talking about associate degree students graduating in four years or bachelor students who graduate in eight years. Even using the ED's own web page can be tricky. According to the ED's site, UOP's online division, which is roughly 90% of revenue, had 359,464 undergraduate students in 2011-12 with 39,000 associate graduating and 32,000 bachelors', or about a 19% graduation rate.[12]

* * * *

September 18, 2009: I interviewed Cheddar Boy and another enrollment counselor on the opposite side of the country. Both sources confirmed that as of September 1, management was abandoning the policy of reducing enrollment counselor salary for failing to meet enrollment quotas. The decline in "free tuition" could cut into sales growth and enrollment growth as those ECs that had been hanging around for the free tuition would no longer have an incentive to do so. Again, outside of multi-level marketing companies, it's uncommon for a company to have employees as its customers at the same time. With the ED working on its program review started in February, management may have intentionally altered their compensation system to placate the ED. Surely that was a clue to short more stock.

---

12   http://nces.ed.gov/ipeds/datacenter/Default.aspx. The ED search engine.

If true, this new policy would alter the financial statements. Bonuses and commission are variable costs, whereas salaries alone are fixed costs. If enrollment counselors are earning more money from salary, APOL won't be able to lower its fixed costs fast enough. That means when the sales slow, earnings will go down at a much faster rate.

Cheddar told me the company was requiring enrollment counselors to generate referrals. In Phoenix the referral quota was ten per week; however, away from Phoenix, Cheddar Boy said his referral quota was only 18 per month. When pressed, he indicated that it was easy to get around the referral quota by simply opening the White Pages and copying down random names. Or, if he actually approached a student, the student often supplied names of family members or friends with little or no knowledge of UOP. I discounted this information from Cheddar.

When investors hear management on calls say that "lead flow" was strong, investors will assume that lead flow was coming from the Internet, where the company has much of its advertising. The number and quality of a "lead flow" coming from the company's banner advertising campaign was likely to be significantly better than random names pulled from a phone book. I was on the lookout for comments from management about lead flow on the next call. With the definition conveniently being altered, it will be interesting to hear how management talks about it to investors, which they may not bother doing.

CHAPTER 7

The GAO Goes Undercover

September 9, 2009. There were several rumors floating around about a scathing study conducted by the General Accountability Office (GAO). A few journalists mentioned it to me. Investors were starting to get more information out of the ED's negotiated rule-making process. Eventually, the 45-page GAO report investors were expecting was finally made public. [1,2]

Below are several of their comments:

"Through separate investigations at proprietary schools, we found test administrators or school officials violating rules to ensure prospective students without high school diplomas passed required tests and obtained access to Title IV aid. In addition to giving out test answers and falsifying test results, test administrators and officials at proprietary schools have violated other test rules, impairing the independence of the testing process and allowing ineligible students to access federal financial aid."

Students without a high school diploma or GED can qualify for Title IV loans, grants, and campus-based aid if they pass an independently administered test of basic math and English skills, called an "ability-to-benefit," or

1   "Stronger Department of Education Oversight Needed to Help Ensure Only Eligible Students Receive Federal Student Aid GAO-09-600," *Government Accountability Office,* August 17, 2009. However, the public didn't see it until September 21.

2   "Final Audit Report to Wonderlic," *Dept. of Education, http://www.ed.gov/about/offices/list/oig/auditreports/a03b0022.pdf,* Feb. 5, 2002. Unfortunately, ATB test manipulation was not something new. OIG wrote a scathing report in 2002 regarding the improper administration of the tests.

ATB test. The intent of the test was to measure whether students have the basic skills needed to benefit from higher education and succeed in school.

GAO said they conducted their own investigation of compliance with ATB requirements. (Paraphrasing) They found improper activities that compromised the integrity of the test process. They sent two GAO analysts, who posed as prospective students, to a local branch of a publicly traded proprietary school to deliberately flunk an ATB test. Each analyst was sent separately to the school and on both occasions, the independent test administrator gave them and all the test takers in the room—about 20 in total—answers to some of the test questions. They obtained copies of the analysts' test forms and found that they had been tampered with— their actual answers had been crossed out and changed—to ensure the analysts passed and would become eligible to receive Title IV funds.

"In the 2007-2008 school year, private for-profit schools—also known as proprietary schools—received over *$16 billion in loans, grants*, and campus-based aid for disbursement to students under Title IV of the Higher Education Act. Title IV funds for the proprietary sector have increased *164* percent since the 2001-2002 school year, and grown at a substantially faster rate than Title IV funds for the public and private non-profit sectors."

"More recently, from 2000 until 2008, four schools were subject to immediate loss, suspension, or termination from the Title IV program due to high default rates, *including three from the proprietary sector.*"

"Though the federal government and taxpayers pick up the majority of the costs on defaulted loans, students who default are also at risk of facing a number of personal and financial burdens. For example, defaulted loans will appear on the student's credit record, which may make it more difficult for them to obtain an auto loan, mortgage, or credit card. A negative credit record could also harm the student's ability to obtain a job or rent an apartment."

"Generally, prospective students without high school diplomas or GEDs must pass ATB tests to become eligible to receive federal financial aid, and test administrators are responsible for administering ATB tests at schools in accordance with test publisher rules. When we conducted our own investigation of compliance with ATB requirements, we found improper activities that compromised the integrity of the ATB test process. Students will also be ineligible for assistance under most federal loan programs and may not receive any additional Title IV federal student aid until the loan was repaid in full. In other words, they are blocked from the very opportunity that the industry claims to be providing."

"In addition to giving out test answers and falsifying test results, test administrators and officials at proprietary schools have violated other ATB test rules, impairing the independence of the testing process and allowing ineligible students to access federal financial aid."

"During our review, we identified cases in which proprietary schools helped students obtain high school diplomas from diploma mills—entities that provide invalid diplomas, usually for a fee and little academic work—in order to obtain access to federal student loans. Through one site visit and interview with students we learned of cases where recruiters at two separate publicly traded proprietary schools referred students to diploma mills for invalid high school diplomas in order to gain access to federal loans without having to take an ATB test."

"However, students who attend proprietary schools are more likely to default on their federal student loans, which can tarnish their credit records, make it difficult for them to obtain employment, and jeopardize their long-term financial well-being. Students from lower-income backgrounds can be particularly hurt when they default on their loans. In addition, *taxpayers and the government, which guarantees the loans, are left with the cost when students default on their school loans.*"

"Education officials told us that the department's official policy is that high school diplomas from diploma mills are not acceptable for Title IV eligibility and the department prosecutes diploma mill cases. Education officials told us they do not explicitly assert this policy in any written form… Education officials have acknowledged that the use of high school diplomas from diploma mills to obtain access to federal student aid is a problem and that *more guidance would be helpful.*"

* * * *

September 22, 2009: The report titled, "Proprietary Schools: Stronger Department of Education Oversight Needed to Help Ensure Only Eligible Students Receive Federal Student Aid," had a very narrow focus (i.e. default rates and eligibility requirements). Representative George Miller, Chairman of the House Education Committee, indicated in an emailed statement to Bloomberg that the GAO report's findings are "extremely troubling and warrant further examination by Congress" and that "the panel's subcommittee on higher education will hold hearings on whether for-profit schools are 'gaming the system' to enroll 'students who may not be fully ready for college and may be more likely to default' on loans."

* * * *

September 22, 2009: Yesterday has to be one of the most insane days I've ever seen in the stock market. The long-awaited GAO report came out. I was in New York City most of the day visiting with potential clients, and one mentioned in passing in our meeting that the GAO report came out. I didn't think too much of it until I arrived at home, where I found I had been inundated with messages. The stocks across the sector were up drastically. Apollo was up six or seven points to $74; ITT was up $10 or $11 to $115. Strayer was up in the $220 plus range. We were all incredulous. In reading through the report, the whole discussion was so one-sided; the for-profits were a total scam. I couldn't account for the rally.

* * * *

September 30, 2009: APOL announced they will release their earnings release for the fiscal year on October 27. The upcoming earnings report represents a significant threat to the stock price, not simply because of the actual earnings, but because the company would likely be releasing its 10-K. Because the ED program review had not been released yet, it was possible that the program review triggered an audit by the Office of Inspector General, and that a disclosure would represent serious "headline risk" to the stock price.

CHAPTER 8

Intra-quarter Churn

Over the weekend I was hiking in the woods, as I do when I have a lot of clutter in my head. On the trail I had a sudden epiphany. I could see in my mind's eye the "intra-quarter churn" model. It meant there must be a massive skim from students dropping in and out. After my hike in the woods that Sunday afternoon, I was so taken by the thought that I pulled out a crumpled piece of paper on the floor of my car and began to write a graphical representation of it (like inventing the flux capacitor in *Back to the Future*). After I came home, I scanned the diagram into a file and emailed it off to the SEC. Clients understood the magnitude of it better when I emailed them the graphic version. I had to think about its ramifications, but the "picture worth a thousand words" type response was having a strong effect on my clients, especially Steve Eisman. His level of understanding was on a higher level than most of my other clients.

* * * *

I was constantly checking complaints on ripoffreport.com. Especially when a former employee made a post, sometimes I would get lucky, as it would lead to new, smarter questions, or I was really lucky getting answers to questions. I found this: "I was in a meeting with all of the Online Finance Counselor [at UOP] Last Quarter the University started 100,000 students by the end of the Quarter only 50,000 students were still enrolled." My epiphany was that UOP and probably the other schools realized that if they enrolled a large percentage of low-income students with access to the Pell program, they could "skim" a portion of the money as revenue from students who dropped out over a couple of days or weeks. Poor students could come in, get their grant and loan, and not show up for class, allowing UOP some revenue, and putting the kid into collections.

This made me think. How was it possible that UOP could recruit 100,000 students during the quarter and only 50,000 remained? With that kind of revolving door, could management be skimming revenue from the students, charging them for a portion of the class they took, just a couple thousand dollars, and putting them in collections? Who would be the wiser? It was one thing to generate a little income from failed students, but something else entirely to systematically squeeze profits from dropped students, especially if the percentage of students dropping was anywhere near 50%, as I was beginning to believe.

In theory, if those numbers are right, it means that a significant portion of Apollo's revenue per quarter was being derived from students who dropped out intra-quarter, not just students who stayed in school. They could be recognizing revenue from 50,000 students per month who were recruited but dropped out somewhere along the way, as well as 50,000 students who were enrolled and stayed during the quarter. That means on an annual basis, there could be 600,000 students from whom Apollo was deriving revenue even though they dropped out each month.[1] That's probably high, but it illustrates the point. That's when things were going great, but now that enrollments are slowing, the issues are magnified as business slows.

It also meant that if their business slowed for any number of reasons, the new enrollment and total enrollment would inexplicably drop. Sure enough, that happened. In the fourth quarter of 2010 new enrollments were 92,000 down 10% year over year. However, because of some of the changes, like stopping incentive compensation, new enrollments in 2011 on average were down 40%, taking total enrollment down about 15% as well.

---

1   A separate source said UOP gets 81-87,000 applicants per month with about 50,000 enrolling.

Cheddar Boy told me that the each EC was expected to enroll ten students per month. At nearly 6,000 ECs x 10 x 12 months, that's 720,000 students, if everyone was making quota. While that's a stretch, the current enrollment is only 400,000, so the chances are reasonably high that there was some number between the two representing their true number of registrations.

* * * *

September 30, 2009: I wrote a report with APOL at $73. The upcoming earnings report represented a significant threat to the stock price, not simply because of the actual earnings, but because the company may be releasing its 10-K. Because the ED program review has not been released yet, it was possible it was being upgraded to an audit, and that disclosure would represent serious "headline risk" to the stock price. Management will deflect questions about the review on the call. Any mere mention of more scrutiny was enough to drive the stock price down. I expect the review to find multiple violations that are repeats from the 2003 program review, relating to incentive compensation, late refunds, and incorrect refunds, etc. While I am not aware of any other enforcement action by a state or federal agency, if the management was aware of any action, it should be disclosed in the 10-K.

Without the boiler shop mentality, and with a greater emphasis on retention, APOL's business model will fall apart. It's possible there could be a slight up-tick in retention, but I am confident that the reduced focus on making the enrollment quotas will offset short-term retention gains.

In the 2008-09 award years, the University of Phoenix earned $656 million dollars of Pell grant awards, $726 million the following year, and the year after that, $1.0 billion. If each Pell award was $5,000, it means that 200,000 students came into the school (or more students with lower grants per student). In the year with $656 million there were approximately 230,000 Pell recipients; by 2010 UOP had over 400,000 students. It leaves open the possibility that they have a rich source of revenue from Pell recipients because not only are those students getting grants, but they are getting loans, too, perhaps as high $10,000, which would lead to a lot of revenue as long as the machine worked. Multiple former employees verified this practice of showing students how to game the system.

APOL Pell recipients jumped to 243,949 from 161,146. In FY2009, the company had over 400,000 students, peaking at 476,500 in the third quarter of 2010. That means that over 50% of UOP's enrollments could have been Pell recipients, with a large percentage of those being Pell Runners.

The Pell grant program has lost its way, as it suddenly became a welfare program. The trends in revenue from Pell grants are disturbing. I am fearful that access to college for the poor may cause the Administration or Congress to overlook the impropriety of the Pell Runners. The government will assume some abuse or slippage in the program (which APOL was taking full advantage of) as an acceptable cost to ensuring access to college. I would argue—though politicized Congressmen may disagree—that the "Pell Runner" phenomenon was bleeding so much money that it was really a welfare program and not an education program.

If our enrollment counselor was accurate and approximately 50% of enrollments are Pell Runners, then it would follow that the government would slow or deny schools from abusing the Pell Program. This was a battle Bob Shireman was now fighting. He wants to reallocate student loan program money away from the for-profits, knowing that the level of abuse was substantial and not in the taxpayers' best interest. Rational minds prevailing was not a given. There was a political threat to the short in the above manner, as the whole industry will parade itself as providing a public service to benefit the lowest-class students.

October 2009

My clients, meanwhile, were concerned about the possibility of a settlement in *Hendow*. There was a whistleblower against Westwood College (another for-profit school) that was settled for $7 million. I called Jay Majors at the DOJ upon first reading about the case in June. He told me (paraphrasing) that--there is a formula for the settlement but I am not telling you what it is, and hung up. I called Jillian and asked her to assign a value to the APOL settlement if there is a trial. She indicated a judgment could be "in the hundreds of millions" because the Westwood case only involved three out of 17 schools. Hence, given UOP's size, the settlement would likely exceed $100 million. Around this same time two more whistleblower lawsuits were filed against the industry, one against ESI and the other against COCO; both were similar to *Hendow*.

* * * *

October 7, 2009: Last night, the House Higher Education, Lifelong Learning, and Competitiveness Subcommittee announced a hearing on "Ensuring Student Eligibility Requirements for Federal Aid" scheduled for October 14, 2009. These hearings are in response to the Government Accountability Office's (GAO) September 21 report. In reaction to the GAO's release, Representative George Miller, Chairman of the House Education Committee, indicated that the House would hold hearings on whether for-profit schools are "gaming the system" to enroll "students who may not be fully ready for college and may be more likely to default" on Federal loans.

* * * *

October 7, 2009: Cheddar walked me through the Pell Runner issue, citing the frustration of a student who he enrolled recently. He contacted the student, who had received a $3,000 Pell grant check. The student said, "Oh, I spent that" on a computer, rent, and some other belongings. I asked Cheddar about the number of Pell grant students who actually apply the Pell money to the cost of their education. The answer was an emphatic "Zero!" Cheddar indicated that in July of 2009, enrollment counselors went through an hour and a half "Responsible Borrowing" training course at UOP. The training was a half-hearted attempt to prevent the Pell Runner sales tactics. Enrollment Counselors are told *not* to tell the student the exact amount of Pell money that would be coming in, but rather, only tell them that based on experience, Pell money would be coming in at a later date. Everyone knows the training is bullshit, a mere smokescreen so UOP can say they trained ECs to not recruit Pell Runners.

I pressed him on whether or not this has had the impact of slowing enrollment of students with no intention of attending. "No," he said, to my surprise. Many of the students being recruited "from the 'hood" can still be steered into enrolling using loans, he explained. The whole financial process with the student takes about 15 minutes to walk through. Because the prospective students are generally limited in their financial knowledge, they often don't understand the loan documents they are signing. A mother of three from the projects on welfare with only $8,000 of annual income can typically be talked into $5,000 or $10,000 worth of loans. The new "Responsible Borrowing" program prevents the ECs from telling the prospective student the precise amount of Pell money they will be receiving, reducing the use of Pell money as what amounts to a signing bonus. Again, the school wants to make it look like they didn't know what was going on, but they did.

Cheddar used this example: If classes cost $8,800 and the student will likely get $5,000 from Pell, the student will borrow $3,800, as opposed to the maximum amount, closer to $10,000. Now, enrollment counselors are supposed to enroll students with 50% of their financing secured, and then if the Pell amount doesn't come through as expected, the EC goes back to the student and forces them to borrow more money, at which point the student either drops out under the threat of collections or borrows more money. In essence, every enrollment counselor doubles as a collections agent. I again asked if he is the only enrollment counselor to pursue Pell Runners so aggressively. He indicated that he was the only one who was willing to talk about it, but everyone does it. What he said made sense but I was starting to question his value as a source.

Technically, there was no law to prevent the industry from going into the low-income projects recruiting single moms with lavish promises of grant money. Who would make it a law to restrict schools from enrolling unqualified students just to get access to the grant money? That makes no sense unless you are a publicly traded company booking a lot of grant and loan revenue from federally guaranteed loans.

Cheddar explained what the homework was that he had to do to help his enrollment. We went through the homework assignment together. How bad could it be? Now, I would see if Cheddar was being dramatic.

The homework assignment instructions read: "View the story below and construct a 350-400 word scenario in which you explain distance learning to a friend. Explain how Axia courses work and use the following terms at least once: Threaded Discussion, Forums, Asynchronous Communication and Feedback." Not exactly something one would see at a real college.

Then it has a point system, 60 points for using each word correctly, explaining the concept of distance education, and effectively incorporating how the online courses work. There are an additional ten points available for "mechanics." There are seven points possible for rules of grammar and punctuation and three points for spelling. That's the homework they are making these kids do and the taxpayers are subsidizing this crap? Are you kidding me? I was being reminded why I am writing the book for all to see. I bet that is still going on and no one is the wiser. For-profit education has no business model to speak of if they haven't invested in properly qualified teachers.

* * * *

At a Congressional hearing on the GAO report, GAO director George Scott told that the agency had "identified potential fraud at a few (for-profit) schools." After attending the hearing, Wedbush wrote that it reinforced its positive outlook on the for-profit education sector. The firm noted that government officials had said that fraud was not widespread among for-profit institutions. Wedbush, a brokerage firm, stated that concerns about the sector could be overdone, and thought that government officials were able to understand the difference between quality and "subprime" for-profit postsecondary schools.

On October 14, 2009 Mary Mitchelson, Acting Inspector General, testified before the HELP subcommittee. "Currently, we have 15 open ATB-related investigative matters," she said. "Our closed ATB investigations have resulted in jail sentences, restitutions, fines, and other significant penalties for wrongdoers." That was in reaction to the GAO.

She continued, "In order to receive federal student aid, an individual must be a 'regular student,' that is, someone 'enrolled for . . . the purpose of obtaining a degree, certificate, or other recognized credential.' *A student must also certify that the aid will be used solely for education-related expenses.* For their part, institutions are obligated to return any Federal student aid received if a student does not begin attendance during the period for which aid was awarded. Institutions must be able to document attendance in at least one class during a payment period."

So the for-profit industry wants to argue plausible deniability and cry ignorance? They are innocent if students are lying about their intentions? The school keeps itself ignorant of students' desire to go to school? And they call that capitalism?

"If a student begins attendance and later drops out or withdraws, institutions must determine what funds must be repaid to the Federal student aid programs or to the student. The HEA and Department regulations require the return of funds in proportion to the uncompleted portion of the payment period. This framework provides unique *management challenges and opportunities for abuse* in programs that are offered through distance or on-line instruction."

The 2008 audit of Capella University found that the school did not have adequate controls to determine whether students actually began attendance in on-line classes. Capella then failed to return funds for students who dropped out *before their first day of class*, and continued to disburse funds for students who did not return for subsequent payment periods. Capella failed to return over $500,000 in federal student aid from 2002 to 2005. Clearly, they didn't look hard enough if that's all they found.

But the OIG was all over UOP's Axia division, thankfully. "As of September 30, six individuals have been sentenced and another has pled guilty for their roles in an on-line fraud scheme at Axia College, a two-year on-line college of the University of Phoenix. The scheme's two ringleaders were former employees of ACS, a third party servicer to the school, who recruited individuals to enroll at Axia in order to fraudulently obtain student financial aid. The former employees assisted the individual in completing the enrollment forms and student aid applications, then enrolled the individuals in the classes and posted homework assignments for them in order for it to appear as though the individuals were attending the online courses. When the individuals received their student aid checks, they would kick back a portion to the two ringleaders. Axia College referred this matter to us for investigation."[2] If this was happening on a small level, why not look at the whole company to ensure it is not just a few bad actors?

* * * *

On the OIG's investigative reports web page, I noticed a steady increase in student loan enforcement activities. If the OIG were to be successful in proving intent to defraud the government, the case could encourage future legal action against Pell Runners. "In one investigation, 64 of the 65 defendants charged in the 130-count indictment from June 2009 have appeared in federal court to face charges that they were part of a scheme to defraud the U.S. Government out of more than a half-million dollars in student loans."

"A conviction for each count of Conspiracy or Financial Aid Fraud carries a maximum *penalty of five years in federal prison*, a $250,000 fine or both. Every conviction for False Statements in Connection With Financial Aid carries a maximum penalty of one year, $100,000 fine or both. Each conviction for Mail Fraud carries a maximum penalty of 20 years, a $250,000 fine or both." Keep going!

* * * *

I pressed Cheddar Boy regarding the allegation in the IG report that former employees of a subcontractor filled out FAFSA forms on behalf of potential students. He said that sometimes students don't know how to operate

2   "Statement of Mary Mitchelson Before the Subcommittee on Higher Education, Lifelong Learning, and Competitiveness," *Dept. of Education,* http://www2.ed.gov/about/offices/list/oig/auditrpts/stmt102009.pdf, October 14, 2009.

a computer. When pressed as to whether management specifically tells ECs to engage in illegal or unethical business practices, he indicated that management doesn't have to tell ECs how to behave; in order to survive ECs have to do things the school would say were against company policy. "They know what we are saying, after all, they brag about spending a ton of money on monitoring ECs' phone conversations."

I've paraphrased his account as follows: The enrollment managers are mostly former successful enrollment counselors and you can only become successful by engaging in behavior where management looks the other way. The bad behavior that occurs regularly was a function of the EC quotas. There was no specific smoking gun. Source said that if pressed, management can document that ECs were trained, but everyone knows that the training documents are a joke.[3]

He went on to say that in reality, no one would be making quota without engaging in illegal practices. "We purposefully go after these people [the poor] that don't stand a chance of staying in class. I had no business admitting a couple students. It's just a never-ending battle. I enrolled 13 people for the month of October. Half of them don't have an eighth grade reading level. UOP doesn't say don't enroll them; they just look the other way. I enroll guys and women at the [homeless] shelter all the time. They want their Pell money. Last week, I enrolled two sisters and a boyfriend. They call every day because they want their Pell money so they can move. Another enrollee keeps calling because she wants the Pell money for a down payment on a house. We are not allowed to tell them when they might get the money."

* * * *

October 18, 2009: Donna emailed me, "Regardless of whether a school is required to take attendance, the withdrawal date (date from which refunds are calculated) for a student who provide notice of withdrawal is the date on which the notice is provided. This is why the issue of whether

---

3   Fiscal year 2010—For example, cash used for investing activities primarily consisted of $168.2 million for capital expenditures principally related to investments in our computer equipment and software. He's got a point. For extra credit, I recommend investigators find out where all that money really went.

a student provides notice of withdrawal becomes critical. If the student says they want to withdraw, but then the school subsequently talks the student into "thinking it over" and "trying a few more days," then the record of the notice of withdrawal can be murky."

"Students who simply quit attending, with no notice that they are withdrawing, are the problem. If a school is required (by state or accrediting agency rules) to take attendance, the withdrawal date is the last date of attendance, regardless of notice of withdrawal. But for schools that are not required to take attendance, the school is allowed to treat the 50% point as the date of withdrawal."

* * * *

I decided to do some hands-on investigation myself and send someone to my local UOP office in Connecticut to pose as a potential student. They said his work experience could be converted to credits, which could later be transferred to the University of Connecticut or Yale. Total Pell money available was $5,350, and tuition was $8,840 per year or roughly $17,000 for an associate's degree. My investigator said, "I am poor. I have two kids on child support. I am broke." The enrollment counselor said that with $9,500 of student loan money the school would write a check for the overage from loans plus Pell grants.

"How do the classrooms work?" he asked. The UOP rep responded: It works the same as email except it's a chat room. The enrollment counselor was currently in a graduate program. She logged on to show her classroom. She said, you only have to attend four out seven classes and you only have to send email to two other students. The teacher posts a question and you send email back and forth with the other students or call them to discuss the answer. There are no right or wrong answers for the class. I just tell others how I feel about the question. The papers only have to be 750 words long. For the first two classes there are no tests. There are seven students in the class; two in Georgia, one in New York, and another in California, and the enrollment counselor in Connecticut. On-ground courses only meet once a week for four hours. The enrollment counselor only takes one class every six weeks. But you can take "breaks" of up to 29 days if you are on financial aid. For every class the enrollment counselor takes, she takes a week off. In class you learn how to write. As long as you know how to read and write you'll do great, she told us.

* * * *

October 26, 2009: Steve Burd wrote a blistering account of what he called "The subprime student loan racket":

"While researching her options online, Student A stumbled on the web site for Everest College, part of the Corinthian Colleges chain, which pictured students in lab coats and scrubs probing a replica of a human heart and a string of glowing testimonials from graduates."

"When she contacted the admissions office, she was told she would receive hands-on training from experienced nurses in state-of-the-art labs with the most modern equipment… She also says recruiters told her that she would be able to do rotations at the University of California, Los Angeles Medical Center, one of the nation's best hospitals…She was intrigued, though she was initially put off by the $29,000 tuition. But the school's recruiters assured her there was nothing to be concerned about: Everest had an exceptional track record of helping students find employment…"

She decided to enroll. The day she came in to fill out her paperwork, the recruiters rushed her through the process and discouraged her from taking the forms home to look over. They told her that she would be taking out private loans in addition to federal loans. But the EC did not explain what the terms of those loans would be. 'They just kept telling me that "we're with you," and that they would try to get me the maximum amount of federal loans allowed,' she says. Only later did she learn that those private loans—which made up two-thirds of her "financial aid" package— carried double-digit interest rates and other onerous terms.

The program did not come close to delivering on the promises that had been made. The instructors had little recent medical experience. They usually just read textbooks aloud in class and sometimes offered students the answers on tests ahead of time instead of teaching.

Since graduating in 2008, Student A has been unable to find a nursing job, because she never learned how to perform basic tasks such as giving shots. Instead, she works as an occasional home health care aid earning at the most $1,200 a month—not enough to pay her rent on the cramped apartment she shares with her sister. She can't afford gas in her car, much less pay off her student loans. Her loan balance has ballooned to $40,000, and she has no idea how she will ever pay it off. 'My credit is ruined,' she says. 'I made one mistake, and I will be paying for it for the rest of my life.'"

Sixty percent of bachelor's degree recipients at for-profit colleges graduate with $30,000 or more in student loans—one and a half times the percentage of those at traditional private colleges and three times more than those at four-year public colleges and universities, according to the College Board. *Similarly, those who earn two-year degrees from proprietary schools rack up nearly three times as much debt as those at community colleges*, which serve a similar student population. Proprietary school students are more likely to take on private student loans, which, are not guaranteed by the federal government, offer scant consumer protections, and tend to charge astronomical interest as high as 20%.

"Sallie Mae clearly understood that these private loans were going mostly to subprime borrowers who might not be able to pay them back; in 2007, Senate investigators uncovered internal company documents showing that executives expected a staggering *70 percent of its private student loans at one for-profit school to end in default*. Investigators concluded that Sallie Mae viewed these loans as a 'marketing expense'—a token sum to be paid in exchange for the chance to gorge on federal funds."

To the school, as long as students were enrolled long enough to be considered a 'start,' meaning that they attended classes for a week or two, the schools got to keep some of the money, and they got to include students in their official enrollment tally, which gave Wall Street the impression they were expanding. It didn't matter whether students would be able to pay off their debt.

"The frenzy only intensified after Congress passed the Bankruptcy Abuse Prevention and Consumer Protection Act in 2005. This made it almost impossible for those who took out private student loans to discharge them in bankruptcy and, not surprisingly, turned the private student loan market into a much more appealing for lenders."

Sallie Mae quit offering subprime private loans to students at for-profit colleges because the astronomical default rates had helped throw its stock price into a nosedive. By making private loans directly to students, much the way used-car lots loan money to buyers rather than going through a third party, the proprietary college industry has found a way around this roadblock. Corinthian said on a recent conference call that it plans to dole out roughly $130 million in "institutional loans" this year, while Career Education and ITT Educational Services Inc., another for-profit chain, have reported that they expect to lend a combined total of $125 million."

October 28, 2009: In an earnings report, APOL acknowledged, "During October 2009, we received notification from the Enforcement Division of the Securities and Exchange Commission indicating that they had commenced an informal inquiry into our *revenue recognition practices.*" Later, they expanded that investigation to include insider trading. Several years later the SEC closed both investigations of Apollo without consequence. I tried to use the FOIA for the investigation results. The SEC had 63 cases of legal boxes costing $14,000 to get them.

APOL closed at $73 before the earnings and was trading at $57 range after the close of the market. I recommended pressing the short at these levels, saying the for-profit sector was likely tainted by APOL's announcement that the SEC was investigating the company's revenue recognition. Until investors are given more clarity as to the SEC's intentions, the uncertainty will weigh the stocks across the space. APOL reported accounts receivables up over $100 million to $298 million versus $192 million sequentially on a $25 million increase in sales. APOL has not disclosed or discussed making loans directly to students, as their private loan exposure was low (4%) when SLM cut back private loan volume in 1Q08.[4] Perhaps the SEC was looking at this new practice of buying one's revenue stream across the space. As long as there is conjecture, the group may remain compressed. It would follow that the SEC may have further inquiries from former management working at other companies, like LOPE, BPI, and EDMC.

The SEC investigation announcement hit the stocks in the sector, but I was surprised at the relatively low revenue number. Increased competition had an impact as well. Twice during the call, management alluded to preferring slower sales growth in return for higher retention. That's the first crack of the revenue unwinding itself, turning negative, especially if several students are being counted as currently enrolled and are in fact not attending classes. APOL claimed, "Over the last several months we've embarked on a companywide initiative to enhance our strategic plan and position ourselves for responsible growth...while balancing this against our responsibility to ensure that only students who have a reasonable chance to succeed enroll in our universities." Management was hounded by the Street regarding tracking attendance, refunds, etc. As these issues wash out, this relatively new management will find itself unable to maintain retention at the expense of student quality.

The following week the ED was holding its first negotiated rule-making hearing. I spoke to a member of the committee, who told me that the discussion would be about the Safe Harbor provisions. Specifically, the Committee would be reviewing incentive compensation, misrepresenta-

---

4   Note that DV reported after the close as well, with A/R increasing to $156.9 million from $104 million sequentially on sales of $396M to $431M. Year over year the A/R was nearly flat at $154; however, in 2Q08, A/R was $55 million, which was approximately when direct loans were ramping up.

tion of information by enrollment counselors (graduation/placement & transfer of credits), and the way schools report start and stop dates for students.

* * * *

October 22, 2009: ITT Education also reported earnings, with some rather negative news. ESI had a trading range of $107 to $114 two days before the earnings. It looked like it was going to run to $125 on a good earnings number, which hurts if you are the short guy. Look out! The next day it rolled to $110, but then the stock was crushed, trading as low as $96 before closing at $103. I didn't have the guts to recommend shorting the stock in front of that earnings report because I did so the prior quarter and was killed. I can't win. (I redeemed myself later in January 2010)

* * * *

October 30, 2009: Dan Golden of Bloomberg wrote a great article, titled "Apollo Weakness for Phoenix Revenues Spurring Short Sellers": "The University of Phoenix, the largest for-profit college in the U.S., may have set off on a collision course with the federal government and investors in 2001. Now, the SEC was investigating how Apollo books revenue, the company said Oct. 27. Apollo recorded a charge of $80.5 million to cover costs it expects to pay to settle a lawsuit alleging that it violated federal student recruitment rules. Apollo shares, which had more than doubled since 2006, may have difficulty rebounding from an 18 percent decline the day after the SEC probe was disclosed. Phoenix may also face scrutiny as the U.S. Education Department examines for-profit universities that rely heavily on taxpayer-supported financial aid. In fiscal 2009, Phoenix derived 86 percent of its $3.77 billion in revenue from federal grants and loans, up from 48 percent in 2001, and approaching a federal limit of 90 percent."

November 2009

November 5, 2009: CECO's conference call dragged the group down: Management said on their last call that they expected AIU to be able to introduce new programs in early 2010. At this point, it appeared new program introductions would take longer than expected. In May 2008, the HLC made certain recommendations to AIU as part its initial grant of accreditation. After submitting new programs for approval, the HLC advised AIU in October that the granting of new program approvals would be subject to satisfying certain recommendation that were associated with the initial grant of accreditation including the completion of the focus visit. As a result, the introduction of new programs at AIU would be delayed beyond the previous estimate.[5]

The accreditors look the other way most of the time when it comes to enforcement. The HLC has the worst reputation in the industry and the ED IG has written about the corruption of accreditors, specifically the HLC. Therefore, for the HLC to take issue with anything regarding CECO would possibly signal a shift in their position toward regulation—realizing the ED was about to crack the whip on them. Since the HLC was an APOL accreditor, this move could benefit the short thesis.

As with other schools, the HLC has also been the target of criticism over transfer of credit policies. The HLC's official policy (3.8) on transfer of credits (as of June 2008) reads: "Each institution shall determine its own policies and procedures for accepting transfer credits, including credits from accredited and non-accredited institutions, from foreign institutions, and from institutions which grant credit for experiential learning and for non-traditional adult learner programs."

In another OIG audit in July of 2003, the IG sharply criticized the department's lack of oversight over the accrediting agencies, and the problem has hardly improved since then. The department relies on the accrediting agencies for quality of education. The ED needs to improve management controls over accrediting agencies recognized by the Secretary. The improvements are needed to ensure that the accrediting agen-

---

5   COCO was another school that attracted a lot of attention from its accreditor in Tsai vs. COCO and other lawsuits for shady business practices (*Satz v. COCO* and *Conway v. COCO*).

cies have established standards to address institutions' success with respect to student achievement and measures of program length, and that the agencies monitor adherence to the standards and take enforcement action when institutions are not in compliance with the standards.

* * * *

November 11, 2009: JP Morgan stated, "[APOL's] management's tone around compliance and accounting was comforting to us. While co-CEO Cappelli did not give any updates to the timeframe or the scope of the SEC inquiry, he sounded credible and engaged in the business. Mr. Cappelli repeated his confidence with APOL's accounting policies particularly related to revenue recognition and internal controls in various parts of the firm. The current senior management team had first worked with APOL in a consulting capacity tasked with (along with forensic accountants) scrubbing its financial statements. Since then, management made numerous operational enhancements, including finance and HR functions. Furthermore, senior management and the company's auditors signed off on the 10-K."

* * * *

November 20, 2009: Cheddar Boy and I talked about retention. He said only 16% of students he recruits show up for the second class (not much different from others in the office). Now, the school is making people sign a paper telling them they have the right to hold back their excess funds. This is to get away from the Pell Runner issue. The school is supposed to disburse grant money to the student. "All of my students are unemployed."

Q: In general, how many leads/people that come through the Internet are unemployed?

A: 75%. We have been told to mark down that they are unemployed so they can get more money. It's terrible working here. All of the responsibility falls on the counselors. There are no qualifications.

Q: Don't you tell the students that they are going to have to pay back the loans?

A: These people care about keeping their lights on, not their FICO score. I enrolled a girl yesterday. She borrowed $9,500 + $5,300 Pell. I explained the difference between a grant and the loan. She doesn't care about the loan. She'll never pay it back. If I told them that it may be cheaper to go to a community college, I would be fired immediately.

The official policy reads: "To enter an associate or bachelor degree program, you must have earned a high school diploma, GED, California High School Proficiency Examination certificate, or foreign secondary school equivalent. You must be currently employed. If you are not employed, *you must have access to an organizational environment that allows you to apply the concepts you learn in our courses.* Selected undergraduate programs require applicants entering with less than 24 transferable credits to have current employment or access to an organizational environment and one year of full-time work experience."

* * * *

November 25, 2009: APOL ($55): APOL's upcoming quarter will be the last quarter positive year over year revenue growth for several years. The for-profit sector was particularly vulnerable to regulatory changes given that they have pushed the envelope so far for so long. With the focus now on the legislative and regulatory changes, it is worth noting the financial statements will be negatively affected by these changes. I have heard through the grapevine that the company has discontinued the practice of lowering the salary for enrollment counselors who miss their quota. This was a preemptive move to placate the ED that will slow growth in the current and upcoming quarters. At a recent analyst meeting, APOL management told investors of their intention to move back toward higher quality students with lower dropout rates. Similarly, I view this as pre-emptive. The relatively new management may be unaware of the full extent of the Pell Runner issue. Had they been informed, they would probably not have signed on as new executives. They think they are making the prudent move to stem the Pell Runners, not realizing that the unwinding impact of the math will be near fatal. Fifty percent or more of their enrollments will dropout.

December 2009

Near the close of 2009, the Safe Harbors issue began to receive scrutiny again. *The Chronicle of Higher Education* reported, the ED is eliminating the Safe Harbor provisions on incentive compensation, reverting back to 2002. I called the ED's General Counsel to ask if the ED removes the Safe Harbors, whether they would be removing the Hansen memo as well, which limited the liability for enrolling students using commission. No answer.

Then, BMO Capital Markets forecast, "Eliminating the Safe Harbors (i.e., exemptions), which had allowed some incentive compensation to be paid, could have some disruptive operating impact on the for-profit post-secondary schools, should it lead to the loss of some highly productive recruiters who would 'lose' their bonuses."

"While this change could hurt margins (e.g., cost of training replacements) and enrollment growth, we nevertheless believe *the impact would be minimal* (a few quarters) and would not materially change long-term growth projections. Other proposed changes include significantly increasing the number and types of 'misrepresentations' to students, adding more aspects of the institution's academic requirements, state approval of specific academic programs, and information about the availability of financial aid. Another round of NegReg continues next week. Final regulations are expected to be effective July 1, 2011. While we believe these proposals were expected, including eliminating incentive compensation, the group could nevertheless see some pressure this morning."

* * * *

December 2nd, 2009 "Congress is moving ahead on a proposal to improve credit protections for consumers that may lead lawmakers to examine the merits and dangers behind a growing practice: colleges that lend directly to their own students. The legislation (HR 3126), scheduled for a vote next week, calls for the creation of a new federal watchdog agency, known as the Consumer Financial Protection Agency, that would be responsible for ensuring the fair treatment of student borrowers. Its area of jurisdiction would cover banks and other companies and companies providing student loans."

"The agency as currently proposed, however, would *explicitly exclude* for-profit colleges from its oversight authority and may not apply to some other types of colleges, at a time when institutions in the for-profit sector and beyond are being encouraged by some financial strategists to accelerate the practice of issuing their own student loans. Many of those for-profit colleges are now lending money directly to their students, as a way of coping in the absence of banks that, in the face of the current economic downturn, have been increasingly unable or unwilling to lend to their students, Mr. Williams said."[6]

* * * *

December 14, 2009: Apollo announced the settlement of the *Hendow* suit, which they settled for $78.5 million, $1.5 million less than the $80 million, which was the amount they reserved at the end of last quarter. John Sperling, the chairman of APOL, was deposed in the case. I really wanted to get it after reading his last depositions. It was put under protective order, so I couldn't get it.

The news of the settlement drove Apollo prices from $55 to $62. The Company came out with some PR noise saying it was confident it would not face any further civil or administrative exposure relating to its compliance with the HEA provision relating to incentive compensation for the period of March 1997 through the present as a result of the various releases and related agreements it had obtained from the DOE, DOJ, and the plaintiffs.

According to one reliable source, the Obama Administration insisted on, and rammed through, a nominal sum the Administration wanted to see the *Hendow* case settle for, letting the UOP get off the hook for less than a penny on the dollar of actual treble damages and penalties. For

---

6   Paul Basken, "Congress Mulls Consumer Protections as Colleges Increasingly Lend to Their Own Students," *Chronicle of Higher Education,* http://chronicle.com/article/Congress-Mulls-Consumer/49319/, Dec. 2, 2009.

people fighting the fraud, the $78.5 million nominal settlement of *Hendow* was simply a joke after the $9.8 million token administrative fine levied by the Bush Administration Department of Education following the scathing 2004 Program Review of UOP. Under both administrations, UOP has wielded enormous political power, effectively immunizing itself and its executives from civil and criminal liability for conduct in violation of the Higher Education Act and the False Claims Act.

* * * *

Paul Basken of the *Chronicle of Higher Education* wrote an interesting article about the rise student loan defaults.[7] "Among more than 5,000 colleges with students receiving federal financial assistance in the 2007, 221 colleges had default rates of 30 percent or greater on the three-year measure, the data showed, according to new Education Department figures."

"That's more than six times the number exceeding the current limit, in which the department considers defaults over a two-year period and makes colleges ineligible for federal aid—a source of money that is critical to the survival of most institutions—if too many of their past students fail to pay back their loans on time."

"'The only thing that explains default rate is the socioeconomic background' of the student, said Harris N. Miller, president of the Career College Association, which represents for-profit institutions. 'By using that as the metric of quality, you will always be discriminating against low-income students.'"

* * * *

More news came out late yesterday on default rates from the DOE. Estimated lifetime rates for two-year for-profit schools are at *47%*. Consider that number for a moment…approximately half of the young kids

---

7　　Paul Basken, "New Measure of Student-Loan Defaults Could Threaten Hundreds of Colleges," *Chronicle of Higher Education, http://chronicle.com/article/New-Measure-of-Student-Loan/49484/?sid=at&utm_source=at&utm_medium=en, Dec. 14, 2009.*

entering these schools will have their credit destroyed by defaulting. Why are these schools allowed to continue bilking students and taxpayers at such a staggering rate? It's inexcusable.[8]

Recently Department of Education numbers also show that the estimated default rates spiked to 21.2% (up 93%) at the average for-profit school when calculating defaults over a three-year, rather than two-year period.[9] If two-year programs at for-profits were at 47%, then a large pool of schools must have been very low, possibly around 10%, to get to the average of 21%.

Several schools are at high default levels and risk losing Title IV eligibility. These schools will ramp up default rate management programs to reduce recorded defaults before they result in any action by DOE. Rather than slowing down inappropriate enrollments and selecting only quality students, profit-oriented schools promise to implement the fix by managing the back-end.

* * * *

December 17, 2010: Late in the day, there was a document circulated around the Street, an OIG report that was suggesting the HLC's license should be revoked, suspended, or terminated because of the lax enforcement of the for-profit colleges, specifically CECO. The document talked about how CECO had moved from SACS over to the HLC and how their programs were weak. At this time, Apollo was down 5% to $57.38.

January 2010

I had taken flak from some of my clients, who were claiming that Cheddar was but one rogue enrollment counselor, a bad apple that I was placing too much value on. So I tried to crank him up a bit, playing the Devil's advocate and being argumentative. He said, "I just put in a person today

---

8   Daniel Golden, "Marine Can't Recall His Lessons at For-Profit College," *Bloomberg*, http://www.bloomberg.com/apps/news?pid=20601109&sid=aGMaO24.IPO8&pos=10, Dec. 15, 2009.

9   "Default Rates," *Dept. of Education, http://ifap.ed.gov/eannouncements/attach-ments/121409EACDRlifetimerateattachment2ratechartPPD.pdf, Nov. 13, 2009.*

that has a sixth grade reading level. It took forever to do the application. He can barely read. No one cares. Nobody asks."

Passionately he reacted to me, saying, "What is the assurance that these people can do some semblance of the work? If I don't meet my enrollment goals I get written up. If I don't have to make my quota then I don't care if you show up. You don't understand the boiler room effect here. The graduation rates show how unsuccessful students are. If I am an anomaly then why is the school overrun with all of these poor people? Someone needs to justify why a student doesn't have to show aptitude to succeed at the school." He was fired up, for sure, and passionate about his feelings toward UOP.

I asked him how many enrollment counselors at his campus behave like him, recruiting poor students (Pell Runners) so aggressively. Answer: "Anyone who has had my tenure here, three years, (the vast majority of them) behave the way I do toward recruiting. Everyone in enrollment is a Pell Runner [they are students as well as enrollment counselors]. Everybody does it. Everyone knows this. Students are intrigued by the amount of Pell money they can get when they are out of work. We go through compliance training to say we don't do that but that's how it is done."

Cheddar was ranting a little: The hard numbers show that students are not benefiting from a UOP education because so many of them drop out. There should be no discussion about graduation and salary correlation when none graduate. APOL has an 18% graduation rate for full-time first-time students and 25% retention for the first year. Those are the numbers we are told quote to students. Twenty-five percent is companywide! There are no numbers for the second year because no one completes the second year! Why is no one talking about that? Why isn't the government asking those questions?

* * * *

January 4, 2010: Apollo ($61). In the absence of short-term catalysts, excluding the Program Review, I am moderately concerned about what unseen risk exists in the APOL short. Today, short investors (and bulls) are facing the same issues in APOL: that on an earnings basis the group looks cheap. Many potential investors are unaware of the issues at UOP and could possibly step up to buy the shares, reflected in the rally from $53 to $62. If one believes that the NegRegs and associated regulatory events are already "in the stock," then I fail to see the next big short-term catalyst that would drive the stock price down. For this reason, I am inclined to believe the stock could rally after its next earnings report.

The risk to the bulls was more disclosure from the company regarding the SEC investigation (which I doubt) and information requests from other regulatory or accrediting bodies. Some of the peripheral changes the company was rumored to have made over the last couple of months could impact the financial statements in the upcoming quarter. In theory, there was an inverse relationship between retention and enrollments. Fewer Pell Runners lowers enrollments and averages up better quality students (retention, in theory). The quarter should have a mix shift in full swing. It doesn't follow that higher enrollments and higher retention students would occur simultaneously, within the same quarter, or year, as the new policy goes into effect. The NegReg risk to the company was *not* enough to drive the shares down further on the earnings call.

* * * *

I interviewed an APOL enrollment counselor who said there are many low-credit quality people coming to UOP. These are not necessarily low-end students being recruited intentionally by aggressive enrollment counselors, but unemployed people who want to beat the system by getting Pell grants. However, the conflict of interest for ECs to meet their quotas, coupled with the rapid rise in Pell money being awarded, suggestions that enrollment counselors have little incentive to turn away questionable students. She expressed regret over the rampant exploitation and bad corporate behavior by the company.

I shared with her some of Cheddar Boy's comments, prompting this response regarding Pell Runners: "That does happen, but I am not sure it's the rule." Too many people would drop out and that person would be fired—unless they can convince the student to show up for the second class, in which case that enrollment was credited toward the EC's quota. He clearly has the ability to succeed in keeping students in class long enough to make quota. She refuses to pressure students for referrals, knowing once the student's family member or friend is in the system, they are fair game for relentless cold-calling (ignoring Do Not Call limitations) and emails. Ironically, source taught Human Resource Management at UOP. APOL's outsourced EAP firm was being overrun by anxiety-ridden employees stressed by the high-pressure environment. Enrollment counselors are struggling to make quota as a result of the company's effort to improve retention.

* * * *

A lot of mud-slinging was going on in the press around this time. Steve Burd wrote extensively about the fraud in the sector, particularly at Corinthian College. Harris Miller of the Career College Association was the industry's chief lobbyist. He was obnoxious and arrogant, the perfect personification of the for-profit education sector, defending their practices virtually to the death until caving to the GAO report. He often complained about the naysayers. In one instance he went after Steve Burd. Miller said in an interview, "We are gratified to learn that Stephen Burd has nothing against for-profit higher education per se," and fully recognizes that there "are some good players" in our sector. Miller continues, "Our institutions are growing in the double digits because students are finding value and the word about the value proposition of this education is spreading." And lastly, "In my almost three years heading CCA, I continue to have extensive dialogue with both supporters and legitimate critics of our sector who have concerns that need to be addressed better. But with Stephen, there is no dialogue because his criticism is not legitimate—it comes from his heart not his head, from what he 'knows' to be true and not what the world around him represents."[10] Miller was eventually fired for incompetence—just desserts. I heard his for-profit handlers were upset about job he was doing to protect them.

* * * *

---

10   http://www.apscunow.com/2010/01/ccas-harris-miller-comments-on-bias-of.html

APOL reported earnings generally in line with the Street's estimates. Some fractures appeared in the growth numbers, leading to some trepidation and lukewarm comments from the Street. In their press release, APOL stated that they posted a letter of credit for $125 million, representing 25% of the prior year's estimated refunds due back to the DOE. That's $500 million versus approximately $3.8 billion of revenue or a potential revenue overstatement of 13%. The timing of late refunds was distorting their financial statements. Management cited the reason for the L/C in this way: "A preliminary program review report cites untimely returns of unearned Title IV funds for more than 10% of the student sampled." This vague reference doesn't rule out the possibility that the number of students for whom refunds have been mishandled was substantially higher.[11]

They reported a 70% increase in accounts receivables versus a 30% increase in revenue; nearly half of APOL's revenue growth was from this A/R increase. For a school that claims not to make loans directly to students, that seems high. I guess they are following ESI and the others, getting into direct lending in some form or another.

My revenue recognition overstatement thesis began to take shape with the earnings report. APOL commented in their 10-Q, "On December 31, 2009, University of Phoenix received the DOE's Program Review Report, which is a preliminary report of the Department's findings from its February 2009 program review of University of Phoenix's policies and procedures involving Title IV programs. The report contains six findings and one concern. In addition, the Department's regulations require certain institutions to post a letter of credit where a preliminary program review report cites untimely return of unearned Title IV funds for more than 10% of the sampled students. Absent relief from this requirement, the University of Phoenix will be required to post by January 30, 2010, a letter of credit in the amount of approximately $125 million."[12]

They were caught making "untimely return of unearned Title IV funds

---

11   Sec. 668.173. Refund reserve standards Chapter VI, Office of Postsecondary Education, Department Of Education and "25% of the total amount of unearned Title IV, HEA program funds that the institution was required to return under Sec. 668.22 during the institution's most recently completed fiscal year."

12   "Form 10-Q: Apollo Group," *Securities and Exchange Commission,* http://www.sec.gov/Archives/edgar/data/929887/000095012310000976/p16479e10vq.htm, Nov. 30, 2009.

for more than 10% of the sample students" has meaning buried in it. Of course this has revenue recognition written all over it. The math was pretty straightforward: $125 million represents 25% of the amount of unearned money, and then $125/25% is $500 million or just over 10% of the company's revenue. That meant over 10% of the company's reported revenue was money that was being refunded to the government late. I instinctually thought that $500 million was actually low.[13]

Reality check: Cheddar Boy indicated APOL's effort to improve retention was to eliminate an introductory math class that too many people are failing. Instead, they introduced a personal finance class to teach them about managing student debt...a class they pay for! Oh, and they have another introductory course students pay for, on how to use Facebook. A manager prevented him from dropping a student who could not read. Cheddar indicated that student comes to his office daily for help reading class assignments. No one gets paid overtime unless they make quota, but they can't make quota without working over 40 hours a week.

* * * *

January 14, 2010: Cheddar Boy said he had to tell me about one student, as it was like a microcosm for the way the company operates. "The man can't read. My manager won't let me drop him. I sit with him every day to go over his homework assignments, helping him understand the class work. He is going to get a tutor. The point is that no one cares that he can't read. They ask me, 'How do you know he can't read?' Seventy percent of enrollments can't read at a 10th grade level. They can read words, but their comprehension is at an 8th or 10th grade level. There is no way that they understand the student loan agreement. Ninety percent of the students being enrolled don't understand the loan agreement terms. They understand that they are borrowing money, but that's it. The other enrollment counselors doing a lot of the financial aid work can't explain the terms of student loans either."

---

13 "Amendment No. 1 Letter to SEC from Bridgeport Education," *Securities and Exchange Commission,* http://sec.gov/Archives/edgar/data/1305323/000104746909001537/file-name1.htm, Feb. 17, 2009. The SEC also wrote a letter to Bridgepoint (BPI) regarding its revenue recognition policies.

CHAPTER 9

Temporary Drop Status

January 13, 2010: On this day I found what was to become one of my best sources of information. This source provided a great picture of the inner workings of UOP and corroborated much of what Cheddar Boy and others had said. And he has a deep knowledge of many questionable business practices I hadn't heard of before.

Source was a former Director of Operations for UOP ground campuses. He left three years prior to my interview, so his knowledge may be somewhat out of date, but everything else about him suggests to me he's a credible source. I'll call him Rockstar to respect his anonymity.

The following are excerpts from my notes taken during conversations with him:

"Students might appear to be scheduled but in reality they have no intention of coming back. Enrolling for a course isn't like what is done at a 'traditional' university where the student logs into a system and picks/enrolls in courses. It's rare to find a student who doesn't have a full schedule built out all the way to graduation."

"When Phoenix counts Active Students (i.e. total enrollment), they include ones who are scheduled regardless of whether that course is scheduled for tomorrow or next year, not just those who are actually taking a course. This inflates the Total Enrollment dramatically."

Q: How does UOP take attendance? How do they verify the person logging in for class is who they say they are?

A: They use bar code scan for attendance. The ground campuses use the course roster that is faxed in. In the online division, the school can't verify if the person logging in is actually who they say they are. It could potentially hire someone to login and take the classes. Employers and regulators have a lot of interest in this, of course. There is no verification.

Q: What if I take one course, but get loans for four classes?

A: UOP will return whole 4-course disbursement and then seek funds directly from the student for one course that is owed. The student is entitled to funds for that one course. So UOP should only be returning three courses but they are returning four to manage their default rate down. They try to collect for that one course directly from the student so the lender just assumes they never attended at all. Finance counselors try to collect for 90 days then goes to formalized collections department.

Academic counselors and finance counselors are also receiving incentive compensation, to keep students in school. UOP created a bottleneck by having an insufficient number of financial aid counselors; making it impossible for students to get out…I was responsible for retention after students were already in the program. Enrollment counselors are responsible for getting students started through the first three or four weeks/nights of their first course. They are handed off during the first course.

Q: How do you maintain retention after the third or fourth class?

A: The academic counselor has a call plan set up that tells the counselor what to say to keep them in school. (I heard this includes threat of loss of credit score and heavy-handed tactics.)

Q: I heard 10% of students only finish the first year?

A: That number is going to vary greatly from one campus to the next. UOP has a term called "temporary drop" or (TDRP-S status). The academic counselor has a mandatory caseload. That means at any given time 80% of students they are responsible for must be "active" (in class). If one student drops out, the counselor has to go find another student who has already dropped and get them back into the system, or have new enrollments channeled to them. You can't fall below 80%, but it doesn't have to be the same 80% pool over time. For example, you can have 15 or 20 drops, but you use new students coming in to keep you above that 80%.

Your caseload is always increasing. For example, out of 100 students in my caseload, I may have 81 active and 19 inactive. If three people drop, I have to take three of the 19 and get them back into the school. The number of students in your portfolio is expanding over time. You may have 100 today and 105 or 110 the next day.

Q: You could have a lot of new enrollments making up that 80% number?

A: YOU GOT IT! That is a big part of their model for stated retention and stated enrollment. New enrollment growth is holding up that number.

Q: Can you walk me through how the temporary drop process works?

A: The student contacts the academic counselor to drop temporarily. The academic counselor is as much a sales position as the enrollment counselor. They do everything they can from the standpoint of a salesperson to keep you in the school. If you are getting a divorce or a death in the family—we can still fit you into class somehow.

Q: Do you mean that there is a quota for the academic counselor?

A: Yes. Their salary is not directly adjusted up and down. This is very similar to the semantics of the whistleblower. (The "solely" argument.) The performance matrix does influence the performance review, which affects compensation. There is a qualitative impact on the performance review, which is subjective. Mixed with other qualitative variables that are subjective, your subjective evaluation is not going be very good if you are not making quota. Senior management declared to academic counselors that they are a performance-based system and if you don't like it, you can leave.

Q: How many of the students are "temporary drops?" How much of it is automated?

A: In online, you are allowed to miss one week of attendance. If you failed to post a second week attendance, the system automatically drops you from the class and changes you to a "temporary drop." That flags the academic counselors to get you back in class. On the undergrad side, courses are five weeks long. You post two nights per week and that counts as attending for that week.

Q: At that point the alert goes off, how long can you keep them in "temporary drops"?

A: We are told 28 days in temporary drop status, and then they need to be in class or it's "return to lender." Return to lender does not happen right away.

Q: What percentage of students are temporary drops at any given time?

A: *30-35% is inactive population at any given time.* It's a big number especially with so much financial aid involved.

Q: How many times can a student drop? Several times a year?

A: There is no limit to temporary withdrawal. However, if you are not enrolled in a course for more than one year, then you need to write to the dean to get an extension and stay in the current version of a course/program.

A: UOP is always changing the classes. They have people whose job it is to just spend their time changing the curriculum. So they have a rolling curriculum. What might have been coursework to graduate two years ago won't be the same if you drop for a year and then come back. The system of prerequisites is designed to make you start all over again. So you are forced to take several classes not originally in your curriculum. At day 366 of being an inactive student, you can only enter into a new curriculum. All legit schools do change curricula as well, but not nearly as often as UOP… UOP is constantly adding and subtracting entire classes, making it harder to graduate on time. It's written into the fine print that they can do this. It traps the students. As long as you stay active and don't take more than a year off, you can stay in the same curriculum.

I tried to get this source to speak directly with my SEC contact, to no avail. But the concept of temporary drop would add an important piece to the puzzle.

In an email several months later, Rockstar informed me that Brian Mueller unveiled his concept for the "Executive Academic Counselor," i.e. pay-for-performance, in October 2006. This system created a tiered compensation structure for academic counselors and directors of operations. He said, we didn't get to see what the pay would be but the highest compensated academic counselors would have a list of 800+ students and must keep 85% of them actively taking classes at any given time.

Regarding incentive compensation for academic counselors and directors of operations: Identifying and reporting total enrollment was fantastically difficult. This is because the number of students in a class and/or any specific student status (TDRP versus a number of "active" statuses) changed daily. Regarding Temporary Drop and Permanent Drop (P-Drop) status, the guidance (emphasize guidance) from corporate was that TDRP could be converted to PDRP after a couple of years of not taking classes. *In practice, it wasn't uncommon for people to linger in TDRP indefinitely because of that small chance that they may start taking classes again with enough follow up from the AC.*

Once someone is in permanent drop, they literally fall off the reporting/recruitment radar. DOOs and above were the only ones who could update the status to PDRP. Lingering Temporary Drops often frustrated many academic counselors (below the Directors of Operation) because they negatively impacted their numbers and the academic counselors knew that the student wasn't coming back…yet many DOOs wouldn't change those to PDRP and kept them in the total enrollment.

I had an email conversation about this with Donna all the way back in September of 2005, but didn't find it until much later. Donna writes to me, "I have not studied Sarbanes enough to know the specifics. I am aware of increased concern in the accuracy of enrollment numbers and Accounts Receivables due to Sarbanes. Consider the fact that some institutions were somewhat creative in who they considered an enrollment for purposes of reporting to shareholders. Terms like "temporary drop" for example. *One school used this to apply to a student who had indicated that they withdrew, but where the sales staff or retention staff logged that the student indicated that they hoped to return someday and complete their program.* This kept enrollments up for purposes of shareholder reporting since the school considered this an active enrollment *for years*, even though revenues were not received for students with a "temporary drop" status. This is a student who would be considered a withdrawn student under TIV [Title IV]. As long as the school treats the student as a withdrawal for TIV [Title IV] purposes, ED has no jurisdiction to address the differing definitions it chooses to use for other purposes. Under Sarbanes, there is concern that such shenanigans might be problematic, however, to the SEC." Aside from not having or remembering that I had this email, there was no reasonable way to assume she was speaking about APOL. Therefore, any of the APOL children also could have been using "T-drop" internally.

I don't think it's a stretch to say that most Wall Street analysts would assume some amount of revenue based upon the enrollment. If enrollments are up 10%, then revenue should be up 10%. But if they have students in T-drop that are not generating revenue, where is the extra money coming from? I guessed new students and Pell Runners with a high dropout rate. That means they can manipulate their enrollment to correspond with the revenue, masking the fact that many of those students are long gone; however, investors can't see that or know the churn underneath. It's a perfect Ponzi scheme until real enrollments started falling later.

* * * *

On January 18, there were several discussions, press releases, opinions, etc. about what came to be known as "Gainful Employment." Aside from revoking the Safe Harbors and other legal changes, the ED was looking to introduce restrictions on the level of debt a student could carry by having it linked it to an expected salary for that field. Through Gainful Employment the ED developed a few ratio requirements that would likely lower debt—and lower tuition. Thus, the short idea quickly focused on the idea of lower tuition.

I hated the idea of Gainful Employment from the start, thinking it would be too hard to enforce. While it plagued the sector following its introduction here in January 2010, it was later pushed off. Of course, it presupposes that students actually graduate. It was a waste of time because the graduation rate was so low on the frontend, and emphasis need not placed on the backend. I will mention G/E in passing; however, I've omitted large sections of it beyond January 2010. Congress hated it, too, so there was a lot of chatter about its faults in the press and in Washington.

* * * *

January 19, 2010: "Apollo Suffers New York Snub as SEC Probes For-Profit Phoenix" (Bloomberg by Dan Golden): "Apollo Group Inc., whose for-profit University of Phoenix is the largest college in the U.S. with campuses in 29 of the 30 most populous states, faces one long-standing obstacle to staking its claim as the future of higher education: New York has blocked Phoenix's bid for a Manhattan campus, questioning its academic quality, its dropout rate, how it compensates recruiters, and even its right to call itself a university, according to interviews and documents obtained under a state Freedom of Information Act request... Apollo shares have fallen 17 percent since Oct. 27, when the company said the SEC opened an informal probe into its accounting practices. Apollo said its accounting is appropriate, and it intends to cooperate with the inquiry."

U.S. Education Department also is prodding Phoenix to disclose more information about costs and course requirements, which could deter some of them from enrolling. In Texas, with the support of then-Governor George W. Bush and his education adviser, Margaret Spellings, later U.S. Secretary of Education, it outlasted the state higher education commissioner who tried to block its entry. 'For-profits are freer than most nonprofit colleges to form political action committees and donate to candidates for state office,' said Miriam Galston, a law professor at George Washington University in Washington.

"State officials remain concerned that Phoenix's dropout rate is too high, said Saul Cohen, a regent and a former president of Queens College in New York. *Only 8.9 percent of first-time, full-time college students who enrolled at Phoenix in 2001 completed their degrees in six years*, according to the National Center for Education Statistics, in Washington."

In order to prove my theory that University of Phoenix was operating a virtual revolving door on its enrollments, I needed to track the Pell recipients. I felt the aggressive recruitment of poor students would provide a roadmap for their strategy. The industry spun this exploitation, arguing their schools were recruiting many students whose parents had never had access to college, as if the schools were providing a public service. That may have been true on some level, but unfortunately, not everyone is ready for college. During January, the National Consumer Law Center published "For-profit education by the numbers," authored by Deanne Loonin. According to that report, in 2008, students received a record $18.3 billion in Pell grants. Proprietary schools collected about $4.3 billion of that amount, or about 24% of all Pell grant funding, about double the proportion from ten years ago.

* * * *

January 21, 2010: Deutsche Bank published "ESI 4Q is all positives, no negatives," by Paul Ginocchio. "*Raising* FY10E EPS on better growth and PEAKS lending program. ESI has a new private student loan program, under which it will continue to assume all of the risk associated with loans made to its students while another party provides the cash to students for the gap between available Title IV funds and the tuition price."

Much later the SEC issued subpoenas about ESI's "Peaks" program. The new Consumer Financial Protection Bureau contacted me for documents in 2012. I told clients, "ESI call not going well, talking about average revenue student flat to down and they are announcing a 5% tuition increase in March, but don't expect there to be a revenue increase. Short it!"

I found this post on an Internet web site: "Teachers at ITT Tech must reach a quota of student attendance AND pass a certain number of students in each class to keep teaching the class. For example, the first class a student takes at ITT must have student attendance and success rates (total number of students that started the class and passed) of around 75%. This practice started about two years ago and the ramifications of not making the number have increased. What started as a gauge to see where improvements could be made to instruction has escalated into teachers being reassigned or let go. This information has been sent to ITT's accrediting body ACICS around a year ago, but no action has been taken by them to date."[1]

---

1   Marat, "ITT Technical Institute Complaint," *RipoffReport.com*, http://www.ripoffreport.com/adult-career-continuing-education/itt-technical-instit/itt-technical-institute-teach-bb393.htm, March 3, 2010.

February 2010

February 1, 2010: On this day, Morgan Stanley published a seemingly harmless research report about the impact of Gainful Employment. In its 20-page downgrade of ESI, Suzy Stein wrote, "We are downgrading shares of ESI to equal-weight and eliminating our price target. The specter of harsh Gainful Employment regulations…puts ESI's programs at high risk for tuition cuts."

In a spreadsheet attached to the report, they walk investors through various scenarios. The report addresses ESI in particular, but the same scenario applies to the entire sector. The idea was to show the impact on ESI's financial statements should they have to reduce tuition by a meaningful amount to be in compliance with the mandates of Gainful Employment. Gainful Employment sought match tuition for a degree with the salary of a person in their field of study.

She nailed it right on the head by showing investors what would happen if they had to cut tuition by 25%. 2010 revenue was $1.5 billion, 2011 would be $1.2 billion (the down 25% scenario). Gross margin was 63% in 2011 and 58% in 2012. Operating margin held in 2010 at 38%; however, at the end of 2011 it was 33%, and in 2012 it was only 19%. I'll take it! I need more reports like that to help my cause. Clients didn't need me to beat on them to short ESI on this.

* * * *

In February 2010, a company named Quinstreet (QNST) was in the process of coming public. Quinstreet was something I was very interested in following. It is an Internet lead flow generation company. According to their prospectus, they were also registered mortgage brokers in 25 states. However, aside from providing Internet leads to the mortgage industry they also supplied leads to the for-profit education industry. Oh my God! Could it be possible they are using subprime mortgage borrower leads as leads to the for-profit education industry? And the company was not small. It had $260 million of revenue in 2009, up from $109 million in 2005. For 2009, education represented 51% of the company's revenue (down from 78% in 2007) with DeVry University representing 19% of revenue for the fiscal year 2009 and only 12% for the first six months of 2010. Financial services—the mortgage industry—represented 41% of revenue in 2009. By 2010 no customer accounted for more than 10% of revenue.

The ban on incentive compensation for schools extended to Quinstreet. I was so bearish on QNST that I wrote a short sale research report *prior* to the company coming public. It was in early February 2010 that I wrote my report. That's not something that short sellers normally do. Newly priced IPOs have limitations on borrowing shares, which one must do in order to short a stock. And if things are as bad as they look, the investment bankers may have difficulty "pricing" the IPO.

The first prospectus was filed all the way back in August of 2009 and simply said they expected to raise $250 million. The seven month delay was red flag number 1. The next prospectus had no number for shares offered or money expected to be raised. There were several letters exchanged back and forth between the company and the SEC. It's not fatal but let's call that a pink flag. In the January 26th prospectus it said they intended to offer 10 million shared to the public and they expected to price the deal between $17 and $19. Another prospectus filed on February 11th said they lowered the expected pricing to $15 per share and 10 million shares. They went from trying to raise $250 million to $150 million. Another red flag! On March 17th the next prospectus raised the number of shares to 12.2 million but lower the pricing to a range of $9.63 to $14.95, raising $121 million. With the stock priced so low, around $14.50, it was less interesting as a short. I suggested to clients that they get out if they got in and wait for a better entry.

I wrote in my report: QNST is at severe risk of having nearly 50% of its revenue legislated away completely or restricted. The recent acquisitions are in financial services—a weak attempt to get away from education concentration. Regardless of the timing of the NegReg implementation, a black cloud will hang over the shares as investors worry about the possible implications of removing incentive compensation for lead flow aggregators. Cyclicality will start to play a role if we are truly coming out of recession. I believe there are saturation issues on the horizon given the low barriers to entry in online education. Still, short sellers need to be alerted to the fact that insiders are retaining most of their shares. Therefore, I would expect perhaps a quarter or two of making numbers while management tees up the stock for a secondary offering, the announcement of which in itself could crater the stock. They may not have that luxury though as the education issue looms large on the horizon. The stock was priced in the mid-teens, and then walked itself up toward the mid to high 20's. But I am fearful at those prices liquidity could be low and the shares may be hard to borrow as others see what I see.

From 2008 to 2009 QNST's education revenue stream went from $142 million to $151 million, 58% of total revenue of $260 million. However, over the same period, financial services revenue went from $21 million to $79 million year over year. The company made several small acquisitions. Clearly, their strategy was to drive growth before coming public to give investor the appearance of organic growth. Once the company compared revenue and earnings of the financial service revenue stream, growth should slow to a more normalized organic growth rate. By 2011, the revenue was $403 million versus $334 million, up only 20%, not the 35% growth reported in 2009 versus 2008. Twenty percent even seemed high to me. I knew I was on the right track when I started comparing the quarterly year over year numbers. In the first quarter ended September 2010, revenue growth was 32% compared to September 2009. However, by the fourth quarter which ended June 2011 growth slowed to $94 million versus $88 million or only 6.8%. That linear decline in the growth rate represented the year over year comparisons becoming more difficult because of the anniversary of the acquisitions. The company cited a steep slowdown in revenue from the education vertical due to regulatory changes. The stock hit $5.50 in the first quarter of 2013.

By December the stock was in the low $20's but I forgot to re-recommend it.

* * * *

February 11, 2010: EDMC was the first for-profit school to report earnings following the announcement regarding Gainful Employment. EDMC is run by Todd Nelson, said, "It's our hope we can continue to work with the department to achieve more specificity on what would be considered appropriate adjustments in salaries for admissions personnel. Our request is then simply that the criteria are clear and consistent with the intent of the Congressional language on which the limitations are based. That said, we can comply with whatever language that is finally included in the regulation."

(Paraphrasing) It would reduce opportunities for students at a time of high unemployment for those without skills. This is not a good policy for our young people. It would also reduce the number of programs available to educate the additional students who will need higher education if the President is to achieve his goal of having America have the highest percentage of adults with degrees by 2020.

* * * *

On February 19, 2010, APOL lowered earnings guidance, causing the stock to fall from $61 to $55: Bad debt expense will be higher than in recent quarters due to the economic downturn and the effects of the mix shift to associate students in recent years, as well as the previously disclosed operational changes the Company implemented beginning in late fiscal year 2009. That's BS. Cappelli said, "…we continue to transition the business in an effort to shift our student mix towards bachelors and graduate programs, and believe over time this will have many positive effects on the business, including reducing bad debt expense." Whenever you hear the word "transition," sell short more stock.

In fact, bad debt for Apollo skyrocketed to $282.6 million in 2010, up from just $104.2 million in 2008—presumably the result of recruiting more risky students who were unlikely to pay for their tuition.

As the company puts more assets toward recruiting bachelor students, the company will be spending more to recruit students than in years past and will lose revenue from the migration from Pell Runners to bachelor. Cynically, UOP should make all of their students Pell Runners to maximize growth. Perhaps the ED scrutiny was influencing their marketing strategy. Regardless, the state of the economy was not a valid excuse for the lowered guidance.

* * * *

February 23, 2010: The GAO released a new report to the Senate HELP Committee based on information gathered from December 2009 to February 2010. In summary, they found substantiated violations of incentive compensation and other HEA regulations at 32 schools. Seventeen schools were found to have violated the ban in the five years prior to the implementation of Safe Harbors. Many of the violations involved commissions to enrollment staff for successfully securing enrollments. Between 1998 and 2009, the Department of Education found that 32 schools had violated the incentive compensation ban, but the total number of incentive compensation reviews and audits conducted over this time period was unknown.

March 2010

March 3, 2010: Education Secretary Duncan responded to a question from Rep. Buck McKeon (R-CA) about the gainful employment rule and how it might force closure of programs at proprietary schools. Secretary Duncan commented that while the ED wants to hold schools at the end of the spectrum accountable, he does not want to be heavy-handed and thinks the free-market can punish bad actors. That was enough to drive the shares of Apollo from $58 to $65 in the following two weeks.

* * * *

March 4, 2010: Bloomberg News, Dan Golden, published a negative article on the sector. "Companies are buying accreditation," said Kevin Kinser, an associate professor at the State University of New York at Albany, who studies for-profit higher education. "You can get accreditation a lot of ways, but all of the others take time."[2]

The nation's for-profit higher education companies have tripled enrollment to 1.4 million students and revenue to $26 billion in the past decade, in part through the recruitment of low-income students and active-duty military. By exploiting loopholes in government regulation and an accreditation system that wasn't designed to evaluate for-profit takeovers, they're acquiring struggling nonprofit and religious colleges—and their coveted accreditation. Typically, the goal was to transform the schools into online behemoths at taxpayer expense.

Golden continued, "By acquiring regional accreditation, trade and online colleges gain a credential usually associated with the traditional academic culture of liberal arts, faculty scholarship and selective admissions. Normally the accreditation process takes about five years and requires evaluations by outside professors."

Enrollment at Grand Canyon University has soared to 41,500 in December 2010, up from 3,000 in 2003. GCU was a Christian college in Phoenix bought by investors in 2004. Ninety-two percent of students now take classes online. Based in San Diego, Bridgepoint Education Inc., has boosted enrollment of two regionally accredited colleges it bought in 2005 and 2007 to 53,688 students as of December 2010, up from 12,623 in December of 2007. That's strong demand for a college, isn't it?

---

2   Dan Golden, "Your Taxes Supporting For-Profit Firms as They Acquire Colleges" March 4th, 2010

In December 2009 the OIG urged the ED to contemplate terminating recognition of the Higher Learning Commission, which has approved more for-profit colleges than its counterparts around the country. The OIG criticized the commission's decision to accredit Career Education Corp.'s online American Intercontinental University, citing concerns about how much time students spent in class. According to the commission and Hoffman Estates, Illinois-based Career Education, the approval was appropriate."

* * * *

March 5, 2010: Cheddar Boy indicated changes were occurring at APOL. The management had implemented training seminars for enrollment counselors, whereby enrollment counselors with high retention rates instruct other ECs about how to retain more students. Cheddar was skeptical of such efforts. The EC trainers boasted a 97% retention rate. He indicated that enrollment counselors with such a high retention rate only recruit students who are white, not black.

His drop rates were going up because students couldn't do the work. He said UOP was going to have to change its business model and start from scratch if it thinks it wants all of its ECs to have a 97% retention rate. As it was now, everyone just recruits as many as they can no matter what.

The company was going to implement a new program called "University 101," designed to filter out some of its low-quality enrollees, later that year. The idea was to enroll prospective students for three weeks for *free* to take a couple of courses to sharpen their skills and prepare them for college. In his estimation, it was a matter of engrained corporate culture: that the company would have to wipe clean the enrollment counselors and start over again. The standard practices of enrollment counselors was still, in the end, encouraging the recruitment of the least educated and highest failure risk students. Whether management was fully aware of it or not, their business model was changing.

* * * *

March 8, 2010: With APOL at $62.25, I published a report titled "Cracks Beginning to Show." APOL lowered guidance a few weeks back due to unexpected high bad debt expense. They said, "Importantly, as we outlined on our last earnings call, we continue to transition the business in an effort to shift our student mix towards bachelors and graduate programs, …while we are still in the early phases of these efforts, we are pleased with the initial results, particularly the continued strong enrollment in our bachelor programs."

I am not hanging my short thesis on the SEC's potential enforcement action, but rather on the rapidly changing dynamics of enrollment and revenue as the company migrates from front-end to back-end. The company was taking action to slow the recruitment of unqualified students with a chance of dropping out in favor of putting more resources into retaining higher quality students on the back-end. The short thesis was just starting to ripen, as the company battles the mathematical realities of transitioning from associate degree to bachelor degree students. Total enrollments will show negative sequential growth through 2011, with associates' enrollments declining steadily in the second half of 2010. Whether they should be allowed to count high drop students as actual enrollments was up for some debate, though management should be disclosing the massive turnover occurring. This systematic churn was a profit-center in itself with lots of government funding and little in the way true education.

* * * *

Two additional former UOP employees began to speak to me: one was an enrollment counselor, the other a financial aid manager. The EC believed that over 50% of his enrollments were not prepared to attend the school. When pressed if the students could read, source argued it wasn't an EC's job to know that—there was a policy of "don't ask, don't tell." Source indicated a very low level of computer literacy as well: students didn't know basic tasks such as email, cutting and pasting, etc. Again, it was don't ask, don't tell. When pressed how exactly they knew this, source indicated that applicants were unable to fill in the FAFSA form without step-by-step verbal instructions. At the bottom of the FAFSA is an "I agree" checkbox for the student to check to take out federal loans. Students checking the box didn't know or didn't understand, even if it was explained in detail multiple times, that they were, if fact, agreeing to pay back sizable federal loans.

If a potential student asks how much it costs to go to school, he was supposed to tell the student only how to pay for it, not how much it costs. "We just kind of danced around that…We were taught to pump them up, telling them how much money they would make with a college degree. It was sad. They had no business being in college. People shouldn't be allowed to sign up for school on an impulse. They didn't understand what they were signing even after I explained the loan documents several times."

Source left the company due to moral objections with these policies. He talked about heavy-handed tactics to keep the students in school no matter what, often finding private loans with 12% interest instead of 6% with federal loans. In many cases, the students didn't understand that concept of interest on loans. Source indicated that well over 50% of the loans would be in default almost from day one of the repayment period. The school routinely paid back the loans and put the student in collections to keep their default rate a secret.

Finance counselors are given incentive compensation based on collections for students heading into default. Finance counselors pull double duty as collections people, hence the stories we've heard of unreachable financial aid people. They are too busy doing collections.

This source had been in financial aid for several years. I indicated that I had heard from two separate sources that UOP was enrolling approximately 50,000 students per month over a three-month period, but that by the end of the quarter the number of students actually still enrolled was down to 50,000. So 100,000 students dropped "intra-quarter," with each student getting hit for a couple thousand dollars? If either number was close to accurate, enrollment growth should be much higher. I pressed— do you have any guesses on how close those numbers are to reality?

Paraphrasing: I'd say that's probably pretty accurate. UOP has been able to do a good job of hiding low retention rates by showing a high total enrollment that was sustained by new starts. Now that the HLC, the ED, and the SEC are taking a closer look, the retention issue is more apparent.

Q: I've heard that for the Pell students—that the dropout rate can be upwards of 50% after the second or third class.

A: I've heard stories of students being told that they can take classes that cost $10,000, but the—and then they can borrow $15,000, and use the other $5,000 to do whatever it is they feel like, with the Pell grant money… we could tell them that they're really the only ones that could decide what a 'school expense' was…because, if a person is about to lose their house, and they're not able to attend school, because of that, well— you know: is that a school expense? There are a lot of different things that can be looked at as, 'OK, well if I don't—if I don't use my car, then I'm not going to be able to go to school anymore, and therefore fixing the car is a school expense.'"

The thing that really muddies the issue of retention was that most students don't "formally withdraw"; they just stop enrolling and don't return phone calls. UOP puts them in TDRP (temporary drop) or TDRP-S (temporary drop—scheduled) and from an outsider's perspective, those students look like they're simply "taking a break." In actuality, most of those students are long gone and never coming back, but they are still counted in the enrollments, according to source.

* * * *

March 19, 2010: The APOL price was now back up to $64.23. With earnings coming up in a few days, I wanted some juicy bullet points for my report. In my ongoing battle to put the pieces of the APOL puzzle together, I am seeking out more information on the "intra-quarter churn" thesis I believe can now be quantified. With a big disclaimer attached because of the multiple volatile variables at work, my numbers are likely to be off, but still useful. Sometimes investing requires guessing and there's no way around it.

Should competition go up or marketing dollars lose traction because of the economy or regulatory enforcement, the pyramid scheme could fall apart quickly without new students to cover dropouts. Since management guided lower for enrollment growth, whether it's by design or a forced choice, putting on the brakes will cause a much greater level of revenue and enrollment decline than management was prepared to deal with.

I was less interested in knowing if these churned students were legal, but was more interested in knowing what would happen if they dried up. The SEC may be looking at this for revenue recognition fraud. Again, short sellers were not counting on the SEC action to make the idea work. However, evaporating enrollment will be near fatal to the company and the stock price was going a lot lower. Once it starts, it will never stop, no matter how much they spend on advertising.

People were looking at me as if I had two heads. Some of my clients, like Eisman, who also sunk a lot of intellectual energy into the research, understood. Some just bought into the short despite regarding my theory as a little whacky. This wasn't like predicting an earnings miss, or a product transition issue, or slowing comp store sales at a retailer like most other short ideas. Some of my clients were working on similar calculations, trying to explain the discrepancy in the enrollments by analyzing the ED data and the SEC filings. At the risk of appearing weak, I told my clients that they shouldn't even bother trying to do that; the company was sophisticated enough in its reporting that there would be no discernible trend that they could rely on. In fact, I was arguing the financials were pure fiction. There were some very heated discussions with existing and prospective clients over my suggestions. I didn't care. They respected a high level of conviction of one's beliefs. The prospective clients were the worst to deal with.

* * * *

One client pressed me on the APOL quarterly earnings release being reported the following day. I told him I would be looking for the guidance to be weak. The stock was up eight points since guiding lower. If enroll-ment growth was 20%-ish the stock probably does nothing, maybe trends up a little on this quarter's number. However, if enrollment growth was forecasted to fall toward 15%, the stock should fall back toward $55 from $64. However, if enrollment growth was headed back toward 10%, back up the truck and sell short every share you can borrow, it will go down 20 points. I'd be inclined to have a decent-sized put options position on, maybe a handful of April 65 calls, throw-a-ways just in case, and buy May / Aug 65 puts.

* * * *

March 29, 2010: APOL reported earnings with the stock at $63.38, but didn't really go up or down. *"Many of our associates aren't with us very long as you can tell from the operating statistics that we provide. Although we're generating some revenue from them, there's many of them that we don't generate a lot of revenue from…"* How many students are in that pool? How are they being accounted for in the enrollments? How much money are they skimming from that pool of students? To me, management's statement smacks of Pell Runners. The slowing of the associates degree enrollments was a forced choice.[3]

* * * *

APOL was claiming that since January 2008, when SLM pulled back from the private loan market, that only 4% of revenue came from private loans. Similar questions were posed to the other for-profit, who immediately sought to fill that gap with their own loans made directly to students, and which fell under the general category of private loans. So if APOL has 4% private loans, then why would they have a steady increase in accounts receivables and the corresponding bad debt alluded to in the lowered guidance, issued last month? If APOL was paying off loans on behalf of

---

3   The10-Q: "In addition, the U.S. Department of Education expressed a concern that some students enroll and begin attending classes before completely understanding the implications of enrollment, including their eligibility for student financial aid."

students in order to understate default rates, then they are, in essence, making loans to students and putting them into collections. Management could argue that bad debt was up because collections are down, and that collections are down due to the economy. However, they could also be recruiting correspondingly high-velocity short-term students, which are showing up in the accounts receivables. Not including the economy's impact on collections, APOL must be making more loans to students. That thought made me ecstatic. Checkmate!

April 2010

April 8, 2010: From Deutsche Bank, the Career College Association (CCA) released its report showing 34% of for-profit students would lose Title IV eligibility under the ED's proposed Gainful Employment regulation. Two- to four-year degrees, women, and minorities would be disproportionally affected. There was no change to our view that G/E in its current form has almost no chance of becoming final, a view we are more confident of to-day than even last week. The CCA report questions the logic of the metrics and its purpose, as well as the issue G/E was supposed to address, and contends that programs enrolling 360,000 for profit students, including 147,000 minorities, would be affected. It also suggests that differences in student demographics account for over half of the difference between for-profit and not-for-profit school default rates. I agreed with that ana-lyst's sentiment about G/E.

* * * *

April 13, 2010: Kelly Flynn at Credit Suisse: upgraded ESI and DV to outper-form from neutral due to new insights on the ED's G/E stance. ESI rallied from $109 to $119 overnight. I am not having much success recom-mending that stock short, for some reason. She raised the ITT price target to $135 from $105 and the DeVry price target to $75 from $55 to "reflect perceived decreased Gainful Employment risks."

A Bloomberg report caused the group to rise 10%, stating "the U.S. government may loosen proposed rules that would restrict companies' eligibility for federal student aid. Proposed rules would require education companies to show that graduates earn enough to afford repayment of their student loans."

* * * *

April 13, 2010: Two new sources (former enrollment counselors) spoke to me candidly. Apart from corroborating information from other sources, they brought up new issues of which I was unaware. APOL, they said, was increasingly recruiting students with no chance of success, a practice that had the blessing of the senior management. Up to this point, I only suspected that these recruiting practices stopped at the level of enrollment managers. Now, it seemed more likely that management was fully aware of them.

Source BM started as an admission counselor for master's and doctorate programs. BM was concurrently a student at UOP. Source graduated, and later taught at Axia.

At first, source had a lot of belief in UOP, but came to realize it was all about the numbers. Source tried to be an ethical EC and was looked down on for it. "Currently, as a teacher, I pray for them to drop." As a former EC, she knows that they shouldn't have been recruited. "You want them to drop, because they are under-qualified. You can tell from their biography that they have 12 children, are 22 years old and in school for no good reason." The school was not screening new students' basic reading and writing skills. Some of the emails source receives from students indicate that they are illiterate. They don't belong in school—a fact that the EC could (and should) have inferred during the enrollment process merely from email correspondence with the students.

"There are certain people that will do anything to make their numbers. *Those are some of the people that advanced to management positions...* I've seen it all. It's hard to say [to the prospect], 'You are too stupid to be a student.'"

Q: Can you tell me what it is like to teach at UOP? What is the attendance like?

A: "What will happen is: I will get 20 students at the beginning and wind up with 11 at the end of the class." Some never show and the rest drop out over the remaining weeks. She teaches a lot of classes. In almost every class she teaches, this 20:11 ratio holds true. She indicated that the retention numbers are much, much worse in the online segment.

I asked source to walk me through how it works: Students click for information on a banner ad on the Internet and don't realize that they are filling out an application. During the process an EC steps in and says you'll get money for signing up for classes. When people hear that, they then want to sign up. Source said her pitch to graduate students was: "You can get $18,500 for master's degree loans per academic year, and it's not going to cost you that much. The difference is yours to put in your pocket." The differential was a couple grand.

Q: That's "walking around money"?

A: "Yes!" When prospects find out that they could/would get money from signing up, they become really interested. The ECs have figured this out, and tell that to every prospect right away.

A: "Everybody knows that! That is a key selling point."

Q: And the management is aware of this?

A: "Management…were admission counselors who succeeded."

Q: Even above the enrollment counselor manager? Are you talking about higher ups, mid-level managers, not the CEO, but close? It sounds like Amway.

A: "*[That's] exactly like what it is, only your product is education….it's the same pyramid concept.*" (At this point, I explained the growth in Pell grant students.) "They are now going toward a more stupid population. That confirms my students…They are getting more stupid as times goes by."

I recounted to source the stories of ECs going into the "hood" and recruiting welfare moms, who then use the money to pay for rent or crack, who sign up right away and say, "Where is my money?"

A: "That's exactly what happens…[a]gain, I didn't comb the hood. I was given names… I was given names of people clicking on the banner and didn't realize until the end [that] they were enrolling."

Source told me that teachers are also tracked. If they don't log into the chat room a certain number of times or post on the chat room, they get in trouble. They are treated the way students are. If you don't have ten posts per week you get written up. Faculty are graded on the number of posts per day…there was no measure of the quality of the post or what was being said. The post has to be in the main forum. Source's students don't know that a paragraph is supposed to begin with a capital letter and end with a period. Source says that she has seen the level of quality of the student go down over the last five years. The whole company is on incentive compensation.

* * * *

In a lawsuit against UOP, it was disclosed that, in fact the whole company was on incentive compensation. "The other factor, which was not as important a drive but played into it, was they were transferring the control of the system into the human relations department because they had a new HR computer system and they were now going to automate the entire compensation system, not just for enrollment counselors but for the company…"[4] It sounds a pyramid scheme or a little like Amway doesn't it?

* * * *

The following are notes from a conversation with FA, one of my sources:

Source wondered aloud, if one were to look at stated enrollments, how many are actively enrolled in a class? "For example, if you have a baby, you may not be able to get back into your program for 12 to 16 weeks, and you are still counted as a student." If you lose your job, you mom dies, etc., you can apply for temporary dropout. "They did a lot of things that were [on the] fringe, but not necessarily illegal."

---

4   Case 2:04-cv-02147 Document 574, *Sekuk Global Ent, et al v. Apollo Group Inc, et al*, Aug. 25, 2008, p. 128

Q: "Is the upper-level management in the know or is it just the enrollment managers? Are the enrollment managers looking the other way or condoning the behavior?"

A: "They are looking the other way. UOP promoted the people who were best at hitting numbers—talk time and number of calls—but not necessarily the most ethical person. It doesn't surprise me to hear that [all of this] is going on."

Q: We have heard up to 50% of students drop after the first few weeks. Is that accurate?

A: "Oh yeah, I am not surprised." Source said that ECs were required to ensure that prospects attended one class; beyond that, no one cared. I pressed source regarding comments from another source about the size and scope of "temporary drops." A prior source indicated that roughly 30% of students are "temporary drops" at any given time and for no more than 28 days. This source, interviewed a few weeks ago, who works at another college, said Pell Runners would not be included in enrollments.

Q: Roughly 30% are in a "temporary drop" pool, is this true?

A: "It wouldn't surprise me." Source said that classes are not offered as frequently as they should be. Initially, they had to have a minimum of five students for a class online, but this was increased to 15. Some specialty programs are just not offered every six weeks; trying to find 15 students to attend can be difficult, so classes are not offered. So, the students drop until a class is being offered that they can apply towards their degree, and they had to wait eight or nine weeks until the next section started. However, "they are still listed as a student."

She ended up moving away from the Phoenix, AZ area. She said that people in Phoenix couldn't get another job if they worked at UOP. You are blackballed by other businesses in Phoenix, because UOP employees are considered to be so sleazy. No other educational institution in Phoenix will hire a former UOP rep, except Grand Canyon or another for-profit school.

* * * *

April 20, 2010: With ESI at $114, I wrote a report recommending investors sell short the shares in front of the quarter on April 22. ESI was expected to report earnings prior to the open on April 22, so it's really only one day advance warning. By quarter, starting in Q1 in 2010, the year over year growth was expected to be: 44%, 37%, 28%, and 18% for an average of 31%, down from 51% in 2009. Clearly, a very big slowdown was expected. 2011 EPS growth was expected to slow further to 12%. Despite a 2011 estimate of $11.63, ESI shares are increasingly vulnerable to slowing. This was a perfect time to jump on ESI. I have to be right sometime.

A new lawsuit provided me with a quick introduction to ESI's bad behavior, in which it was alleged that, "Halasa observed ITT staff alter and destroy files required to be maintained by state and federal law to maintain ITT's status as an accredited institution and its ability to participate in federally subsidized student aid programs."[5]

"Shortly after Halasa began work at ITT, he observed violations of state and federal laws by ITT at the Lathrop campus. Halasa observed ITT staff changing failing scores to passing grades on placement tests so that consumers could attend ITT and benefit from federally subsidized financial aid." Halasa observed inaccurate job placement figures being compiled by staff and those numbers were being conveyed to potential students and its accrediting agency. "Xxx, Vice President of ITT Operations, fired Halasa on September 9, 2009, because Halasa complained about ITT's fraudulent conduct and statutory violations."

On February 22, 2010, ESI management stated: "…quickly touching on grants and scholarships. Pell grants, we've seen increases there over the couple of years, not only in the amounts, but also in the eligibility percentages because of some changes in the calculation criteria. So that's been a very positive thing for us, increased levels of Pell grants for our students. And that probably hasn't completely played itself out, so you'll likely see some incremental increases there versus the numbers we disclosed in our 10-K that we just filed."

ESI has $300 million available for what I call "bridge loans." The standard repayment term for a private education loan made under the Private

---

5   Jason Halasa, who was hired in February 2009 as director of the ITT campus at Lathrop, CA and was fired in September. *Halasa vs. ITT Educational Service,* Southern District of Indiana 1:10-cv-0437WTL-JMS.

Student Loan Program was ten years, with repayment generally beginning six months after a student graduates or three months after a student withdraws or was terminated from his or her program of study.

It's well advertised that ESI was buying its revenue stream by filling a relatively small gap between tuition costs and federal loans. The company, and the industry, is more than willing to make loans directly to students to grow their business, even though the collectability of the bridge loan of $2,500 may be slim to none. Then why do it? The school obviously wants the Title IV for revenue recognition purposes. They are willing to write them off completely much later or collect a fraction of the bridge directly from the student. Like at APOL, how many students are withdrawing?

* * * *

And still, the deluge of Internet complaints continued: "I am working for ITT and I know what's going on, everybody knows ITT TECH and their fabricated information and invented reports… The only concern of the management in the HQ is to increase profits and do not care about students …They claim to be changing students' lives at ITT TECH. You are not a student—you are a 'start number.' Absolutely, no good reasons to work for this unethical institute, most horrible management practices, bogus and fake reports and information about the company. Who would have thought that ITT TECH can be permitted to be up and running with so many morals complaints, ethics violations, and educational deception and hoax?"[6]

The accrediting bodies were themselves corrupt, under the sway of the very schools they were supposed to be regulating. At one point in 2010, for example, six of the sixteen commissioners at the ACICS worked at for-profit education companies including ITT, Kaplan, Career Education, Lincoln Education, Apollo College (DeVry), and Corinthian. No wonder the complaints by the Inspector General fell on deaf ears. The fox was guarding the hen house. Now I get it.

---

6   "ITT Tech Is a Scam!" *Indeed.com* http://www.indeed.com/forum/cmp/ITT-Technical-Institute/ITT-Tech-Is-SCAM-DON-T-DO-IT/t42772, accessed July 8, 2014.

* * * *

April 22, 2010: I was killed again by the ESI earnings report. The stock was indicated up $4 in the pre-market trading at $121. Even if the quality of the earnings was subpar, sometimes you just get killed on the short side. I was the sheep instead of the wolf that day. Sometimes I have to debate with myself whether to stick to my guns and tell clients to keep shorting or add to it and say "Cover!" and hide under my desk, hoping they don't send a hit squad out to waste me for losing so much money. Luckily, most hedge fund managers are seasoned veterans and understand that's part of the game. Frankly, I've been a little privileged in my career. I have fired customers who became too verbally abusive over losses. The trick was to try to be objective and not to get overly emotional or take it personally when a stock goes against you and people are upset. Otherwise, you are just setting yourself up for giving poor investment advice and probably having a stroke at an early age.

I wrote at the top of my report, "Short into the pre-market rally, reported EPS; beat by $0.17, guidance range up, new enroll slowing, up only 21.8% down from 30%, receivables up 71% vs. 33% increase in sales. That's easy for me to say. And then I stared at my monitors and prayed! True to form, management continued to waste taxpayer money by aggressively repurchasing its shares during the quarter, such that cash actually dropped from $219 million to $165 million year over year, though still up from $128 million sequentially. Management spent $95 million buying back stock in the quarter. They crushed the stock late in the day down to $111." A week after that it was $100.

* * * *

In the spring of 2010, I received a call from a *Frontline* producer. They wanted to shoot a documentary on for-profit education. I eagerly anticipated the May 4 airing of *Frontline*, which could be a game-changer. It was possible we would get a repeat of the CECO experience following the *60 Minutes* piece about the industry a few years back. This Congress was more likely to follow through and dig deeper into the issues. Sometimes the stocks would have rapid moves up or down as rumors spread loudly through trading desks about the timing of such a report. *Frontline* published a press release on its site announcing the airing of its documentary on May 4.[7] Maybe I'll get a reprieve in ESI.

In *College, Inc.*, airing Tuesday, May 4, 2010, "*FRONTLINE* correspondent Martin Smith investigates the promise and explosive growth of the for-profit higher education industry. Through interviews with school executives, government officials, admissions counselors, former students and industry observers, this film explores the tension between the industry—which says it's helping an underserved student population obtain a quality education and marketable job skills—and critics who charge the for-profits with churning out worthless degrees that leave students with a mountain of debt."

"Even in lean times, the $400 billion business of higher education is booming. Nowhere is this more true than in one of the fastest-growing—and most controversial—sectors of the industry: for-profit colleges and universities that cater to non-traditional students, often confer degrees over the Internet, and, along the way, successfully capture billions of federal financial aid dollars."

"At the center of it all stands a vulnerable population of potential students, often working adults eager for a university degree to move up the career ladder. *Frontline* talks to a former staffer at a California-based for-profit university who says she was under pressure to sign up growing numbers of new students.'I didn't realize just how many students we were expected to recruit,' says the former enrollment counselor. 'They used to tell us, you know, "Dig deep. Get to their pain. Get to what's bothering them. So, that way, you can convince them that a college degree is going to solve all their problems."'

"Graduates of another for-profit school—a college nursing program in California—tell *Frontline* that they received their diplomas without ever setting foot in a hospital. Graduates at other for-profit schools report being unable to find a job, or make their student loan payments, because

7   "College Inc.", *PBS.org,* http://www.pbs.org/frontline/collegeinc, last accessed July 8, 2014.

their degree was perceived to be of little worth by prospective employers. One woman who enrolled in a for-profit doctorate program in Dallas later learned that the school never acquired the proper accreditation she would need to get the job she trained for. She is now sinking in over $200,000 in student debt."

The biggest player in the for-profit sector is the University of Phoenix— the largest college in the U.S., with total enrollment approaching half a million students. Its staggering $2 billion in profits last year has made it the darling of Wall Street.

* * * *

April 29, 2010: *Inside Higher Education*[8] wrote, "…Robert Shireman, offered a much more critical assessment of the private sector institutions than he has in his public comments to date, according to accounts given by several people who were in the room. He compared the institutions repeatedly to the Wall Street firms whose behavior led to the financial meltdown and called them out individually, one by one, for the vast and quickly increasing sums of federal student aid money they are drawing down."

While Shireman's comments were aimed directly at the for-profit colleges themselves, they may be most noteworthy for his indictment of accreditation. In Shireman's narrative before the annual meeting of the National Association of State Administrators and Supervisors of Private Schools, the accrediting agencies are to the for-profit colleges what the Wall Street ratings agencies were to the misbehaving financial firms: entities charged with regulating an industry that has grown too quickly and too complex for them to control, and that have an "inherent conflict of interest" because their existence depends on financial contributions from those they regulate.

Accreditors lack the "firepower" to regulate the for-profit sector, and the states and the federal government doesn't necessarily have all the tools they need to do it either, Shireman said, according to the notes of

---

8   Doug Lederman, "Comparing Higher Ed to Wall Street," *Inside Higher Ed,* http://www. insidehighered.com/news/2010/04/29/shireman, April 29, 2010.

several in the audience. That, he suggested, is why the Education Department must toughen its rules in the way it is now proposing.

* * * *

April 30, 2010: Bloomberg's Dan Golden wrote an article titled "Homeless Dropouts from High School Lured by For-Profit Colleges."

Driven by a political consensus that all Americans need more than a high school diploma, the quest to recruit the homeless has increased. Disadvantaged students are preyed upon because they qualify for federal grants and loans, which are largely responsible for the profiteering of for-profit colleges. Federal aid to students at for-profit colleges jumped to $26.5 billion in 2009, from $4.6 billion in 2000. Higher education companies that trade in the public markets derive nearly 80% of their revenue from federal funds, with Phoenix at *86%*, up from just 48% in 2001.

"Chancellor University in Cleveland explicitly focused recruiting efforts on local homeless shelters after it realized that Phoenix, owned by Apollo Group Inc., was doing the same thing. Chancellor has stopped pursuing the homeless, and Phoenix says any recruiting by its employees in Cleveland shelters was unauthorized. UOP's so-called business code prohibits recruiting students at shelters. Any employee violating the ban could face termination, Apollo says."

Phoenix promotes "only students who have a reasonable chance to succeed enroll in our programs," Apollo spokesman Manny Rivera said in an e-mail.

Last year, in Cleveland, Chancellor and Phoenix were both recruiting at the homeless shelters. A recruiter who joined Phoenix in 2009 soon made presentations at Y Haven, Salvation Army Harbor Light, and Transitional Housing, all of which serve the city's homeless.

"Because they don't have to repay their educational loans until they leave school, some homeless students spend beyond their means. Kim Rose, a recovering crack cocaine addict and ex-offender in Raleigh, North Carolina, began pursuing an online bachelor's degree in business last

November at Capella Education Co.'s Capella University, based in Minneapolis. At the time she was staying in a drug-free program with Internet access."

"Rose, 38, receives almost $4,000 each academic quarter in federal grants and loans for tuition and living expenses. She splurged last Christmas, spending $700 of her financial aid on presents for her seven-year-old son, who has lived with his grandmother. 'I got him everything he wanted,' Rose said in a telephone interview. Rose moved into a shelter in February where the only computer was broken. She has struggled to keep up, dropping an English composition course."

Suddenly Cheddar Boy doesn't sound so much like a rogue, does he?

May 2010

May 4, 2010: The *Frontline* documentary was perfect. It put a face on the complaints from so many former employees and students. It made people realize the human tragedy of mass-recruiting unsuspecting students unprepared for the avalanche of debt they were about to incur (and all for naught). The show provoked a flurry of emails and calls with clients and some of my Washington contacts. Joanna Serra, an aid for Congressman Tim Bishop, was particularly interested in the issues raised.

Arne Duncan, the Secretary of Education, seemed uninformed, not misinformed. The documentary will create earthquakes across Washington. One would think Duncan would be on the phone this morning to Shireman wanting to get up to speed a little better.

Rep. George Miller talked about the student being trapped in the middle as a "pawn." Miller gets money from the industry, but now he may be forced to do what he supposed to do—the right thing. This was where educating Congress became important now that they know they are misinformed.

The Wall Street analysts looked terrible, talking about how much the for-profits have been recruiting students who shouldn't be recruited over the last couple of years. Where have they talked about that in their printed garbage investors read?

* * * *

May 5, 2010: Apollo wrote an official statement to the *Frontline* piece claiming, "University of Phoenix is committed to doing the right thing for students. Along with a renewed dedication to making high-quality, practical and accessible educational offerings available to working learners, we are focused on maintaining a responsible growth strategy and on implementing financial aid practices that ensure government funds are responsibly utilized and student debt is minimized."

APOL management responded to *Frontline* with some dismal graduation figures. They reported APOL's dismal completion rates. Associate degree students in a 2 year program have a graduation rate of 26.38% after 3 years, and for those attending a 2 year program for more than 3 years the completion rate was 31.67%. For a four year bachelor degree program, the graduation rate within six years was 36.06% and only 39.32% after 6 years.[9]

Management went on to say that it would be against school policy to start a student regardless of whether they were academically ready or not. "Should the University find an enrollment advisor purposely misadvising or misleading students, prompt and appropriate action would be taken, up to and including termination." There's more, but the readers get the drift.

* * * *

Corinthian was not a primary target of mine. It was too small for my clients to sell short. Corinthian prepared its own attack on *Frontline*, accusing the program of getting information from the short sellers as part "of a scheme" to manipulate the shares of Corinthian's stock. Short sellers, they argued, make their profit by manipulating media outlets, government agencies, and others with false and misleading information. I filed a FOIA with the ED for documents related to Heald College, which Corinthian bought several years ago. In those documents they talk about chronic late refunds, high dropout rates (>30%), excessive awards of financial aid, and incorrect refunds.

In any event, the impact of the story was apparent. Since the press release previewing the *Frontline* program appeared last week, Corinthian's

---

9   UOP official statement in response to *Frontline* documentary.

stock fell by more than 10%. Management went on to say they believe that the sources *Frontline* used may be short sellers who provided false statements and inaccurate and misleading information concerning Corinthian.[10]

I didn't help *Frontline* to make my short idea work. Short sellers don't need to promote their ideas to make them work. In fact, if a short idea has to be forced, through attempts at manipulating the media or some other means, it isn't a good short to begin with. Alerting the public to dishonesty meant merely exposing what was already there. It's annoying when companies make noise and level baseless accusations at the short sellers; plus, the stock was already down. Every seasoned short seller knows to never bet on a potential press article coming out because if it doesn't come out, the stock goes right back up again, or if it does, people might say it wasn't that bad and the stock goes right back again. Good short sellers look at broken business models and bad behavior.

Ironically, Corinthian's 10-Q came out May 4, 2010. COCO's stock price could've fallen because of this statement: "In April 2010, we received the ED's program review report, including the online division and the two ground campuses in Phoenix and Mesa, AZ. There were a total of 5,647 students in these three operations as of March 31, 2010. The Report maintains that the school failed to make students aware of the total amounts of financial aid for which they were entitled, failed to accurately inform students of the program costs, and delayed disbursements. The report also contains findings regarding inadequate documentation, verification and availability of records for ED review, and the failure to make certain disbursements. In the report, the ED characterizes certain of these findings as misrepresentations by the school to its students, as a *breach of fiduciary duty* and as evidencing an intentional evasion of the 90/10 requirements."

Maybe the release of the 10-Q caused the stock to go down, not *Frontline* or short sellers! By 2014 COCO was trading at less than $1 and closing almost all of its schools.

---

10   See also *Conway Investment Club vs. Corinthian* Central District of California CV-04-5025; *Douglas Rose vs. Corinthian* Central District of California; *Nancy Tsai vs. Corinthian* BC-326573 Superior Court of California; *Scott Levy vs. Corinthian* Central District of California CV-07-01984; *Jaclyn Fisher vs. Corinthian,* Superior Court of Washington 05-2-06620-8; *Satz vs. Corinthian College.* There are more, as well as several OIG audits.

* * * *

May 7, 2010: Steve Burd wrote that Harris Miller, the president of the Career College Association, often claims that his organization doesn't have any tolerance for proprietary schools that engage in unscrupulous practices that harm students. "Hang them high," he likes to say.[11]

This week, the association had the opportunity to live up to its word. The latest issue of *BusinessWeek* includes startling revelations that some for-profit colleges are once again trolling homeless shelters, trying to lure their residents by promising them rich financial aid awards—while at least in some cases, pushing these extremely vulnerable students to take on heavy amounts of student loan debt. Harris Miller did include one line in a letter he wrote to *BusinessWeek*'s executive editor acknowledging the seriousness of the allegations. "Let's be clear: recruiting at homeless shelters is not acceptable. Period," he wrote. But in the very next breath, he tried to undermine the article by criticizing the negative press.

* * * *

May 7, 2010: I called Cheddar Boy following the *Frontline* piece, knowing he'd be riled up. He indicated that 40% of his enrollments are GED students. He indicated there was no person inside his campus whose job function it was to verify students have a GED. He said no one checks because students are enrolled in as little as a few hours. There's no time to check all of them even if there was someone to do it. He said that financial aid counselors are required to approve an application within four hours. The financial aid rep was responsible for enrolling new students for 3,000 enrollment counselors—"they receive so many applications that nothing is verified." I showed Cheddar UOP's responses to the Frontline questions.[12] He angrily took issue with UOP's insistence that "We are also committed to ensuring

---

11   Steve Burd, "Blaming the Messenger at the Career College Association," *Higher Ed Watch,* http://higheredwatch.newamerica.net/blogposts/2010/blaming_the_messenger_at_the_career_college_association-31450, May 7, 2010.

12   University of Phoenix, "Statement," *PBS.org,* http://www.pbs.org/wgbh/pages/frontline/collegeinc/responses/apollo.pdf , accessed July 8, 2014.

that we attract and enroll only those students who believe have a reason-able chance of success at the University of Phoenix, and we have taken several important steps to help ensure that all students are prepared for the challenges and rigor of our programs."This was a false and misleading statement, he countered. No such verification exists. In practice, ensuring students are prepared for higher education does not exist despite what the company's web site says regarding requirements.[13]

* * * *

Then something totally unexpected happened after *Frontline*. The producer called to tell me they received over 800 responses to the program on their web site, well beyond the norm. Most of the responses were negative and attributed to students or employees (much of it corrob-orating some of my assertions about the heavy-handed tactics involved in recruiting unqualified students).[14]

There were also a number of letters objecting to the report. Being skeptical, I looked more closely at the letters, which came in batches of a hundred here, two hundred there, all reading exactly the same as if writ-ten by one person just with a different person's name on it, as if someone mail merged the letter to a database of students. In fact, the schools told their students the ED was going to cut off their financial aid, which was what prompted the negative response. Despite that being incorrect, it did have an effect on the players in the ED who were contemplating the mer-its of Gainful Employment.

Career Education hired a company called "CREDO Action," which is a social change organization that supports activism and funds progressive nonprofits. Incredibly, they submitted *19,346 complaints from students*. Each complaint has the same couple of sentences with different students' names at the bottom.

---

13   "Admissions Requirements," *University of Phoenix*, http://www.phoenix.edu/admis-sions/admission_requirements.html, accessed July 8, 2014.

14   "Join the Discussion," *PBS.org*, http://www.pbs.org/wgbh/pages/frontline/college-inc/talk/, accessed July 8, 2014.

* * * *

Another post from the *Frontline* boards: "I worked for one of the mentioned for-profit schools in the program for nearly 3 years; the first year in Enrollment, the rest in Financial Services. The primary problem is the 'target market' and tactics used to deceive already struggling Americans into enrolling. High pressure sales tactics, misleading information, encouragement to enter a degree program that is not what the student requests, but what the school has that is 'close enough' or 'better.' If students were even required to write a complete paragraph with accurate spelling and punctuation the enrollment numbers would be about half of what they are."

Another commenter called the industry "the new mortgage crisis and it's the former mortgage brokers who lost their jobs selling this new misuse of federal funds, using the same tactics, to the same people who are already in over their heads." Actually, that's not too far off.

A third individual stated, "I have taught at University of Phoenix, and I believe it is much worse than *Frontline* uncovered. They could do a whole show about the poor quality of the courses and the incredible problems of plagiarism. I strongly believe the University of Phoenix should not be accredited. There are no tests in the science class I taught. Students, therefore, do not need to know any information very thoroughly. They have no lectures either, so the information is not even explained to them. The combination of no testing and poorly worded assignments allows students to go through entire courses without hardly needing to open a book."

* * * *

I can't recall which for-profit company this post referenced; however, it is entertaining enough to share. One poster said this, which I thought was kind of humorous: "They offered Public Speaking over the Internet —you gave your final speech on your computer's webcam— which anyone can see is not at all the same as speaking in front of a room full of people. They offered a CSI program in Criminal Justice, but neglected to tell students that you can't be a crime scene investigator with a CJ degree. They offered nursing programs that had no clinical or real world component; therefore our graduates would have a hard time finding work."

* * * *

May 12, 2010: EDMC filed their 10-Q on May 6, 2010. A whistleblower action captioned *Buchanan v. South University Online and Education Management Corporation* that was filed under the False Claims Act in July 2007 was unsealed due to the U.S. Department of Justice's decision to not intervene in the action at this time.[15]

Buchanan was an enrollment counselor from 2005 to 2007. Enrollment counselors were told to "seat" students at all costs. Enrollment counselors pushed potential students through the financial aid paperwork and loan agreements right away to get them signed up. He says the school did not reprimand enrollment counselors who openly coached students on the admissions test. "Defendant will also manipulate prospective students' transcripts to achieve an admissible GPA."

"Defendant SOU [EDMC] encourages admissions representatives to 'walk' students through the first 3 assignments within seven days of the start of class. Federal funds are provided for fraudulently enrolled students, students that are not qualified."

"...Defendants EDMC demand that all admissions representatives remove any evidence of sales figures, salary matrixes, student seated goals, and/or anything that could be construed as 'sales materials.'"

EDMC was accused of "...submitting fake proctor forms for ability to benefit tests; allowing students to take ability to benefit tests repeatedly until they passed; and offering free trips, iPods, and gift cards to representatives who enroll the highest number of students."

The quota system was enforced by the defendants by immediate termination of the recruiter for not enrolling enough students. "The term 'slamming' was well known at the Art Institute. That term means that the

---

15   *Brian Buchanan vs. Education Management* 2:07-cv-00971-AJS Western District of Pennsylvania.

recruiter enrolls any prospective student who walks through the door, without regard to their qualifications or expectations…Those pressures also make recruiters 'create' or embellish the prospects for the employment and salary expectations of students upon graduation" (Doc 46-13).

May 24, 2010: A similar case was filed against the EDMC, this time in the District Court of Minnesota.[16] "Arthur Andersen knew or deliberately turned a blind eye to the red flags which indicated that Art Institute's compensation program was illegal," the plaintiffs alleged. "Arthur Andersen refused to see the obvious, to investigate the doubtful, and its accounting judgments were such that no reasonable accountants would have made the same decision if confronted with the same facts. Arthur Andersen's work on the financial statements was so deficient that the audits amounted to no audit at all."

"Arthur Andersen directly participated in the dissemination of the false quarterly and year end results which Art Institute released to the U.S. Department of Education in 1995, 1996, 1997, 1998, and 1999" (Doc 46-13).

Then EDMC was required to post a letter of credit with the DOE, which was $173.2 million at March 31, 2010, or currently set at 10% of the Title IV aid received by students attending the company's schools. The reason for the Letter of Credit was triggered "because it did not return unearned funds in a timely manner…"[17] If that's true, then how sizable is the percentage of funds returned late? It could be substantial, putting the integrity of the financial statements into question. On May 7, 2010, the ED requested EDMC to increase the letter of credit to $259.8 million by June 4, 2010 based on projected Title IV aid to be received by students attending EDMC institutions during fiscal year 2011. The stock meandered under $5 for much of 2012 and 2013. By late 2013, somehow it managed to rally to $16; however, by August of 2014 EDMC was $1.20 falling in unison with ESI, COCO, and CECO.

---

16   *John Bunn vs. Education Management* was submitted as an exhibit to *Buchanan*. This lawsuit was originally filed in 2000 and covers 1995 through 1999 before Todd Nelson joined the company. His official employment agreement was signed in February 2007. 2010 10-K.

17   Sec. 668.173 Refund reserve standards.

CHAPTER 10

Continuous Enrollment

A
t this point, I was talking to clients about individual for-profits almost interchangeably; from my perspective, they were *all* more or less equally bad. After the "solely" loophole was established in the early 2000s, the companies followed suit, not wanting to miss out on robbing the government piggybank. Making late and incorrect refunds suddenly became trendy. Consequently, there was a continuous flow of lawsuits against the industry, which underscored my point. The *Hendow* lawsuit was the first big suit and opened the floodgates for other legal actions targeting the rest of the group, which provided a wealth of information for me.

May 13, 2010: I received a big break, blowing the short story wide open that fit well with the whole T-Drop issue taking shape. Ben Elgin, a reporter from *BusinessWeek*, called me one evening. I had chatted with him several times over the prior year. He had been doing some work for a story on the for-profits and received several documents from a FOIA but didn't know how to interpret them and asked for my take. It was late in the day, as he was on California time, and I was beat, so I planned on reading them the next morning. It was a series of emails between Dale Hillard, who works in the ED's San Francisco office, and the HLC, the accreditor for Grand Canyon, APOL, and several others.

In a letter from Dale Hillard on October 30, 2007, she writes to the HLC and the Arizona State Board of Education, "In resolving a student complaint we encountered a situation with Grand Canyon University that I wanted to run by each of you...to see if either of your agencies would have any concerns."

"The enrollment agreement that is signed by the students contains the following two statements: 1. 'and I agree to grant permission for continuous enrollment, unless I request formally to withdraw from the program or request a formal leave of absence.' 2. 'I understand that...non-attendance in my classes does not constitute an official withdrawal from my classes or the university....'"

She says, "The student in question was enrolled in two courses in two different terms (the student contends that she never intended to enroll in the second term), but posted attendance in only one course each term. In accordance with the policies above the student was charged for two courses each term."

"Theoretically, a student who never intended to be enrolled in a given term could be enrolled by the University (under their continuous enrollment policy), never attend any classes and be charged for the courses (because they never officially withdrew)."

In a second letter Dale Hillard writes to the HLC back in April 2008. "In November of 2007 I sent a packet of information regarding two policies of Grand Canyon [remember Grand Canyon is run by Brian Mueller former CEO of Apollo] for your review and possible comment. The two policies could be characterized as 'continuous enrollment' and 'non-attendance = attendance.' The continuous enrollment policy was in the Enrollment Agreement and by signing the Enrollment Agreement the student grants permission for the University to continuously enroll the student in two classes every term without any action initiated by the student term-to-term. The non-attendance-attendance policy was found in the Credit Agreement signed by the student. In this agreement the student acknowledges that 'non-attendance in my classes does not constitute an official withdrawal.' *These two policies together lead to a student who does not intend to enroll for a term being charged for the term even though he or she never attends one class session.*"

Hillard writes, "If the Higher Learning Commission or State licensing agency has any concerns or comments regarding these two policies, or any policies or practices at Grand Canyon University, we would appreciate hearing from you."

The HLC wrote back to Dale Hillard, "The Commission has no policy that would forbid this institutional approach to enrollment."

My blood quickly came to a full boil once I realized the implications for revenue recognition and overstatement of enrollments. Continuous enrollment and T-Drops were intertwined with each other. I brought this to the attention of the SEC immediately. They were aloof because the student signed those agreements. Had the contract told students they would be robbed at gunpoint, at the beginning of each class, would that be ok too, if it was in the agreement? I expressed my disdain for their lack of interest and vision.

Even though the email about continuous enrollment referenced Grand Canyon and not Apollo, I had to assume that because there were so many overlapping questionable procedures among the players in the industry, that Apollo may have a similar policy in place. Proving that, however, became a priority when talking to sources going forward.

Another letter came in Elgin's FOIA, the OIG Hotline wrote to an ED regional office: "The U.S. Department of Education, Office of Inspector General Hotline has received several calls from an employee of the University of Phoenix in xxx. One of her allegation is that counselors are being instructed to lie to HLC representatives during the upcoming visit."

The OIG hotline also wrote, "The school is asking Financial Aid Counselors to meet a certain quota each month, and if they do not meet the quota, the school threatens to cut the counselors' pay. Also, HLC is coming to school next month, and the school is already asking the counselors to *lie* to HLC."

* * * *

Rockstar reached out to me again regarding the Temporary-Drops Status. "Students are automatically withdrawn from a course after missing two nights of class. They are not automatically withdrawn from the program.

Academic counselors try to follow up with the student and get them rescheduled. These are counted as active students. The reporting of total enrollment gets skewed when these TDRP-S students have no intention of taking the scheduled course but haven't voiced that to the counselor. Due to sales pressure, they [the students] didn't actually give permission to be scheduled, etc."

He continued, "Here's what the standard process would look like: At some point, student changes his/her mind about UOP and decides that they aren't going to any more classes. They don't tell their academic counselor; they just stop going to classes and don't return phone calls/emails. They aren't required at UOP to officially withdraw and it's actually in *UOP's financial interests that they don't*. Academic counselor calls student and may or may not make contact. Often, they will schedule a course for the student to hold them a 'seat.' Student status becomes TDRP-S, an 'active status' counted in total enrollment."[1]

I ran this scenario by another former employee of Apollo: "You can see how they can get away with counting these TDRP-S as active because as he said many of them are just either switching a course because 'life happened' and they need a re-schedule or they can see they are going to fail and rather drop out than get an F and lower their GPA. *But the sad part is the enrollment and academic counselors will reschedule courses for them without talking to them and keep doing so.*" This was the proof I was looking for that it wasn't just Grand Canyon engaging in 'continuous enrollment,' but also UOP and perhaps others.

The source continued, "I have seen enrollment managers ask their team to follow up with ACs about these TDRP-S to make sure they are re-scheduled and can be counted, this is only when the students are in their first two classes after this it's just the AC's job to keep the enrollment up. It is a sad cycle and what he [Rockstar] said is extremely accurate. If the AC has not made contact with a student they should...not be rescheduled for another course. What do you think a student thinks when they hop online knowing they have no intention of coming back and see they are scheduled out for 6 classes? They can see the change right online. They can see

---

1   In another letter to ED complaining about UOP, the employee says, "The University [UOP] systematically keeps itself ignorant of 'problems' if that benefit them."

that they dropped the class and their whole schedule changed from what it once was to what it is now and if they kept watching their schedule they would see it change again after they didn't start the next course."

* * * *

May 17, 2010: Shireman announced he was quitting his position at DOE, which caused the stocks to rally. APOL went from $53 to $58. It was disappointing, to say the least. James Kvaal, Senior Director at the White House National Economic Council, who worked on higher education, training, and labor issues, was slated to take over.

* * * *

May 20, 2010: Also on this date, a letter signed by about 25 consumer advocacy organizations was submitted to Secretary of Education Duncan regarding the practices of for-profit schools: "In particular, we urge you to propose regulations on incentive compensation and gainful employment that will more effectively protect students from high pressure and deceptive sales tactics for educational programs of little or no benefit to them, and will ensure that taxpayer dollars do not subsidize such practices and programs."

* * * *

May 24, 2010: On this day the ED's Inspector General's Office released a highly critical audit of the Higher Learning Commission. In particular they took issue with the HLC's move to accredit CECO's AIU School, which had lost its accreditation a few years back. CECO's online division, CTU, changed accreditors to the HLC to get around the more stringent rules imposed by their former accreditor. The OIG writes, "This decision to grant accreditation to AIU, an institution it found to have an 'egregious' credit policy, is not in the best interests of students and calls into question whether the accrediting decisions made by HLC should be relied upon by the Department when assisting students in obtaining quality education through the Title IV programs."

The HLC stated that they do not consider themselves an inspecting body that applies a single yardstick or matrix, but as a reviewing body that assures the public that academic programming at an accredited institution occurs within the continuum of good practice in higher education. The HLC expects institutions and peer reviewers to understand good practices, but it does *not* provide institutions or peer reviewers with guidance on the lowest acceptable threshold. (In other words, they basically told the OIG to take a hike that it's not their job to regulate the schools they accredit. It sounds like more of an honor system than a legitimate regulatory body.)

The OIG fired back in the letter, "…HLC cannot ensure that the programs and courses offered are of sufficient quality and quantity to be considered postsecondary education at the level represented to students, especially with regard to asynchronous, accelerated, and other programs delivered through nontraditional formats. HLC's reliance on an understanding of 'good practice' without establishing minimum requirements for program length and…*could result in inflated credit hours, the improper designation of full-time student status, and the improper awarding of Title IV funds.*"

"Our report states that HLC granted AIU full initial accreditation with no limitations on the programs it offered at the time of initial accreditation… This allows AIU to represent that these programs are accredited despite the significant findings in the AIU Team Report. HLC did not prevent AIU from continuing to enroll students in the courses peer reviewers identified as having credit inflation problems and it did not require AIU to disclose the nature of those problems to students."

The HLC peer review team identified significant problems with AIU, yet HLC granted AIU full initial accreditation with no limitations on the programs it offered at that time of initial accreditation. The decision to grant accreditation to an institution found to have an "egregious" credit policy was not in the best interest of students. It calls into question whether the HLC should be relied upon by the Department when assisting students in obtaining quality education.

* * * *

May 26, 2010: With Education Management at $23.27, I started coverage of the stock as a short. The market capitalization was substantial; the number of shares sold short was quite low, giving it a high risk/reward. The estimate for 2011 was $2.06, up 22% from 2010 earnings expectation. If the stock sold at 22 times the estimate for 2011, it should go to $44. EDMC came public in October 2009, raising approximately $400 million.

EDMC had outstanding letters of credit of $210.7 million at March 31, 2010. The ED required the company to maintain a letter of credit due to its failure to satisfy certain regulatory financial ratios after a merger. On May 7, 2010, the ED requested EDMC to increase the letter of credit to $259.8 million by June 4, 2010, based on projected Title IV aid to be received by students attending institutions during fiscal year 2011. To participate in federal student financial aid programs, an institution must either satisfy certain quantitative standards of financial responsibility on an annual basis or post a letter of credit in favor of the ED and possibly accept other conditions or limitations on its participation in the federal student financial aid programs. As of June 30, 2009, EDMC did not meet the required quantitative measures of financial responsibility on a consolidated basis. Like LOPE, here was another situation with regulatory issues at the company prior to the IPO.

EDMC introduced a new student loan program with a private lender in August 2008, referred to as the Education Finance Loan program, which enables students to finance a portion of their tuition and other educational expenses. During fiscal year 2009, disbursements under the program were approximately $19 million. EDMC estimates that additional loans to students will be approximately $75 million. Clearly, they were in a rush to catch up the other schools with this new game of lending to students directly.

* * * *

May 26, 2010: Bridgepoint Education (NYSE: BPI) announced that on May 24, 2010, Ashford University received an audit report from the OIG regarding its compliance audit of the University. The OIG draft audit report varies from what the University received in connection with its September 2009 OIG exit interview, when the auditors communicated a tentative finding that the enrollment advisor salary plan was not in compliance with the incentive compensation provision laws. The OIG could not determine whether Ashford University was in compliance with the HEA because the University did not provide sufficient documentation to support its compliance with the Safe Harbor permitting salary adjustment based in part on the securing of enrollments.

* * * *

May 26, 2010: "Steve Eisman's Next Big Short: For-Profit Colleges" by Andy Kroll: [2] Steve Eisman has set sights on a new target: for-profit colleges of the kind of you might see advertised on daytime TV and at bus stops. In a speech Eisman criticized the for-profit education industry, comparing the companies to the sleazy mortgage brokers who peddled subprime loans over the past two decades. Eisman said driving much of the growth was the sector's easy access to guaranteed debt through Title IV student loans. For-profit educators raked in almost one-quarter of the $89 billion in available Title IV loans and grants in 2009 despite having only 10% of the nation's postsecondary students.

Eisman cited the industry's success to a Bush administration that stripped away regulations and increased the private sector's access to public funds. "The government, the students, and the taxpayer bear all the risk and the for-profit industry reaps all the rewards," Eisman said. "This is similar to the subprime mortgage sector in that the subprime originators bore far less risk than the investors in their mortgage paper. (Calls to several for-profit colleges, including ITT and Corinthian, were not immediately returned.)"

---

2   Andy Kroll, "Steve Eisman's Next Big Short: For-Profit Colleges," *Mother Jones,* http://www.motherjones.com/mojo/2010/05/steve-eisman-big-short-michael-lewis,   May   27, 2010.

June 2010

June 7, 2010: Apollo at $50.36. I wrote: APOL is expected to report on June 30. Associates revenue last year increased 25%, while bachelor grew 20%. I ran a variety of models plugging in various growth rates for associate versus bachelor. Putting the brakes on the lower-cost associate and stepping on the marketing gas for bachelor should offset each other. The company line is that bachelor students have a greater level of retention. I don't really buy that. It is just that the associate student have such high turnover. They have to stop recruiting associate students. At 40% of revenue that will drag the total enrollments down almost indefinitely. That won't happen in a smooth fashion sufficient enough to meet earnings expectations. Have enrollment standards increased enough to slow new enrollment growth? Given their low-quality education, do they have a more competitive product? With BPI, EDMC, and LOPE quickly catching up, I expect a loss of advertising leverage. Any "transition" is not likely to be smooth. Stay short!

Over time, any unscrupulous behavior will be increasingly difficult to perpetuate; hopefully, long investors will see through an upside earnings report and sell the stocks. Investors should expect an increase in accounts receivables to reflect the growing pool of "temporary drops," whether it consists of fewer students with greater dollar amounts (bachelor drops) or more students with lower amounts (associate drops). Regardless, the bad debt should be indicators of APOL's potentially increased difficulty keeping students enrolled who are long gone.

* * * *

June 8, 2010: With EDMC's stock now $18.60 I published a report describing an interview with a former managing director of admissions, "SA," at Brown Mackie College, a division of EDMC. I am documenting this interview with a lot of quotes because of the egregiousness of the unethical behavior by EDMC:

SA left the company because "the environment changed and I couldn't live with myself ruining people's lives…Even if BMC [a division of EDMC] doesn't have the program that the student wants, get an in-person in-terview with the prospective student and sell them on anything…Draw a picture of your dream and then sell them on being able to have everything in the picture. A degree from our school will allow you to achieve all of the dreams."

She said, "*The school forces students to sign waivers regarding employment post-graduation to be excluded from EDMC's placement ratio*… EDMC hires many graduates to help boost the placement ratio."

Like UOP and others, EDMC was supposedly recruiting extensively in the projects, even going door to door, and like the others, graduation rates were abysmally low; student withdrawals was essentially part and parcel of the business plan, a fact that extended, the source claimed, throughout the whole EDMC system.

"Many students were eligible to receive checks for $3,000 and then instead of using it for their education or rent or their needs, they would get their nails done, buy the newest flat screen TV or spend it on other things they cannot afford. EDMC actively targets the population in the lowest socio-economic class because they are easily manipulated—*We went out door-to-door in the projects* that were near the bus stop to recruit students for BMC."

Retention rate there was really low. They had students who were given a *pre-enrollment test* that basically, if they passed it, let them go right into the regular curriculum. If they didn't pass it, they went into "enrichment classes."

Q: "What percentage of people actually finish a course?"

A: "I would say, well, the first class is a really easy class, named 'professional development,' and so I would say probably *the majority of the drop-outs would be in that second month*, where they are taking their curriculum, because the first class is kind of easy, it's like 'welcome to college' class. Yeah, that second class is where they actually get into really doing things."

Q: Have you heard of Pell Runners? When an EC makes a sales pitch to low-income people when they sign up they can get more money than they need and not have to pay it back. Did you ever see that? How often do they have to show up to get their Pell grants?

A: "I know that process is used when they know the student has four kids on welfare. The saying is, 'the poorer you are the better you are'... single, living on welfare will qualify you for grants and student loans and will get overages where you can get a check and use that money however you want; you just have to make sure you come to class so many days in order to keep doing that. You had to come to class once a week. They could miss three classes but had to show up on the fourth day."

"And they can fail that class and take it two more times before they would be academically dismissed. Technically, you could have someone collecting several thousand dollars in financial aid over a quarter and never actually earn a passing grade and show up four times a month."

"Every Friday, we would have a line of students up to 100 to 150 people. For Pell money typically what happens where they receive Pell and student loans, the grant money is what is going toward education and student loan money overage is paid to them. One way or another it's financial aid funds."

"It was so ludicrous. The school sent out a memo to all the students— you have to be in class the day you pick up your check. You have to go to your instructor and have him sign a piece of paper to get your check. So it's basically show up, sign the roster, have the student sign the paper, get your check and we'll see you next check time. The whole thing was a mess...they prey on lower income, we play on their dreams, take out all these loans. If they graduate, if they are lucky they can get a $10.50 per hour."

Q: How far up the food chain does all of this happen? Is this isolated to your school or is this across the system and a very deliberate policy?

A: "It's deliberate. Initially, I just thought it was my campus, but when regional people would come in, in charge of multiple campuses and multiple regions and they are feeding us the same kind of crap. You can realize it's coming from someplace else, not just internally."

Q: I am interested in knowing the number of students who drop after that first class or two. At UOP I believe it's around 50%.

A: That sounds accurate. Brown Mackie would have big meetings, they would have call numbers, enrollment numbers and appointments on the boards and say—you should be ashamed to be taking a paycheck...you are lucky you have a job (to those missing quotas).

"It started out ok, but it quickly picked up speed. When the economy went south they raised tuition. They are facing market saturation, huge enrollment goals that they are not making."

They have entrance counseling for loans but they give the students cheat sheets on how to pass the entrance counseling through Sallie Mae. They realize how much they are taking out per quarter. Beyond that they don't understand how much it will cost ordinarily. There was no reason for the student to be given an overage or any extra money. They could easily have a policy to borrow what you need. No overages or cutting checks. They are facilitating the lender. They don't educate the student enough. They have all this debt. One of the things that pushed me over the edge was at the gas station I stopped at every morning for my coffee. One of my students works there. She graduated with very high marks and now works in a gas station. And I am the one who convinced her to enroll. And she has a lot of debt. We have an intelligent person with a two-year degree. I am the one who told you to do this and you are serving me the coffee? *That's the rule, not the exception.*

Purported employees on www.jobvent.com also voiced their grievances.[3] "I worked for this company [EDMC] for about four years," read one post. "When I started I was promised that the position which I was working in

---

3   "Working at EDMC Education Management Corporation: Reviews by Employees,"*Job-vent.com,*   http://www.jobvent.com/edmc-education-management-corporation-job-re-views-C7602, accessed July 8, 2014. (Typos and grammatical mistakes in this excerpt are part of the original text.)

was only temporary and that once I had learned the business I would be moved up to a position more suited to my experience which never happened….The company is very unethical and littered with favoritism...I also took classes through EDMC which was great, however the curriculum is so far skewed from what the degree is centralized around that you spend most of your time taking classes that are not needed and then when it comes to your specialization classes they are blown over and you never learn what you need to succeed. They only want you to take as many classes as possible to keep you in longer so they get bigger bonuses for having so many students active."

* * * *

June 10, 2010: Today Senator Tom Harkin announced plans to hold hearings to examine the student loan program and for-profit higher education institutions. "The hearing will be on June 24. Pell grants and student loans now provide more than $20 billion to for-profit higher education companies every year. I need to ensure for-profit colleges are working well to meet the needs of students and not just shareholders. I owe it to taxpayers to make sure these dollars are being well spent." Between 1998 and 2008 the for-profit sector has grown from 550,000 students to 1.8 million, a 225% increase. Students at for-profit institutions are borrowing more, and more frequently, than their peers at non-profit schools, and according to the Department of Education, one in five students who left a for-profit college in 2007 defaulted on their loan within three years.

This seemed to be the beginning of the end for the stocks in the group. The negotiated rulemaking was obviously a big catalyst because the schools were in the process of changing their enrollment practices by removing the incentive compensation, a major blow. Sales would be going down immediately and would continue to decline for a long time. Harkin's announcement produced a flurry of bad press all over the country in various media outlets. The industry argued that the bad press itself was causing their enrollments to go down. (Pardon the cynicism, but it's less than likely most of their students even read newspapers.) More likely, more and more students were figuring out what a scam it was and just dropped out. I expected this would produce a *sudden, unexpected drop in enrollments* if shady enrollment counselors stopped promising free money as a reason to sign up.

* * * *

Andrew Steinerman at JP Morgan wrote, "ED released its tough-sounding draft regulations related to the Title IV program integrity initiative.[4] The education stocks should react favorably to this draft regulation, but investors will still recognize the extended DC uncertainty. The proposed rules eliminated all Safe Harbors and changed the scope of the compensation restriction to apply to all activities directly or indirectly related to securing enrollment."

* * * *

June 17, 2010: In another development, the Northeast Ohio Coalition for the Homeless sent a rather alarming letter to Secretary Arne Duncan of the DOE, stating "For-profit-trade schools and career colleges are systematically preying upon our clients. These companies employ predatory recruiting tactics, promising our clients free government money, quality education, rosy job prospects, and the chance for a better life. The companies fail to deliver on the promises they make. Quite the opposite, for-profit schools devastate the financial stability of our clients by initiating a vicious cycle of over-borrowing and student loan default."

"While predatory recruitment and lending to the homeless is not a new problem in the for-profit education industry, it is a substantially larger problem than it was nearly twenty years ago. In 1990, students attending for-profit education companies borrowed less than $5 billion from the Title IV program; in 2009, students attending for-profit education companies borrowed $28 billion from the Title IV program."

---

4   "Negotiated Rulemaking for Higher Education 2009-10," *Dept. of Education,* http://www2.ed.gov/policy/highered/reg/hearulemaking/2009/negreg-summerfall.html, modified Nov. 22, 2013.

* * * *

June 18, 2010: *Good Morning America* reached out to me, wanting information for a possible story. I told them I would ask my former employee
contacts if they wished to be interviewed on television, but none did.

Rockstar would not get involved despite my insistence. He wrote me
a few emails, which I truncated here: It was a tragedy to the American taxpayer…when there was an opportunity for vast personal gain, there will
always be people who push the limits of the law and, regrettably, stay one
step ahead of and beyond an ethical line that shouldn't be crossed. Think
Prohibition, the war on drugs, the war on terror, just to name a few. Each
time the "bad guys" were able to stay one step ahead because it's nearly
impossible to envision all of the potential avenues for pushing the limits.
In business, it's even harder because we have to find the balance between
throttling up capitalism and adequately serving the market… I'll sign off
with a final thought from Adam Smith. For free market capitalism to work,
two things are necessary 1) An educated citizenry (i.e. informed consumers) and 2) a strong moral compass. In the case of for-profit education,
they miss the mark on both counts by the groups that they often target
and their high orientation toward profit. This was capitalism run amok.

I made my case to Rockstar, trying to get him to come forward and
speak to the press. Short sellers are the naysayers, the spoilers, a force to
help create equilibrium. My clients, and hopefully you, and people like
you, realize what I am trying to accomplish in exposing the fraudulent
behavior. I've met the industry executives. Their greed blinds them. They
have committed crimes for so long they forget they are crimes and just
assume they are legal since they haven't been caught.

A client of mine met with APOL management recently. He told me,
they are in total rationalization mode, a state of cognitive dissonance, justifying their behavior into truly believing they are doing society a favor.
They are mentally ill with group narcissism. Hopefully, with your help we
can bring justice and protect the taxpayer from eating billions of dollars
of bad loans. At its peak, APOL may have had as many as a million students going through their revolving doors, incurring debt they may never

get out from under. Or there's a huge pool of a couple hundred thousand students who incurred a couple thousand dollars of debt while trying to quit having just signed up. Do these low-income inner city youths deserve that treatment? Almost every former employee I've encountered feels so strongly that something should be done. I've never been able to do research like this before because so many people find the industry's behavior so abhorrent that they are looking for someone, anyone, to complain to, realizing how detrimental the industry was to society. Usually there are just not enough people out there to complain. Here there are thousands of students and teachers coming out of the woodwork.

CHAPTER 11

UOP the Repeat Offender

June 21, 2010: Apollo Group announced that it has received the Final Program Review Determination Letter from its February 2009 program review by the ED and that the University has successfully completed the corrective actions and satisfied the obligations arising from the review.[1] The bigger question was if the ED found such a high error rate within the relatively small sample size, why doesn't it stand to reason that whole company could be experiencing those same percentages? What if a large percentage of refunds are being made on an untimely basis? But ED doesn't look at it that way. Why not? That makes the whole process of regulating the industry worthless if the schools are only going to be forced to pay a small fine based on the sample size. Donna thought that way, too, but would never be allowed to dig deeper. Almost half of the document was blank. I assumed management was able to convince ED that it revealed trade secrets. I have a different view for why they wouldn't want people to see the truth.

The report said that current student enrollment (2008-2009) was 362,100 as of August 31, 2008. The number of students for whom a return to Title IV calculation was processed during the 2008-09 award year was 139,141. This implies a dropout rate of 38%. The churn thesis quantified. Federal funds received as of August 2009 were $5 billion (page 3). That's

---

1   "Final Program Review Determination," *Dept. of Education,* http://www.sec.gov/Archives/edgar/data/929887/000095012310059465/p17847exv99w2.htm, June 16, 2010.

interesting because according to the 10-K, UOP had revenue of $3.9 billion.

"Out of the 90 files reviewed by the Department, 49 [54%] Title IV recipients withdrew from UOP during the award years reviewed. Unearned Title IV funds were due in the case of 48 Title IV recipients. In the case of eight students, Title IV funds were not returned timely. These late returns represent two out of 23 (9%) for the 2007-2008 award year and six out of 21 (29%) for the 2008-2009 award year."

"Due to the high error rate for the 2008-2009 award year (29%), UOP must reimburse the Department for the *cost of Title IV funds paid untimely* for the 2008-2009 award year.[2] In order to identify such liability, UOP was given the option of performing a full file review of all students for whom the *return to Title IV* was paid for the 2008-2009 award year, of reviewing and reporting for statistically random *sample files* chosen by the Department, or by identifying the liability on the basis of a projection of liability using the data in the statistical sample used in the review." Management was also told to "a reconstruction" because the error rate was so high.

"*During the July 7, 2009* exit conference with UOP officials, UOP indicated that it had taken action to address the concerns of the Department as stated in the March 2008 meeting. UOP stated that it revised its withdrawal process in June 2008 and August 2008 to provide 'more clarity to staff about processing of withdrawals and actions that must be taken by the staff.' On July 14, 2009, UOP provided the program reviewers with copies of documents reflecting the 2008 revisions and described training and directions given to staff to address the problem of failing to treat students' attempts to withdraw as withdrawal notification. Review of the student files in the program review process revealed however, that throughout 2008, *UOP continued to fail to timely withdraw students who expressed a desire to withdraw, resulting in UOP's untimely return of Title IV funds*. Further, the documents reflecting UOP's 2008 revisions and directions to staff were inconsistent and conflicted with existing UOP policies regarding determination of a student's withdrawal."

"*UOP disregarded the regulatory requirement of treating the day* that a

---

2   Note they are not asking for the illegal tuition earned to be refunded as I believe they should've done.

student notifies of his or her intent to withdraw, as the withdrawal date.[3] UOP follows its own written procedure entitled 'Withdrawal Date — Date of Determination of Withdrawal' and, *regardless of the fact that a student actually provided notification of withdrawal at an earlier date, does not treat a student as withdrawn until 30 days of absence.* UOP's procedure of disregarding students' attempts to withdraw is systemic in nature, echoing the student complaints discussed with UOP in the March 2008 meeting. The actions taken by UOP in June 2008 and August 2008 to address the Department's March 2008 stated concerns about disregarding a student's notice of withdrawal and implementing safeguards to prevent the transmittal of credit balance checks *after* a notice of withdrawal *were ineffective as corrective action. UOP's procedures and disregard of student attempts to withdraw results in the untimely return of unearned Title IV funds."*

"This UOP 'Official Withdrawal' policy does not address a date of determination of withdrawal. It simply describes the internal procedure for processing a withdrawal. Neither the 'Official Withdrawal' procedure, nor the 'Date of Determination' procedure provide for treatment of a student's notice of withdrawal as an actual date of withdrawal or date of determination."[4]

Noncompliance: The student files revealed that a student who notifies UOP that he or she is withdrawing is treated as an enrolled student until the student fails to attend at least 30 days. For 22 students who notified UOP that they were withdrawing, UOP *disregarded* the withdrawal notice provided by the students and did not acknowledge the withdrawal until *after several weeks of absence.*

Final Determination: While UOP returned Title IV funds due to student withdrawals, it returned them in an untimely manner (a criminal act, according to Higgins' May 26, 2005 testimony). UOP's liability, therefore, is for the cost to the Department for the delayed return of funds. The Department projected liabilities based on the results of a review of the valid statistical sample used in the PRR. An average liability for the cost of funds was calculated for the statistical sample ($4,738), and this

---

3   34 C.F.R. § 668.22(j).

4   An otherwise eligible student becomes ineligible to receive Title IV funds on the date that the student is no longer enrolled. 34 C.F.R. § 668.164(g)(1).

average was multiplied against the population (139,141) being reviewed. Therefore, the projected liability for the cost of the funds for this finding is $659,296.44 payable to the Department. They are missing 3 digits. That's $659 million they should've owed.

If the error rates were so high and the company failed to make changes from the 2003 program review to the 2009 program review, why wouldn't the Department, instead of looking at a sampling, go and look at all of the refund calculations? Don't forget there were a couple of OIG audits between the two program reviews talking about late refunds, as well, the IG himself testifying that late refunds are a crime.

Due to the number of unpaid and late refunds, UOP was required to have on file with the Department an irrevocable Letter of Credit (LOC) equal to 25% of the total refunds. After May 31, 2010, APOL posted a letter of credit in the amount of approximately $126 million, as required to comply with the Department's standards of financial responsibility. The LOC is fully cash collateralized and must be maintained until at least June 30, 2012.

UOP personnel met with the Department on March 28, 2008. At this meeting, UOP was advised that the Department had received a number of complaints in 2008 that: *Even though students tried to withdraw, UOP refused to acknowledge their withdrawal until weeks after they withdrew.* Students complained that UOP personnel did not provide them with withdrawal information or did not provide withdrawal information in a timely manner. One student complained that after he told the enrollment counselor that he had no money and did not want to start school until his financial aid was finalized, the enrollment counselor told him to go ahead and start, that he "would need no money." When the student's financial aid was not approved, UOP began immediate collection efforts against the student, who complained that he had been misled by UOP.

Student #6 called UOP on April 7, 2008 and notified UOP that she withdrew from the program because she was not happy with the classes. The UOP academic counselor noted: "The student called me because she wants to drop from the program. She said that she is not happy with these classes." When the UOP academic counselor told her that she would be financially responsible for two weeks of attendance, the student replied that she did not care. The UOP finance counselor emailed the student and acknowledged the student's decision to withdraw from the program. The UOP counselor further notified her that "your last day of class will be today," and advised her that after 29 days of absence, a calculation will be made to determine the amount of financial aid earned.

The student did not return to UOP after April 7, 2008. UOP did process the student's account for account collection purposes on April 8, 2008. As for Title IV, however, UOP did not treat the student as a withdrawal until she had 34 days of consecutive absences, and then entered May 11, 2008 as the "date of determination" for return to Title IV (R2T4) purposes. UOP returned unearned Title IV funds to the lender on May 27, 2008, 50 days after the student notified UOP that she was withdrawing.

Here is the official ED policy, "The withdrawal date for a student who ceases attendance at the University, including a student who does not return from an approved leave of absence or scheduled break, is the last date of academic attendance determined from the University's class attendance record. The University will determine the withdrawal date within 30 days of the student's last date of attendance...The University's review will determine if the student re-entered as scheduled, or did not re-enter as scheduled and must be withdrawn for the purposes of the Return to Title IV."[5] My issue with that is whether or not the students are being re-enrolled during the 30 day window and being charged tuition along with it. This official policy was designed for an accelerated program of study where courses last 5 weeks instead of 12.

Student #29's last date of attendance was October 18, 2008. On October 22, 2008, he notified UOP that he withdrew, saying that "I would like to drop out of my classes because I don't have time to do the classes and spend time with my family." UOP withdrew the student from his classes on November 1, 2008 for billing purposes. UOP did not return unearned funds of $4,702.50 of loans and $2,013 in Pell funds until December 8, 2008, 49 days after the student notified UOP that he had withdrawn.

The program reviewers advised UOP that the error rate of late return of Title IV funds for 2008-2009 files (29%) required a determination of the

---

5   HEA 484B: Dear Colleague Letter GEN-98-28 RE: 1998, CFR 668.22(b).

cost to the Department of the funds paid late. UOP was advised that it is the Department's procedure to require a file review of all files or to project the liability based on review of a random statistical sample.

Student #77's last date of attendance was July 22, 2007, according to UOP's attendance records. This online student advised UOP on July 24, 2007 that she was withdrawing because she was moving, would have no Internet service, and would mail back the credit balance check that had been provided to her a week earlier. On August 2, 2007, UOP updated the student's account to "Withdrawn Course" and initiated the automated drop adjustment process for billing purposes. Instead of treating the student as a withdrawal when she gave notice on July 24, 2007, UOP waited until 35 days after the student's last date of attendance and entered August 26, 2007 as the "date of determination" for Title IV purposes. UOP returned unearned funds to the lender on September 17, 2007, 55 days after the student notified UOP that she was withdrawing.

* * * *

After the 2003 program review, APOL only had to pay a nominal fine of $9.8 million. Had the regulation been applied the same way as CLCX, the fine against APOL would have been hundreds of millions of dollars. So that raises the question: will the revocation of the Safe Harbors allow the Department to reapply the existing regulation pre-Safe Harbors against the industry going forward, the way it did Computer Learning Centers? In other words, will the school have to give back all of the money from Title IV if companies are found to have recruited students illegally through incentive compensation and/or other regulatory violations? I don't know yet, but if so, it's a regulatory risk no one has even thought of yet.

At the state level things are different. Don't forget at the beginning I mentioned that there are 32 state attorneys general investigating for-profit education companies. While the federal government has abrogated its responsibilities to protect taxpayers, the states have been more aggressive in seeking protect their citizens. This could be near fatal to the industry as they have a long track record of seeking full tuition refunds.

Going back to Computer Learning Centers in 1998, they settled for $500,000. What was interesting about that was the 500,000 dollar fine only covered tuition refunds for the 55 students that were part of the complaint, NOT the entire school much less the whole company. I went back and looked at CECO's fall from $90 to about $15 and why the stock fell so hard. The reason was because of the activities of the Bureau of Private Post-Secondary Education, an office set up in the California AG's office post-CLC. They received multiple complaints from students at Brooks Institute of Photography. The bureau said, "Brooks Institute will review the assessments made to the Student Tuition Recovery Fund for 2002, 2003, 2004, and year to date 2005" effectively opening them up to a high value liability. The report continued, "No later than August 31st, 2005, Brooks Institute of Photography must provide a plan to the Bureau that provides in detail how it will provide equitable restitution to *all students enrolled from May 4th, 1999 to the present [July 05]*. Investors hate near unlimited liability potential.

In 2007, California Attorney Jerry Brown announced that Corinthian Schools, Inc. and Titan Schools, Inc. will pay *$6.5 million, including $5.8 million in consumer restitution,* to settle a lawsuit alleging that the for-profit vocational operator engaged in false advertising and unlawful business practices by presenting inaccurate salary and employment information to students. The complaint alleges that Corinthian engaged in additional unfair, unlawful or fraudulent business acts and practices, including falsifying records provided to the government...[6]

On October 18th, 2010 the Oregon Attorney General issued a press release saying they were planning to sue Apollo for $10 million. 'The for-profit college allegedly deceived investors about its revenue between 2007 and 2010, a practice that sparked an investigation by the U.S. Securities and Exchange Commission. The loss to the Oregon Public Employee Retirement Fund as a result of the misrepresentation is estimated at roughly $10 million...'The company's financial practices also hurt Oregonians who were pursuing higher education. The company allegedly did

---

6   "Brown Reaches Multi-Million Settlement With Corinthian Vocational School," http://oag.ca.gov/news/press-releases/brown-reaches-multi-million-settlement-corinthian-vocational-school Tuesday, July 31, 2007

not follow the proper steps when dealing with federal student loans, and improperly canceled loans and left students on the hook financially *for classes they did not take."*[7]

Then on May 16th, 2014 Bridgepoint settled its suit over enrollment tactics in Iowa. They agreed to pay $7.25 million regarding its incentive compensation. Bridgepoint denied any wrongdoing but agreed to change the way it enrolls students at Ashford. "The attorney general's office had contended that Ashford misrepresented to students in its College of Education that the program would allow them to become teachers." Then this, "…He said about $7-million of the settlement would reimburse current and former Ashford online students from Iowa."[8] Iowa is one of about two dozen states where attorneys general are investigating or conducting inquiries into for-profit colleges.[9]

In the end the program review was a disappointment.

* * * *

June 23, 2010: A Career College Association attack on short sellers is always a good sign for us. "Dear CCA Member, the Senate Health, Education, Labor and Pensions (HELP) Committee is convening a hearing to examine the career college sector on June 24, 2010. The Career College Association (CCA) has welcomed the hearing as an opportunity to examine the value and benefits of career and professional education in the United States; however, CCA questions why a short seller—Steven Eisman—is testifying before the Committee, especially when Department of Education Secretary Arne Duncan has not been invited to testify."

"Wall Street short sellers, like Eisman, play an ambiguous—both positive and negative—role in society. Eisman's comments should be

---

7   Bill Graves, "Oregon Sues University of Phoenix Parent Apollo Group Alleging Fraud That Hurt PERS," *The Oregonian,* http://www.doj.state.or.us/releases/2010/rel101810.shtml and http://www.oregonlive.com/business/index.ssf/2010/10/oregon_sues_university_ of_phoe.html, Oct. 18, 2010.

8   Goldie Blumenstyk , "Bridgepoint and Ashford U. Settle With Iowa Over Enrollment Tactics" May 16th 2014. http://chronicle.com/article/BridgepointAshford-U/146675/.

9   On March 31st, 2014 Bridgepoint announced it would be unable to file its 10-Q with the SEC due to a letter received by the SEC. The letter related, to the company's revenue recognition policy and its accounting for doubtful accounts.

vigorously examined with an understanding that a short seller's aim above all else was to make money on the decline of stocks, not to protect students or taxpayers. In a speech at the National Press Club today at 2 p.m., CCA President and CEO Harris Miller will address Eisman's previous published and spoken remarks, as well as his submitted testimony" [signed by Harris Miller]. Miller went out of his way to try to paint an ugly picture of hedge funds. He said—a lot of the activity going on, and with other media reports, was being driven by the short sellers, who are hiring people who are semi-disguising who they are and not being candid with people about their role in trying to drive down the stock price of certain companies.

"Short sellers and the industry claim the moral high ground. The industry argues they are performing a social service by making education available to many who have been excluded from traditional four-year colleges. The short sellers argue they are protecting the same groups of people from the lower echelons of society from deceptive and predatory marketing techniques to gain access to federal loan programs."[10]

* * * *

June 24, 2010: Notes from the hearing: Evidence suggests that for-profit schools charge higher tuition than comparable public schools, spend a large share of revenues on expenses unrelated to teaching, experience high dropout rates, and, in some cases, employ abusive recruiting and debt-management practices. What distinguishes for-profit schools from public and non-profit private institutions is that they have an obligation to maximize profits for their shareholders. Indeed, securities law stipulates that each corporation must act in the interest of its shareholders. However, this could conflict with the objective of federal student aid programs, which was simply to increase access to a quality higher education. The potential conflict this situation produces underscores the need

---

10   Sharona Coutts, "Investment Funds Stir Controversy Over Recruiting by For-Profit Colleges," *ProPublica*, http://www.propublica.org/article/investment-funds-stir-controversy-over-recruiting-by-for-profit-colleges, July 9, 2010.

for rigorous government oversight and prudent regulation to safeguard the investments of taxpayers and students.

APOL was at $44.62. I spent the latter part of last week in Washington, attending the Senate HELP Committee hearing. My take-away emanates from the fact that the OIG had only cursory knowledge of the issues. The OIG had a new leader, Kathleen Tighe. Interestingly, she didn't have any background in education, as she came from the Department of Agriculture's OIG. Being suspicious, I wonder who made that decision. Having only been in the Department of Education for a few months, her knowledge was slim at best and "I'll have to get back to you" at worst.[11] That's a good way to sabotage regulating for-profit schools. Eisman and Margaret Reiter made at least some impact about the true magnitude of the issues. Senator Al Franken appeared most receptive, suggesting the bad apples ought to be shut down. Harkin pressed Eisman about the biased position of the short seller. The industry defenders are smearing the short sellers.

Following the Senate HELP Committee hearing, I met with staff on the Post-Secondary Education Committee in the House, where I was stripped of any remaining naïveté. It was pointed out that the industry is very well financed and has stepped up its lobbying efforts to "educate" Congress on how for-profit education was a good thing. The Career College Association recently hired some high-profile PR consultants to aid in this propaganda campaign. There was a rumor that Harris Miller was out. I also heard it was unlikely Congress would do anything to curb the for-profits this year because it was an election year.

* * * *

With APOL reporting in just a few days, I wrote to clients: My internal mental target for APOL was $40 for 2010. With the stock here at $45 heading into the earnings report, it would not be a surprise to see $35 before the year's

---

11   "Kathleen S. Tighe, Inspector General – Biography," *Dept. of Education,* http://www2. ed.gov/news/staff/bios/tighe.html, last modified May 12, 2014. On March 17, 2010, Ms. Tighe was sworn in as the Inspector General for the Department of Education. Prior to this, she was the Deputy Inspector General, United States Department of Agriculture. From 1995 to 2005, she served as Counsel to the Inspector General, GSA and, before that, as an Assistant Counsel for the Office of Inspector General.

end, possibly by the end of this week. The question is: what fundamental forces are driving APOL shares most? On an earnings basis, the stock was cheap and should be bought anywhere under $50—the bullish case. However, if the company discloses an audit by the OIG (perhaps criminal), the HLC, their auditor, or more expanded investigation by the SEC, then the stock was trading off regulatory risk, making earnings irrelevant. On that basis, if there was a risk of criminal prosecutors or suspension of Title IV access or accreditation, similar to what investors saw with CECO in 2004, then the stock could trade sub-$30 either this week or later in 2010. As a reminder, in 2004, CECO dropped from $70 to $54 in light of an earnings report. It was tough to justify staying short through the earnings given the size of the drop, especially with the stock rallying right into the report date. For investors who stuck it out, though, the rewards were high as the stock legged down further to $41 and then $28 a few months later! I estimated there was a 35% chance that APOL trades sub $30 in 2010.

June 29, 2010: A scathing article was published regarding the sector.[12] "The for-profit education industry makes huge profits taking government money and lending it to students, most of whom will never get a degree. And the beauty is that when those poor suckers take the loans and can't repay them, that is the government's problem, not the education company's. Meanwhile, at least one for-profit educator hires sales people to push this money onto the weak—including a dying woman who wouldn't live long enough to complete a single course—and when sales people don't meet their quotas, it cuts their pay to force them to leave."

I learned these and other details from an enrollment advisor at Bridgepoint. My source told me that Bridgepoint enrollment advisers usually last only six months—and if they don't meet their quotas, the company cuts their pay by $15,000. My source also mentioned that the company prefers not to out-and-out fire the salespeople, because otherwise they'd be required to pay into unemployment. Instead, it drives them to quit by cutting their pay so much that they can't afford to stay.

Bridgepoint's filings with the SEC indicate that the company was being

---

12   Peter Cohan, "For-Profit Education Gains from the Pain of Customers and Sales Staff," *Daily Finance,* http://www.dailyfinance.com/story/credit/for-profit-educa-tion-gains-from-the-pain-of-customers-and-sales/19532735/, June 29, 2010.

investigated by the Department of Education's Office of Inspector General for violations of enrollment procedures. Most recently, Bridgepoint issued a press release that claims the Inspector General had yet to issue its final report because Bridgepoint hadn't provided the OIG sufficient information about whether it pays enrollment specialists based on quotas.

*   *   *   *

June 30, 2010: Dick Durbin made harsh comments in the press about the for-profit sector, arguing that many for-profit technical schools rake in federal student-aid dollars while leaving young people poorly trained for jobs and awash in student loan debt. He said these students often are women, many of them single parents, minorities, poor and first-generation college students who are out of work or in low-wage jobs. The Obama administration was drafting new rules that may cut federal aid to for-profits if the schools' graduates have a high default rate.[13]

In another article Durbin said, we could be looking at a repeat of the subprime mortgage fiasco, with low-income, high-risk students mortgaging their futures—not on overpriced homes this time, but on worthless diplomas. Durbin said. "Let me be clear: There are many good trade schools and for-profit colleges, and they serve a vital purpose, supplying job training that helps people take the next step up the economic ladder. But there are also a lot of bad for-profit schools that are raking in huge amounts of federal dollars while leaving students poorly trained and over their heads in debt."[14]

Durbin suggested a number of steps that the Obama Administration and Congress could and should take to address the situation, including changing the "90/10 rule," setting limits on the amount of money schools dependent on federal financial aid could spend on marketing and advertising, and changes regarding regulation of private loans and concerns about schools buying accreditation.

---

13   "Durbin: Many For-Profit Tech Schools Leave Students Poorly Trained," *Chicago Tribune,* http://www.chicagobreakingnews.com/2010/06/durbin-many-for-profit-tech-schools-leave-students-poorly-trained.html. Durbin warns of for-profit colleges rip-offs.

14   Lynn Sweet, "Durbin Warns of For-Profit Colleges Rip Offs," *Chicago Sun-Times,* http://blogs.suntimes.com/sweet/2010/06/durbin_warns_of_for-profit_col.html, June 30, 2010.

July 2010

July 13, 2010: Meanwhile, things started heating up on the legislative front. Higher Ed Watch reported, "Congress is expected to approve landmark legislation this week that would, for the first time, put a single federal agency in charge of regulating private student loans, rather than the patchwork of agencies that have done little to curb the types of predatory private loan practices I have written so much about. The new Consumer Financial Protection Bureau (CFPB) would be in charge of writing rules that apply to all private student loans, including those offered by non-banks, such as Sallie Mae and for-profit colleges. The bureau would have the authority to set standards related to the underwriting and marketing of private loans and to determine the types of disclosures lenders would be required to make to prospective borrowers."[15]

"The final bill includes a provision that was in the House of Representatives version that would give the CFPB regulatory oversight and enforcement authority over the sub-prime private loans that for-profit colleges make to their students. This is important because some schools are making these high-risk loans even though they know full well that many of the low-income and working-class students who take them out won't be able to repay them. Corinthian Colleges, for example, has told investors that it expects nearly *60 percent of the $150 million in 'institutional loans' it is making to students this year to end up in default*. These losses are more than offset by the federal financial aid dollars these students bring in. But for the students, defaulting on these loans could lead to a spiral of debt that could literally ruin their lives."[16]

July 20, 2010: With ESI at $90, I wrote a report: "Consumer Protection Act Should Slow Growth; Bill Passed Last Week; Regulates Private Loans; April Lawsuit Documents Predatory Practices Pell grant dollars up 76%." The new Consumer Financial Protection Bureau (CFPB) would be in charge

---

15   Stephen Burd, "Congress on the Verge of Making Private Loans Safer for Students," *New America Foundation*

16   http://higheredwatch.newamerica.net/blogposts/2010/congress_on_the_verge_of_making_private_loans_safer_for_students-34316, July 13, 2010.

of writing rules that apply to all private student loans, including those of-fered by non-banks, such as Sallie Mae and for-profit colleges.

* * * *

July 21, 2010: Sallie Mae was trading off 7% on weak earnings—sounds good for the for-profit bear case, as they are raising FICO private loans, lower originations, and higher charge-offs. (Paraphrasing) Non-tradi-tional loans *now represent 11% of the total loans in repayment, but contrib-uted nearly 37% of the charge-offs.* The increase in charge-offs this period was largely due to seasonal factors, though current economic conditions continue to negatively impact results.

The charge-offs increased in the quarter to $336 million, up from $284 million in the first quarter, and charge-offs on an annualized basis, totaled 3.7% of traditional loans, up from 3.2% in the first quarter, and 18.7% of non-traditional loans, compared to 15.9% in the prior quarter. Loans un-derwritten in the quarter remain a higher quality; with an average FICO score of 735, and 77% of the loans we made had a co-borrower. Reduced loan availability, i.e. higher FICO requirements, will slow the for-profits down.

After a decade plus of abuse by the for-profit education sector, we will reach a point where vast quantities of student debt will fall into default. The top ten for-profit schools in aggregate may have north of one million students flowing through them per year. How many of those dropped out even before the first year, no one knows. Multiply that by ten years and some amount of debt, several thousand dollars each, and the wave of de-fault will be substantial, well into the hundreds of billions of dollars.

* * * *

July 25, 2010: "Why Do You Think They're Called For-Profit Colleges?"[17] Michael Clifford believes that education is the only path to world peace.

---

17   Kevin Carey, "Why Do You Think They're Called For-Profit Colleges," *Chronicle of High-er Education*, http://chronicle.com/article/Why-Do-You-Think-Theyre/123660/, July 25, 2010.

He never went to college, but sometimes he calls himself "Doctor." Jerry Falwell is one of his heroes. Clifford has made millions of dollars from government programs but doesn't seem to see the windfall that way. He has come to symbolize the contradictions at the heart of the growing national debate over for-profit higher education.

Clifford calls himself an entrepreneur. He and his fellow for-profiteers have been snapping up dying nonprofit colleges and quickly turning them into moneymaking machines. Most of that money comes from the federal government, in the form of Pell and subsidized student loans. Phoenix alone was on pace to reap $1 billion from Pell this year, along with $4 billion from federal loans.

But graduates of for-profit colleges are having trouble paying those loans back, unfortunately. Horror stories of aggressive recruiters' pressing students to take out huge loans for nearly worthless degrees are filling the news. As a born-again Christian, Clifford learned at the knee of the University of Phoenix's founder, John Sperling. In 2004, Clifford led the sale of a destitute Baptist institution called Grand Canyon University to investors.

* * * *

July 25, 2010: With ESI trading at $86, Deutsche Bank downgraded the stock, lowering the price target from $110 to $85, on the expectation that Gainful Employment language will restrict a significant proportion of ESI's programs. ESI will have to increase its admission criteria over time to increase its repayment rates. The restrictions, plus the need to raise admission criteria, will make it difficult for ESI to grow. They cut their fiscal year 2010 and 2011 estimates by 8% and 29%, respectively, due to our assumed business model changes.[18]

---

18   Not to pick on Deutsche too much, but on January 21, 2010 with the stock at $104, he raised estimates and the price target to $125, citing new lending under the company's program of making loans directly to students (PEAKS).

August 2010

It was fairly well known in the short community that the for-profit companies were milking the Department of Defense GI Bill program. It made me ill to think that American veterans were being exploited for their tuition benefits. Again, this was partially driven by another loophole in the legislation. It was nice to see the Senate address this issue, albeit late. Schools are not allowed to gain more than 90% of their revenue from the Title IV program. However, veterans fall under the DoD's GI Bill and are not counted in the 90% but in the 10%, even though it was still coming from a federal agency.

August 4, 2010: Senators request more information on tuition assistance to for-profit colleges—"Concerned about reports of some for-profit colleges aggressively targeting military personnel and veterans, Senators Jim Webb and Dick Durbin asked the Secretaries of the Department of Veterans Affairs and the Department of Defense for detailed information on how veteran and military tuition assistance program funding is being spent. Specifically, Webb and Durbin asked for data on the tuition assistance used for education at for-profit colleges and the standards in place to ensure that veterans, service members and their families are given the best possible options for higher education and that taxpayer funding is being well-spent."

The Senators wrote, "But we have heard reports that some for-profit institutions may be aggressively targeting service members and veterans, signing them up for educational programs that may bring little benefit to future employment opportunities, low graduation rates and high default rates. Finally, with the recent passage of the Post 9/11 GI Bill, which provides for tuition reimbursement, we have heard concerns about excessive tuition being charged at some of these institutions."

Later, in May 2012, Ted Daywalt, CEO of Vetjobs.com testified in Congress. He said, "…Congress needs to redress this issue and provide mechanisms by which those veterans who were victims of fraud by the predatory for-profit schools can have their GI Bill eligibility restored. This can be done by recovering from the predatory for-profit schools funds to restore GI Bill eligibility to the veterans."[19]

---

19   https://veterans.house.gov/submission-for-the-record/mr-theodore-ted-l-daywalt.

* * * *

August 6, 2010: "Education Stocks Fail to Make the Grade" from Barron's: "For-profit universities are going to the back of the class, which is where they belong. Stocks in the sector are down across the board today, continuing Thursday's struggles, following the Government Accountability Office's scathing testimony to the Senate Health, Education, Labor and Pensions Committee on Wednesday that the schools provided 'deceptive and otherwise questionable information.'"

"The GAO showed the committee undercover video of representatives from for-profit schools encouraging prospective students to falsify financial information. The Department of Education will be handling some of the worst cases of fraud-encouraging practices, while several Democrats have noted their concern and hope for further investigation, given the schools' pursuit of taxpayer-funded government loans."

* * * *

August 6, 2010: Next, Kaplan suspended enrollment at campuses in which federal regulators uncovered recruiting abuses, in Pembroke Pines, Florida, and Riverside, California. The Florida campus was where undercover government investigators posing as applicants encountered admissions officers who lied about the college's accreditation, and admissions-test proctors who coached the investigators on the answers. The investigators also encountered recruiters who scolded and mocked them for being hesitant to take out government-subsidized loans to pay the tuition. Scenes from those encounters were videotaped and played at a U.S. Senate hearing earlier this week.

The U.S. Department of Justice weighed in Tuesday on the side of several whistle-blowers who have alleged in lawsuits that various colleges owned by Kaplan Higher Education defrauded the government of hundreds of millions of dollars by paying incentives to recruiters and lying to obtain accreditation. [20]

Top executives from Kaplan and its parent, the Washington Post Com-

---

20   Goldie Blumenstyk, "Justice Department Weighs In for Whistle-Blowers in Cases Against Kaplan," *Chronicle of Higher Education*. July 6th, 2010

pany, issued a joint statement earlier this week saying they were "sickened" by the findings in the GAO report. But Kaplan had been accused of questionable conduct before. Four pending lawsuits by former Kaplan employees raise allegations similar to some of the GAO's findings. Ms. Mack said that the company takes all charges of wrongdoing seriously but that its investigation had found those accusations to be "without merit."[21]

* * * *

August 9, 2010: With EDMC at $12.90, I wrote, my advice would be to respect the fact that the stock was down nearly 50% since May, and recommend to investors the position be closed in front of the next earnings report. However, in this environment, we vote for maintaining a position and cover/boxing on a sharp decline toward $10 and pressing if it rallies into the high teens. The company will report after the close on August 12. I assign a 50% chance of the stock trading to $10 on the earnings later this week, 40% chance of establishing a sideways range between $12 and $15, and only a 10% chance of a move toward high teens.

* * * *

August 10, 2010: Harkin's staff directed the publicly traded companies and 15 privately held for-profit institutions to submit two dossiers in the next few weeks. The first, due August 26, primarily consists of information related to management structures, revenue sources and enrollment totals. The second, due September 16, includes several requests for all documents and e-mail messages related to recruiter performance, financial aid procedures and tuition hikes.[22]

* * * *

---

21   *Charles Jajdelski vs. Kaplan* Case 2:05-cv-01054-KJD-GWF. Document 116, *Jude Gillespie vs. Kaplan* Case: 09-20756-CIV-SEITZ/O'SULLIVAN, June 18, 2010, p. 1.

22   Jennifer Epstein, "What Harkin Wants," *Inside Higher Ed,* http://www.insidehighered.com/news/2010/08/10/forprofit, Aug. 10, 2010.

August 12, 2010: A new and nasty lawsuit was filed in the eastern district of Michigan against Sallie Mae and ITT Education.[23] "On or about March 28, 2006, plaintiff applied to attend ESI… In June of 2006, plaintiff began classes as ESI, and took 12 credit hours in her first semester, paying $2,400 cash and using grant money for those eight credit hours… Plaintiff took minimal credit hours after her second semester but dropped those courses and informed ESI that she would no longer be attending the institution."

It was alleged that, "After 2008, Plaintiff discovered that *ITT Educational Services, Inc. had taken out fifteen or more loans in Plaintiff's name* as identified as Account Nos. (Account numbers intentionally deleted here)… Plaintiff never applied for the fraudulent loans…ESI fraudulently applied for loans and then kept the money." The rest of the suit discusses whether Sallie Mae failed to perform an appropriate investigation to prove that the student was in fact defrauded by ITT. In effect, Azar's credit rating was being negatively affected by outstanding loans.

The trade group representing career colleges was finally acknowledging that member schools have made mistakes as they sought to grow their student populations quickly and should increase transparency in the face of harsh government scrutiny and the threat of new regulations. "My schools have stopped blaming other people for their troubles," Harris Miller, head of the Career College Association, said in an interview with Dow Jones Newswires. "This is a teachable moment." Capitulation--finally.

Last week, the U.S. Government Accountability Office issued a report showing recruiters at *all 30 institutions* involved in an undercover investigation misled students or even encouraged fraudulent activity as they attempted to boost enrollment

Harris Miller said his group, which represents more than 1,400 programs in subjects including beauty, business, health care, and culinary arts for nearly two million students, was considering booting some members for bad behavior. It was Miller, who led the charge attacking short sellers for causing trouble in the interest of profiting from declining stock prices. Schools are beginning to take ownership of some of the problems they now face.

---

23   Case 2:10-cv-13196-ADT *Azar vs. Sallie Mae and ITT Education.*

* * * *

August 13, 2010: EDMC was at $11.90. At the risk of drawing criticism, I recommended to my clients that shares of one of my education shorts be covered. The stock failed to decline further on the earnings announcement earlier this week. The downside was limited and much of the regulatory risk was baked into EDMC, for the time being. I would look to revisit it at higher prices, perhaps $18 if an unforeseen bullish event causes investors on the sidelines to turn bullish on the stock. ESI, STRA, and others in the space should still have more downside, I told clients. Based on the liquidity, and the fact that shares are down 50% since May, it's prudent to take advantage of the downward pressure in EDMC. There was news flashing across the tape that some individuals in the industry could be criminally prosecuted. The ED intends to step up program reviews and undercover investigations.

A legislative initiative would provide solid footing for the short in the near-term. The Senate Education Committee was expected to hold a hearing on August 4—probably not a market mover, but worth tracking, especially since Congress was out of session for August, so there will be no news coming from them. Worst-case scenario: The group switches from trading off legislative risk and back to earnings growth, in the absence of new information, causing the sector to rally. If there was *any* roll back in Gainful Employment, the group will rally. New deep-pocketed institutional money, albeit being very naïve, could step up to buy the low prices.[24]

In Congress, a "bad apple" mentality prevailed, and it's conceivable that APOL will be used as an example of a bad apple. A witch-hunt of APOL will provide a warning shot to the industry that they are next unless they improve their performance. But does Congress know how deep and how severe the misbehavior is in the industry? The JP Morgan conference call also cited the new position of Senators Enzi and Alexander, jumping on the "bad apples" in the industry that need to be shut down.

---

24   I did my best in my reports not talk out of both sides of my mouth while at the same time presenting them with various kinds of risk that could move the stocks in the group up or down.

* * * *

August 14, 2010: The government revealed extraordinarily low repay-ment rates for the industry: 54% at public colleges and universities, 56% at private nonprofit institutions, and only 36% of students at for-profit colleges repay their loans. The numbers for the for-profit industry were sufficiently low to shock the markets. Most of the for-profit education companies dropped on the news that some repayment rates were below the 35% threshold. The entire industry went down in a big way, with the exception of Apollo and Grand Canyon. The other children rallied back. Strayer had closed at $200, opened at $160—rallied back during the day; Education Management fell to $9 and change, down 10%; Corinthian hit $5, down 21%; Capella was down $13 to $61; Washington Post was down 11% for $303. All of them seemed to have rallied back some at some during the course of the day.

"At some for-profit colleges, the repayment rates were startlingly low-er than non-for-profit and private schools. For example, 33 of the 86 Co-rinthian Colleges' Everest locations had repayment rates of less than 20 percent—and at several; the rates were less than 10 percent. At University of Phoenix, the repayment rate was 44 percent, compared with 38 percent at DeVry and 27 percent at Kaplan University."

"Repayment rates have become a concern not just to debt-burdened students and the taxpayers who pick up the tab if they default. For-profit colleges, under proposed regulations the department issued last month, can lose their eligibility for federal financial aid if their repayment rates are too low." Programs with low repayment rates will be able to get feder-al student aid if their graduates earn high incomes. Community colleges, where the majority of students do not take out loans, are unlikely to lose their eligibility, even if their repayment rates are low.

* * * *

Strayer held a conference call, arguing essentially that the ED doesn't understand how to do math and that their ability to calculate their payment rates were wrong. I didn't know or didn't think Strayer was that bad. I have to give credit to clients of mine, Scott and Jim, for really pressing the Strayer short. I didn't find as much wrong with STRA as I did the others in the group. By December 2013, Strayer was $30 down from $250 in 2010.

Even though these repayment rates are extraordinarily low and the ED attached a pretty strong set of disclaimers to their numbers, Apollo stock's was up because people thought their 44% repayment rate was better than everybody else. Forty-four percent, in my mind, was extremely misleading. While I cannot determine what that number should be given currently available data, there should be a correlation between repayment rate and graduation/completion rates. With APOL's low graduation rate, there was no way their repayment rates could be that high. What about the rate for students that don't graduate?

If APOL had been paying off loans on behalf of students to keep their default rate down, at some point, it was no longer an economically viable alternative, especially in a weak economy, where putting students into collections yields lower returns.[25] The recent rise in bad debt expense, 5.4% of revenue versus 3.4% in the previous quarter, signals non-collection. Therefore, the company was becoming handcuffed in its ability to maintain an artificially low default rate. Last quarter gross receivables grew twice as fast as revenue. As of May 31, 2010, Gross A/R was $409 million with $184 million of allowance for doubtful accounts versus $269 million in May 2009 with $99 million of allowance.

* * * *

August 15, 2010: The Senate HELP committee held the second in a series of hearings "For-Profit Schools: The Student Recruiting Experience." Overall, the hearings reflected the fears of the industry. The GAO presented its findings, including video evidence, of instances of improper conduct at all 15 of the 15 visited schools, including four cases of fraud (at privately owned schools). Overall, areas of concern included information

---

25   As previously stated, we believe UOP keeps default rates down as explained in *Angela Russ v. University of Phoenix,* case number 9:2009-CV-00904, Central District, California.

on the student aid forms, misrepresentation of placement and graduation rates, and aggressive marketing, among others. These findings served as an opportunity for Sen. Harkin's call for legislative action to fix systemic problems in the for-profit sector. Low graduation rates and student churn will be one area of focus, which could possibly be the subject of the next hearing.

Reuters reported that the U.S. government investigators found that for-profit colleges encouraged fraudulent practices and made deceptive statements to prospective students, according to a study released. Investigators from the Government Accountability Office posed as students and applied for admission at 15 for-profit colleges across the United States. School personnel encouraged GAO staff to falsify financial aid forms, misled them about costs, and gave false information about accreditation.

* * * *

August 15, 2010: A shareholder class action suit was filed against EDMC.[26] "At the time of the Initial Public Offering of Education Management stock and thereafter throughout the Class Period, defendants issued a series of materially false and misleading statements regarding the growth and foreseeable profitability of Education Management. It was only on August 3, 2010, however, that investors finally began to learn the truth about Education Management after the GAO issued a report that concluded that for-profit educational institutions like Education Management had engaged in an illegal and fraudulent course of action designed to recruit students and overcharge the federal government for the cost of such education. Following these disclosures, shares of the Company collapsed—falling almost 18% in several trading days as this news reached the market."

The defendant was liable as a participant in an illegal scheme and course of business that operated as a deceit on purchasers of Education Management common stock by disseminating materially false and misleading statements and/or concealing material adverse facts that enabled

---

26   Case 2:10-cv-01061-RCM, *Gaer vs. Education Management*.

EDMC to *sell at least $414 million of stock while in possession of material, adverse, non-public information about the Company.*

* * * *

August 16, 2010: Apollo Group, Inc. announced that its subsidiary, University of Phoenix, Inc., has received a letter from the Higher Learning Commission ("HLC") requiring the University to provide certain information and evidence of compliance with HLC accreditation standards. The HLC was a regional accrediting body recognized by the U.S. Department of Education and is the principal accreditor of University of Phoenix and its programs. The HLC letter relates to the recent report published by the U.S. Government Accountability Office ("GAO") of its undercover investigation into the enrollment and recruiting practices of a number of for-profit institutions of higher education, including University of Phoenix.

The language in the earlier lawsuit sounds similar: "Although each student withdrew from UOP within weeks of enrolling, they attended long enough to incur some amount of tuition related debt that UOP was entitled to debit from the students' federal loans. Although UOP was in possession of each student's federal loan money, rather than debiting the amount owed for tuition, UOP, without the knowledge or consent of the students, and without standing to do so, cancelled the loans, returned the federal loan monies to the lenders and immediately thereafter sought to collect the outstanding amount directly from the students."[27]

The way in which UOP returned federal loan monies for educational services rendered is neither mandated nor permitted by applicable federal rules.[28] UOP effectively pays off that student's loan by returning a student's loan money to the lender, eliminating the student's contractual obligation with their lender. Rather than eradicating the debt on their

---

27   *Angela Russ v. University of Phoenix*, case number 9:2009-CV-00904, Central District California.

28   Indeed, the HEA requires the opposite—a borrower is entitled to the applicable percentage of loan funds earned prior to a student's withdrawal 34 CFR 668.22(e)(2).

books, however, UOP then seeks to collect directly from the student the amount owed for tuition that it should have satisfied with federal loan money.

CHAPTER 12

ABC News Report

August 18, 2010: Ahead of another investigative journalism piece on network TV, ABC gave APOL management an opportunity to respond to the findings in advance, to which school president William Pepicello wrote, "It saddens and disappoints me to note that sometimes, these policies are not adhered to by our employees, though I was to stress that we take immediate action to address any such violation, up to and including termination of the employees involved. Let me be clear: even one violation of our student protection policies is one too many, and as president of this University I am committed to ensuring it does not happen."

* * * *

August 19, 2010: *ABC News* Investigates For-Profit Education: Recruiters at the University of Phoenix: "ABC News Gets Answers for Student Who Claims She Was Duped by Online School."

"The University of Phoenix, with nearly 500,000 students, is the biggest for-profit college. But some former students said they were duped into paying big bucks and going deeply in debt by slick and misleading recruiters."

The University told *ABC News* it does not tolerate recruitment at facilities like Y-Haven.

"'I don't want anyone else to be sucked in,' said Melissa Dalmier, 30, of

Noble, Ill. The mother of three had big dreams to be an elementary school teacher, so when she saw ads for the University of Phoenix pop up on her computer, she e-mailed them for more information. A few minutes later, Dalmier received a call from one of the school's recruiters, who she said told her that enrolling in the associate's degree in education program at the University of Phoenix would put her on the fast-track to reaching her dream."

"It's not the first time that the controversial school, which obtains almost 90 percent of its revenues from students paying tuition from federal aid, has come under fire for its recruiting methods. The University of Phoenix was one of 15 for-profit schools whose aggressive recruiting practices were the subject of hearings held by Sen. Tom Harkin, D-Iowa. The Government Accountability Office sent investigators to for-profit schools across the country and found that all of them were misleading potential students."

At the University of Phoenix's, the loan repayment rate was 44%, according to data from 2009 provided by the Department of Education. Students at their Nellis Air Force location had a repayment rate of 36%. At the headquarters of Brown Mackie College, another for-profit school, the repayment rate was 27%. Harris Miller, who heads the for-profit industry's lobby group, told Chris Cuomo that default rates at for profit schools are comparable to other schools that service similar student populations.

* * * *

The television producer interviewed a UOP recruiter:

Recruiter: I tell students to take out the max and whatever you don't need or you don't use then use it [for whatever]. But it's easier to take out more than you need and send back the excess versus you didn't take out enough.

Producer: What are the kinds of things, though? I mean in terms of like that I could use it for? I mean, what if I just...because you're going to have to have money to walk around.

Recruiter: They don't care. Right. They don't. They just tell you use it for educational purposes.

Producer: And they don't ...They don't what?

Recruiter: No one follows up. No one says, "What happened to this money? You received a check for $562, where did you spend it?"

Producer: It's your business.

The university president said that there was no excuse for a recruiter to push someone to borrow to the max. "It's absolutely indefensible. It is not the way that I intend to run this university," Pepicello said.

Experts say recruiters who are misleading students may only be the tip of the iceberg. Students who have attended for-profit schools are defaulting on their loans at an alarming rate, which experts say may be contributing to the next big financial crisis.

Though for-profits get the lion's share of their tuition from financial aid, the default rates on loans for students who attended for profit schools are alarming. About 50% of the students at for-profits drop out, according to Eisman, so schools need to keep adding new students, and have to try to recruit just about anyone—even those most vulnerable in society, he says.

The university told *ABC News* it does not tolerate recruitment at facilities like Y-Haven. "We can assure you that anyone who participated in the recruitment of residents from homeless facilities in Cleveland no longer works for the University," said Alex Clark, a spokesperson for the University of Phoenix. "Any such activity is strictly forbidden by our Code of Business Conduct and Ethics, and employees who violate this policy face disciplinary action up to and including termination."

Harris Miller said even though the schools serve an important role by providing higher education to students who wouldn't ordinarily get one, many schools' recruiting practices need to be changed.

* * * *

August 31, 2010: Everything was moving incredibly fast. Strayer held a conference call after the stock plummeted from $200 to $160. They claimed the ED was calculating their graduation rates incorrectly and that the repayment rate was not 25% but 55%. They defended their calculations, and now Strayer was down to $143. Meanwhile, Durbin says Congress must curb for-profit colleges' practices; he proposes having for-profit colleges bear some loan risk. For-profit colleges get 25% of all federal financial aid but represent only 10% of higher education students.

September 2010

September 1, 2010: Another legal shot was fired at the ailing industry: this time, a whistleblower suit against Kaplan in Florida, which ended up being combined with another suit in Pennsylvania. The individual at the Pennsylvania firm was the lead attorney on the case. Here are some data from the new Florida suit[1:]

Kaplan sought to fraudulently obtain federal financial aid for as many students as possible, instituting a policy whereby it manipulated the students' academic progress in such a way to certify that students receiving financial aid were maintaining satisfactory academic progress. When students failed to perform at the lowest possible standards Kaplan professors were pressured to inflate those students' grades.

Some professors gave into the pressure exerted by Kaplan to inflate grades as recognized by the Dean of Undergraduate Studies, when she commented in an email that "some faculty will give a student a grade of C when they have done no work whatsoever." This pressure to inflate grades resulted in the majority of the students receiving "As" or "Bs," part of the fallacy that students were obtaining satisfactory academic progress. Senior management pressured department chairs not to renew the contracts for those professors who did not grade leniently. Professors were graded on a student survey, reflecting how easily they graded. This forced the professors to inflate grades or risk losing their jobs.

The students could not afford to pay the tuition, so Kaplan would just give/award them the money in what was called the "Gift of Knowledge Scholarship." It was nothing more than diverting legitimate student loan

---

1   Case 09-20756-CIV U.S. District Court of Southern Florida, *Gillespie vs. Kaplan*. There was a second whistleblower suit filed in Western District of Pennsylvania. 06-1524 *U.S./ Victoria Gatsiopoulos vs. Kaplan*. The allegations are similar: placement rate fraud, pressure to inflate grades. *United States/Jude Gillespie vs. Kaplan, Inc.*

monies into the free money account. Kaplan would give employees money so they in turn could pay their tuition. That would give the appearance that they were cash-paying students, thus providing Kaplan with the 10% of students who were not on federal loans, helping them to avoid being in violation of the 90/10 rule.

The most blatant case of fraud by Kaplan in this 90/10 scheme may have been Miss xxxxxxxxx's. She was given the "Gift of Knowledge" in 2005 to pursue an MBA with Kaplan. Ms. xxxxxxxxx never paid a dime of her own money to Kaplan. All of her tuition was paid though the Gift of Knowledge fund and Kaplan reported her to the government and the (HLC) Higher Learning Commission as a cash-paying student. This was very interesting because it implied other schools, such as APOL, that provided classes to employees could've been doing so to manipulate their 90/10 ratio. The more students who were "self-pay" that fell into the 10%, the more students could be recruited who used federal dollars, in the 90%.

Kaplan reported to the IRS that xxxxxxxxx was a cash-paying student. Kaplan also reported the 'income' from Miss xxxxxxxxx's tuition as cash paid by her to the school. She received a $12,000.00 tax credit from the IRS, indicating that Kaplan had reported cash income from her for her MBA tuition; thus she was given a $12,000.00 tax credit for 2006 and 2007 tax returns for 'tuition paid' to Kaplan….This fraud was repeated many, many times with many employees…"

"When the students failed courses, Kaplan kept *re-enrolling the students until the Federal financial aid was cut off.* It was only then that Kaplan would dismiss the student. Kaplan would pursue high-risk students and inform them that the U.S. Government would give them loans that would not have to be repaid for some time, and that they could use the funds leftover after tuition was paid in any way they wished. The fraud is perpetuated when the student uses some of the loan money to buy a car, and does not even go to class."

Senior management put emphasis on doing whatever was necessary to keep the students enrolled, so the cash flow would continue to come to Kaplan…This policy was instituted because to maintain eligibility to receive Title IV funding, students are required to maintain satisfactory academic progress, or a 'C' average…By inflating grades, Kaplan was falsely certifying that its students met the minimum GPA standard. Had it been truthful in its grading, many students would have failed out of the school, rendering Kaplan ineligible to receive funds on their behalf after their first semester.

* * * *

September 1, 2010: EDMC at $8.01, "Cover": I wrote a cover on August 13 with the stock at $11.90 and another report on September 1. The stock continued to trade lower. The risk/reward of being short was not attractive at these levels; however, the 10-K was valuable for other reasons, such as private loan volume that may be drying up as SLM demands higher FICO scores and bigger restrictions on deferment/forbearance abuse. During fiscal year 2010, revenues derived indirectly from private loans to students at our schools, excluding loans under our Education Finance Loan program, represented approximately 4.5% of net revenues, compared to approximately 13.0% and 22.3% of net revenues in fiscal years 2009 and 2008, respectively.

Pell grants were $358 million versus $193 million, up 85% year over year versus total revenue up 25% (more Pell Runners). During fiscal year 2010, the ED performed reviews of two out of thirty institutions. An additional program review was performed at an institution in July 2010. The ED recently notified EDMC that it plans to perform two additional program reviews in September 2010. They must have found something.[2]

* * * *

September 2, 2010: "For-Profit College Helps Employees Complain About U.S. Proposals Education Management Corporation": The company that runs the Art Institutes, Argosy University and other for-profit colleges, has turned to external consultants to help employees craft letters voicing

---

2   See also for entertainment value: *Scholl vs. Education Management* (dba Brown Mackie), Case: 2:10-cv-00343-TLS in the Northern District of Indiana.

opposition to the U.S. There are 7,000 posts on the www.regulations.gov site under "gainful employment."[3]

* * * *

Bank of America: Education: lowering estimates and ratings; APOL was the top pick. They lowered estimates and price targets for the postsecondary education industry. Forecasts are now low on the Street for many stocks to reflect new regulations. Uncertainty was high and rules could change before the November 1 deadline, but they expect consensus estimates to come down over time. Although B of A said--Apollo should fare well on gainful employment. We like its increased focus on quality and note that consensus already incorporates flat earnings in FY11.

* * * *

September 10, 2010: Around this time I obtained a letter dated October 19, 2009 from the State of Wisconsin Education Approval Board (EAB).[4] It was a seven-page certified mail letter sent to the UOP Campus Director of the Milwaukee Campus. Such evidence flies in the face of UOP's insistence that such behavior represents isolated instances rather than a systematic pattern.

The EAB had received several complaints from students. The EAB thanked the school for allowing them to visit and interview employees at three campuses in Wisconsin. While EAB congratulated UOP on some improvements, they specified that some issues remained unaddressed.

This 2009 visit attempted to understand the numbers of "new students, drop, continuing and completed" that Phoenix reports…[a] "surprisingly small number of 'completers/graduates' given the total enrolled students…*Every year many new students enroll, and about the same num-*

---

3   "For-Profit College Helps Employees Complain About U.S. Proposals," *Inside Higher Ed,* http://www.insidehighered.207elmp01.blackmesh.com/quicktakes/2010/09/02/profit-college-helps-employees-complain-about-us-proposals#sthash.7CBiiCWZ.dpbs,   Sept. 2, 2010.

4   State of Wisconsin Educational Approval Board October 19th 2009 certified letter to David Steffen Campus Director University of Phoenix Milwaukee Campus

ber drop as enroll, and a substantial number continue, but a very small number of students actually graduate."

Students reported that counselors did not give a realistic picture of how difficult UOP would be. They reported the "unofficial" credit/transcript review done by enrollment counselors over-estimated the transfer of credits and degree requirement met as compared to the official Phoenix review which happened after enrollment. All students interviewed complained of call centers that provided poor customer service, calls not being returned, staff changes, and academic counselors not being helpful. Students reported their transcripts of classes and grades were misleading, which often meant increased requirements that needed to be fulfilled and more courses needed to be taken.

Students reported they did not have a defined "degree plan" showing when courses would be offered, though they were told, "Your academic advisors will map out your entire program path, including an exact date of your graduation." Students reported it's nearly impossible to do so because of the availability of course offerings. The students also expressed concern pointing to "systematic problems in the Phoenix business model for retaining and graduating a high percentage of the adults enrolled."

The Wisconsin regulators letter continues, over the past six years through a series of visits focused on student retention and graduation, I have developed the following picture of the Phoenix business model— Phoenix spends considerable resources on recruiting students but little on retention and graduation. In Phoenix's business model, few adults who start their program will survive through graduation. The term "graduation team" implies a separate department to help students. In truth, there is no functioning team and Phoenix has no metrics in its system to evaluate and reward the graduation team for graduating students.

It is unlikely Phoenix can improve student retention and has almost no chance of dramatically improving numbers of students who graduate unless there is major redesign of the Phoenix business model. Enrollment counselors should stop making guesses about the number of credits that can be transferred. The graduation team should be disbanded since it apparently doesn't fulfill any real function except to mislead.

Phoenix needs to drop the phrase "degree plan" unless it can prove the graduation date.

There is one more incriminating page in the document. It is a spreadsheet that shows by school and by year the number of enrollments, the number of new enrollments, the number of drops, the number of students who continue, and the number of students who complete the program or are employed (on this last one in the letter it is noted many enrollment counselors are graduates of UOP). For example, in the Business program there were 347 students at the start of 2008, 1,117 new students, 631 of whom dropped, 848 continued, and 39 either graduated or were employed. In the 2009 Business program there were 848 students, 1,044 new students, 832 dropped, 979 continued, and 81 graduated or were employed. Business is one of the better performing programs. In the Criminal Justice program, in 2009 there were 272 students, 350 new students, 279 drops, 321 continued, and 22 graduated/were employed. That's even more egregious than I was estimating.

* * * *

September 9, 2010: Westwood College's flagship campus was placed on probation and its three Texas campuses face losing their state licenses following a federal investigation that uncovered recruiting abuses at Westwood and several other for-profit colleges.[5] The Texas Workforce Commission, a state oversight body, notified Westwood's Dallas, Fort Worth, and Houston South campuses that it would revoke their licenses to operate in the state. The campuses have until mid-September to appeal the decision. Roughly 1,500 of Westwood's 17,000 students attend its three Texas campuses, and 800 attend the Denver-North campus, a college spokesman said. Alta Colleges, Inc., which is headquartered in Denver, is Westwood's parent company.

A week later they were kicked out of Wisconsin for enrolling students without the knowledge of the state regulatory body.

---

5   Kelly Field, "Recruiting Practices Imperil Westwood Campuses in Texas and Denver," *Chronicle of Higher Education*, Sept. 9, 2010.

* * * *

September 10, 2010: There was serious concern building that, if the Democrats lose both houses in the upcoming election, which seems likely, and then the industry will be once again insulated from oversight by the DOE. I am obviously very afraid that the election could run the stocks up, and it could run the stocks up a lot.

* * * *

APOL and its cohorts have been whining that their enrollments are weak because of the bad press they have received. I sought to verify this. I found a web site showing approximately 20 negative articles published nationwide in 2010.[6] It was unlikely such articles would negatively affect enrollment growth. It was more likely that it was caused by the new regulatory concerns, especially if their students can't read, as Cheddar says.

I think management was increasingly concerned about what enrollment counselors are saying, which has the effect of creating an overreaction. The school was probably giving all enrollment counselors a "shape up or ship out" ultimatum, the "pulling the finger from the dike" behavior I've been hoping for. Now, the onus is on management to attempt managing the transition, an attempt they're probably going to fail. The turnover of enrollment counselors was accelerating. Management may be unaware of how many people will be forced to "ship out" or fade into the background, as their enrollments falter due to lack of recruiting marginal students at the low-end, as well as not having any incentive to perform well.

* * * *

September 16, 2010: Apollo was $48.46. Industry representatives are appearing at a BMO Capital Markets conference today. They'll soon be trying to talk about how what a great corporate citizen they are. My clients

---

6　　Chris Morran, "Court Orders For-Profit College To Pay $1,000/Day For Sidestepping Subpoena," *Consumerist,* http://consumerist.com/2013/12/04/court-orders-for-profit-college-to-pay-1000day-for-sidestepping-subpoena/, Dec. 4, 2013.

are all battling the same psychology. We have the election coming up on November 4. Gainful Employment was coming out November 1. Harkin probably will be having a hearing in the next couple of weeks, and Apollo's earnings are released on October 16. I spent my day in the city visiting clients and going over numbers, arguing out thoughts on the quarter with the analysts and portfolio managers.

* * * *

Interview with a former APOL adjunct professor: Source was an adjunct faculty member for a year and taught C++ programming. He left after seeing some of the horrific business practices. Source indicated that only 50% of students enrolled in any given class actually showed up. Teachers were responsible for watching students sign attendance sheets to verify they were there; however, it was school policy that a student only had to stay in the class for 15 minutes for the attendance to count. The school imposed the distasteful task of having teachers call every student who failed to show up for class to ascertain the reason for absences, and faculty soon soured on having to stay late until students were reached. Source could not identify a consistent pattern for absences, though it was clear most students were ill-prepared for the class. As a side note, source indicated that at his current position at a "real" college the course-work he teaches was stretched over three classes, whereas APOL tried to jam the same material into one class, making it that much harder for the student to succeed. Source consistently complained of low-quality of students (and staff) and of rampant cheating, including the theft of mid-term answers.

* * * *

September 17, 2010: For-Profit Education research note by Sterne Agee: "The group has rallied for two days in a row. We attribute this to nervous short covering prior to quarter end. What may be causing nervousness to shorts was speculation of a possible delay in implementation of G/E rules.

Speculation of delays stemming from an article in *The Hill* that mentions renewed pressure from a few Democrats to delay the rules and; Speculation that some of for-profit education executives' discussions with ED officials lead them to believe a delay was possible given the number of comments received (84,000). We believe G/E rules are very much on track to be issued by Nov 1st and the rally in the space may be temporary. Remain cautious."

* * * *

September 18, 2010 (Saturday): I've had a difficult day or two. I have been in the process of writing a research report regarding the upcoming catalysts. I'm about to jump out of my skin over the election upcoming on November 4. The for-profits have convinced their students to write letters against Gainful Employment to the ED. There are now 126,000 comments and they haven't been able to put all them on the website. Obviously, looking at the letters, they are all generic letters written by Phoenix students and God knows who else.

One batch of 76 letters, all written on the same day, began, "I am very concerned about the gainful employment regulation recently proposed by the Department of Education. If implemented, it would eliminate programs and courses for hundreds of thousands of non-traditional students like me." With maybe one or two words changed, they were all the same letter. EDMC was shamelessly sending several thousand complaints on the same day and at the same time plus or minus a few seconds. "At 101 schools in 31 states, Education Management Corporation's (EDMC) faculty and staff prepare students for a successful career in their preferred field.... EDMC-operated schools have seen countless students excel in their classes and leave with practical skills..." I heard the schools told students the ED was cutting off their financial aid.

* * * *

September 22, 2010. More whipsaw action. I published my report warning about the possibility of G/E being delayed. I took a little bit of heat for it. The House Armed Services Committee had a hearing this morning to talk about for-profit education and military students. Congressman Bob Andrews, who was a strong supporter of for-profit education, even though he is a Democrat, is holding a hearing tomorrow to call for a delay in Gainful Employment. That could potentially move the group up. This Washington way of disseminating information was a challenge to try to trade around. I don't think clients know how to handicap it very well.

* * * *

A new development: Education Department May Delay Controversial Rule on Gainful Employment. The U.S. Department of Education will announce on Friday a new "timetable" for the release of rules aimed at the for-profit higher-education industry, a spokesman said today. The announcement came in response to rumors that the department would postpone the release of its controversial "gainful employment" rule.

* * * *

September 23, 2010[7]: Corinthian Colleges, Inc. and Career Education Corp. led a gain in for-profit U.S. education stocks after an analyst said the industry was likely to rally because short sellers will be closing their bearish bets. Corinthian shares surged 5.4% to $6.50 while Career Education jumped 4.9% to $21.76.

Signal Hill Capital Group LLC's Trace Urdan said the bears' exit will encourage investors who shun shorted companies. "We believe the bulk of the buying to date has consisted of short sellers covering positions," Urdan, who is based in San Francisco, wrote in a note to investors today. "If true, this would begin to create conditions that allow longs to begin to reinvest." I was having none of that.

---

7   Nikolaj Gammeltoft, "Education Stocks Rally After Signal Hill Says Shares Bottomed," *Bloomberg*,   http://www.bloomberg.com/news/2010-09-23/corinthian-for-profit-education-stocks-jump-as-analyst-urdan-calls-bottom.html, Sept. 23, 2010.

* * * *

September 24, 2010: Investors have been waiting for the G/E news to come out of the ED. Apollo was as high as $53.53 this morning and had a low at $50.70. They delayed it because of the high volume of critical letters, despite the fact that the company paid a consultant to generate them. The implementation date hasn't changed. I literally sent out an email saying here's my gainful employment rally, back up the truck across the space in options. Please pass the Rolaids.

* * * *

September 28, 2010: EDMC ($11.90) report: Interestingly, via a FOIA document in FY10, EDMC had 198,000 total loan recipients; however, in the fourth quarter 2010 press release, the company reported 112,700 enrollments. Assuming that every EDMC student receives some amount of loans, this could represent a 76% overage. This represents "intra-quarter churn" that was occurring at EDMC. The overage was driven by the loan dollars from short-term students… Referring back to the 10-K for 2010, page 22, we see that Pell grants represented $193 million of FY09 revenue, up 85% to $358 million. Recall the company went public in October 2009. Referring back to the original prospectus, I can see Pell was only $131.4 million in FY08, a 43% increase. So they came public knowing they could jam the Pell Runner revenue. Pretty crafty, Todd!

Through FOIA, I received compliance audits from 30 of EDMC's schools. The majority reported a withdrawal rate of 30% or more. Also, some of the schools were found to be making late refunds, though the amount was not egregious, just shy of 10% of files examined. Refunds that were due within 45 days, of the four out of 50 refunds found for Brown Mackie College, three of the four were *late by 170 days*. "Based on the auditors' definition of a material non-compliance, the auditors expanded the sample by an additional 59 students…the expanded sample testing resulted in 23 students for whom the enrollment status was initially reported incorrectly." That's 39%.[8]

"The auditors found that in 18 of 68 [26.5%]…the students' enrollment

---

8   Brown Mackie College, Findlay, OH, OPE 02616200.

status and *effective dates were reported incorrectly*. Based on the auditors' definition of material non-compliance, the auditors expanded the sample by an additional 59 students…testing which resulted in 33 additional students for whom the enrollment status was initially reported incorrectly."

* * * *

September 28, 2010: The Senate HELP Committee announced it will be holding a hearing to listen to testimony from a career counselor at Education Management Corporation who has accused the company of misleading prospective students, accrediting agencies, and policymakers about its record in placing graduates into jobs. The Republicans boycotted the hearing, with McCain and Enzi popping in to register their complaints that the hearings were part of a liberal conspiracy to single out for-profit education, evidenced by lack of proper representation on the panel of speakers. The panel was weak, with a former student from a for-profit with high debt (they already played that card) and the president of the Counsel for Opportunity in Education, was also weak in my view, stating the obvious that the industry targets minorities (playing the race card). Lauren Asher from TICAS was strong, articulate, and far better qualified than Kathleen Tighe from the OIG last hearing.

Finally, Kathleen Bittel, an employee from EDMC, told horror stories about the placement practices. I sent my interview transcript with a former EDMC enrollment counselor to most of the members of the committee. The hearing resembled a witch-hunt and was marked by a distinct lack of balance.

Bittel's opening comments were entered into the record prior to the hearing. "I am currently employed by EDMC and it was a tough decision to put my livelihood on the line in this current economic situation," she wrote in the letter, "But my conscience will not allow me to remain quiet about what I know."

She provided the following, which are some examples of the misleading tactics EDMC employs: "A graduate only needs to be working at their job for one day for it to 'count' as an employment in their field. I was also shown how to eliminate a document received from a graduate stating she was working in her field, but only earning $8,000, and to subsequently create a document using Salary.com to validate that an employee in that position would be typically earning $25,000, which would meet the salary threshold of $10,500 to 'justify' placement in their field."

She also provided examples of some of these allegedly dubious placements. These include: a Game Art and Design bachelor's student (one who learns how to create video games) with $100,000 in student debt was working at Toys 'R Us in the video game department earning $8.90 an hour. "I was told to 'place' him as employed in his field because his work tangentially involved with video games. He needs to know the knowledge he learned to be able to help his customers decide which games to purchase. I came across Graphic Design students working in places like Starbucks who were expected to agree they were using their 'skills learned' within their employment by making signs for daily specials and menus. A co-worker had a Residential Planning Graduate who was working in a gas station convenience store. He was expected to convince her that she was 'using her skills' by arranging the displays of candy bars!"

Bittel added written comments into the record, which are of interest: (Paraphrasing) when you factor in that the industry was targeting the lower socioeconomic class to enlist them as students; you have an end result of graduates who will never find gainful employment justifying their $50-$100,000 debt. Many of the graduates I have worked with could barely read and had difficulty writing in full sentences. This was at the end of their programs! One bachelor's student with a disability had his sister complete the courses for him! He had no skills of his own! He was a Graphic Design bachelor's graduate who did not know how to open a document in Adobe Reader! Please help those who cannot help themselves. Not every person was "college material." If they do choose to try college, they certainly should not be being coerced into incurring huge debt for questionable skills. By eliminating eligibility to the Federal Financial Aid system for the programs that are the greatest risks, you will eliminate the crushing debt incurred by these students and ensure that the funds are available to those who will benefit most." I left the hearing with trepidation.

October 2010

In a weird new twist in the ever-changing soap opera, a new lawsuit was filed by Keiser College down in Florida, which isn't even a public company, against a competitor.[9] It alleges, "tortuous interference with Keiser's existing and prospective business relationships." Defendants include Steve Eisman, a portfolio manager at FrontPoint Capital, Gilchrist Berg, the founder of Water Street Capital, and Antal Desai of CPMG, as well as Pauline Abernathy, who testified from TICAS, Deanne Loonin, and Rich Williams at U.S. PIRG. Phew. I am glad I am not on that list.

The suit alleges that "In May 2010, Eisman gave a speech regarding his views on proprietary universities. Defendant Lehr, who was a Vice President of government relations for Florida State College, promoted Eisman's speech in advance and tailored a press release to spread Eisman's message that proprietary schools are guilty of 'subpriming students'...In addition to Eisman, Defendant Lehr traded information with Dallas-based CPMG, Inc., another investment firm that had an apparent interest in seeing the value of proprietary schools decline. CPMG's Antal Desai contacted Lehr looking for student stories to use against proprietary schools."

Clearly, this was an act of desperation. Surprisingly, Keiser seems on the fringe. Not being a public company, I can't understand why Keiser would care. Corinthian has a big presence in Florida. It could be negative press about them would actually help Keiser. I doubt the negative press affected their enrollments that much. For them to claim short sellers created gainful employment, hurting their business, speaks to their desperation. The case was withdrawn a few weeks later in mid-November.

* * * *

October 7, 2010: Senator Durbin Takes on Corinthian Colleges[10]: Last Tuesday, Senate Majority Whip Dick Durbin (D-IL) took to the floor of the

---

9   *Keiser School Inc. vs. Florida State College at Jacksonville (2010).*District Court for Broward County, Florida

10   "Senator Durbin Takes on Corinthian Colleges," by Stephen Burd *New America Foundation,* http://higheredwatch.newamerica.net/blogposts/2010/durbin-38098, Oct. 7, 2010.

Senate and lambasted the for-profit college giant Corinthian Colleges for the multi-million dollar advertising campaign it has launched against regulations that the Obama Administration has proposed that would penalize for-profit colleges for saddling students with unmanageable levels of debt.

Senator Durbin: "If one opens the newspaper from the last several weeks, you have probably noticed a large full-page advertisement that has appeared almost every day. It shows, usually, a young person, and it has a caption that reads: 'A hundred thousand working Americans don't count? Put the brakes on the Department of Education's gainful employment rule.'"

CHAPTER 13

"Last Chance to Short APOL North of $50"

October 7, 2010: APOL at $50.70. I wrote a report titled "Reporting on the 13th After the Close — Last Chance to Short APOL North of $50." Their business should be showing more signs of slowing, whether it was behavior modification on the enrollment front, freezing salaries for enrollment counselors, bad press, etc., something was likely going to happen. I was hoping for new enrollment growth to fall and catch the Street by surprise.

* * * *

October 8, 2010 Deutsche Bank wrote: "We are a little cautious on APOL into fourth quarter results next week based on a meaningful number of recent meetings with clients. The bears are now focused on a significant slowdown in new enrollment. The bulls think this is already priced in due to the significant compression of multiples that has already occurred due to Gainful Employment. Who is right will only be known over time. It is safer to play those companies that are less impacted by Gainful Employment, and those companies trading on low current multiples. Thus, we maintain our Buy on Apollo Group."

* * * *

Just a quick email to my other clients: "Don't forget Apollo reports today, recommending minimum 50% position headed into the quarter, pressing any rally. It should blow up, hopefully."

October 13, 4:30 p.m. EST: Apollo reported numbers. They said that they are going to see acceleration in the decline of their enrollments. The stock was down $4.50 after the close, about 10%. They had just a terrible quarter, I feel so happy about that, and I congratulated clients over email before the conference call. Management suspended guidance for 2011 saying that they are going to go through a "transition" period and the conference call was in 15-20 minutes. The market was efficiently pricing in new information.

* * * *

October 14, 2010: Apollo was trading down $12 to $37 prior to the open! The whole group was down 20%. COCO was down from $6 to $4.75. Education Management went from $13 back to $9. STRA went from $158 to a low of $132. CECO went from $20 to $16. You get the point.

* * * *

Signal Hill writes, "Better Company, Worse Stock (For Now) — Downgrade to Hold." Apollo Group announced changes that are nothing less than profound and will likely create ripples across the for-profit post-secondary industry. Better screening processes for prospective students and the re-orientation of the company's approach to enrollment abandons much of its traditional lead sourcing. It promises to elongate the sales cycle and likely depress the overall pace of enrollment growth on a permanent basis should profoundly improve the quality of all the University of Phoenix's outcomes in the long term. Ultimately the changes will result in a more investible asset and a higher-multiple stock. In the short term, in our estimation, the changes almost completely obscure visibility into the company's earnings. And while the company undergoes this transition, we are hard-pressed to judge what investors should pay for the stock. He put a $45 price target "conservatively."

* * * *

October 14, 2010: The most stunning piece of information on yesterday's earnings call was management's guidance that new enrollments would be down at least 40% in the first quarter of 2011, and most likely would be down even more than that in the second quarter. Associates, bachelors, and graduate enrollments all will be turning negative. Management once again tried to blame bad press, but that was a mere scapegoat, ignoring the fundamentally rotten structure underpinning the business model. I refused to believe they didn't know what was going on and they definitely should've known. Ignorance is not a defense. And this was costing Sperling a lot of money, which was just such a great feeling. Hitting him in the wallet was a beautiful thing.

After the GAO report, *Good Morning America*, and other press, management may have assumed they had some bad apple enrollment counselors, but failed to understand that the behavior documented by the hidden camera footage was widespread, as my multiple sources indicated. Once they figured that out, they took steps to stop it, pulling their finger out of the dike and putting the lights out. Now, it was a question of how bad it will get before they can turn it around. It seems they now are willing to take their lumps all at once, rather than slowly—probably a good idea in the long-term, and to the benefit of the short.

Luckily, for APOL's current management, people don't go to jail for being naïve or stupid. This mess was created by Todd Nelson currently at EDMC, Brian Mueller currently at LOPE, and "Dr." Michael Clifford at BPI, with John Sperling still operating behind the scenes. All should be shorted at the open of the market on principal alone. Now, the cat's out of the bag. There was no visibility for the next several quarters. This was a problem APOL will not recover from in calendar year 2011, if ever.

Down 40%, new enrollments may only reflect the changes made in the recruiting practices, Pell Runners, etc., and not the potentially *bigger* problem of "temporary drops." That could add an additional 20% decline to revenue in 2012. Management may not know that—yet. To the shorts, UOP's retention was euphemism for keeping students enrolled against their will. That was a skimming strategy that was likely to evaporate, too, in 2011 and into 2012.

* * * *

When I received the documents from the program review at APOL, nearly 1,900 pages of data, the ED had redacted over 500 pages. Fortunately, the ED provided an explanation for failing to provide the documents. First, they cited "trade secrets," then "pre-decisional internal communication" and "personal information…invasion of privacy." Interestingly, the ED cited another reason for withholding information: "information that was compiled for a law enforcement purpose… [that] could reasonably be expected to interfere with enforcement proceedings."[1] It's possible this withholding relates to on-going OIG audits or even audits outside of ED enforcement bodies. That's new. I've never seen that language come back in a FOIA request.

* * * *

FBR Capital Markets: Downgraded APOL from Market Perform to Under-perform and lowered their target from $49 to $40 to reflect significant declines in enrollment and earnings for what is likely to be the *next several years*. APOL will be forced to alter its business model. "It is important to note that last night's announcement by APOL of at least 40% declines in new student starts in the upcoming quarter has nothing to do, in our

---

1   34 CFR 5.73(b), CFR 552 (b)(7)(c), 34 CFR 5.71(c).

opinion, with any of the new regulatory proposals regarding incentive compensation and gainful employment."

* * * *

October 18, 2010: (CPLA—$68). CPLA was one of the few companies in the group that looks pretty solid on paper. Nevertheless, these squeaky clean players are still expensive stocks and should have more downside to them. It was $100 at the beginning of the year. CPLA dropped from $79 to $60 on the APOL blow-up, and rallied back to $69. Under these circumstances, arguments concerning whether a company makes or misses its quarterly estimates are futile. Due to the regulatory pressures, every stock in the group was fair game to be shorted. While there may be some differentiation in terms of repayments or defaults from one company to the other, with the market in a "throwing the baby out with the bathwater" mode, individual metrics matter less. The GAO makes the point of having found misleading practices across the space, which surely includes CPLA.

At a CPLA analyst conference on the 10th, management (J. Kevin Gilligan) said, "*We expected second half growth to decelerate slightly from the first half*, but we were at a very high level in the first half in part, because timing of new programs." We are now lapping those improvements. So we won't have that benefit. Along the way, through earning seasons I was suggesting some fairly aggressive options trading.

* * * *

The Florida Attorney General's office has launched an investigation into five for-profit colleges, including four publicly traded schools, seeking information on potential misrepresentations in financial aid, recruitment, and other areas.[2] According to a statement from the attorney general's office, the probe was seeking information on "alleged misrepresentations regarding financial aid; alleged unfair/deceptive practices regarding recruitment, enrollment, accreditation, placement, graduation rates, etc."

2　　Melissa Korn, "Florida Attorney General Investigating For-Profit Schools," *Dow Jones Newswire,* http://www.nasdaq.com/aspx/stock-market-news-story.aspx?storyid=201010191815dow-jonesdjonline000556&title=correctflorida-attorney-general-investigating-5-for-profit-schools.

* * * *

October 26, 2010: "APOL announced that it has received from the Enforcement Division of the SEC a request for additional information in connection with the Division's ongoing informal inquiry regarding APOL. The most recent inquiry requests information regarding, among other things, APOL's insider trading policies and procedures, a chronology of the internal processing and availability of information about the ED program review of UOP commenced in early 2009, and certain information relating to non-Title IV revenue sources." The stock actually went up on that news. I assumed the SEC was talking to Donna Wittman, probably through some intermediary at the ED.

* * * *

October 27, 2010: DeVry (DV—$45) reported weak numbers. Management told investors to expect "a modest decline" in undergrad new student enrollment this fall. Management cites tough comps. DV undergraduate total student enrollment growth will be in the mid- to high teens in the fall. Fall enrollment decreased at one of their divisions, Carrington: new student enrollments down by mid-single digits, total students down by low-single digits.

DeVry *climbed* 7%, to $45.75, the steepest climb since July despite management saying new enrollment growth would slow to mid- to high single digits. The shares have declined 17% in 12 months. While DeVry said new student enrollment will fall, the company may be hurt less than other for-profit education providers, said Jeff Silber, an analyst with BMO Capital Markets in New York. That's not a very good reason to buy the stock.

* * * *

I had been working with Gretchen Morgenson of the *New York Times* on an article. I gave her a heads up on the APOL SEC filing talking about the insider trading investigation. Typically, when working with journalists, it was best to stay in the background by providing documentation, not quotes. However, I decided to take a leap into this one. It was important that people know there could be a link between the stock sales in the fourth quarter of 2008 and the first half of 2009 and the program review documents. Journalists *never* tell sources if and when they are planning to publish an article. So I had nothing to gain or lose.

Just like on the long side, there are some unprofessional, sleazy short sellers who might call clients before an article comes out, suggesting they get short the stock in case the article knocks the stock down. That's not the point. My clients are big, long-term short investors. Their investments are years in duration, in fact. They're not day trades. Public companies often think short sellers spread false rumors or generate negative press, but that was a baseless accusation. This couldn't be further from the truth, in my experience.

* * * *

October 30, 2010: The *New York Times*[3] reported: "But back in 2009, the period the S.E.C. is focusing on in its inquiry, Apollo and others in its industry were highfliers. Apollo's shares peaked that year on Jan. 16, at almost $90. By year-end they had fallen to $60.58. Insider sales of Apollo shares spiked twice in 2009—once in January and again in July. What the S.E.C. may want to determine is whether these sales were related to communications from the ED about problems it had identified at the UOP."

"The first batch of sales took place between Jan. 15 and Jan. 23. John G. Sperling, the company's chairman and founder, and Peter V. Sperling, his son and the company's vice chairman, sold almost 1.1 million shares during that period, S.E.C. filings show. Most of the shares were sold for prices ranging between $87 and $89. On Jan. 13, a Department of Education official sent an e-mail to Apollo asking about three student complaints it had received relating to the University of Phoenix's loan disbursement practices. It also noted that the department had received a copy of a class-action lawsuit against Apollo filed by students encountering problems with reimbursements from the company."

"The government raised a series of questions about Apollo's practices. On Feb. 9, about three weeks after the Department of Education sent the e-mail, federal education officials advised Apollo that the government

---

3   Gretchen Morgenson, "For-Profit Schools, Tested Again," *New York Times,* http://www.nytimes.com/2010/10/31/business/31gret.html?_r=3&ref=business&, Oct. 30, 2010.

would be conducting an in-depth program review of the company's financial aid practices. The federal inquiry was to begin on Feb. 23rd and examine Apollo's procedures going back to 2006. Apollo didn't publicly disclose the federal review until March 31, 2009, when it announced its quarterly earnings after the stock market had closed. The next day, Apollo's shares dropped 15 percent, to $66 from around $78."

November 2010

November 1, 2010: The Sperlings issued an interesting response to the article. In an SEC filing that day, it said, "Apollo Group, Inc. (the 'Company') announced that Dr. John G. Sperling, the Executive Chairman of the Company's Board of Directors, and Peter V. Sperling, the Vice Chairman of the Company's Board of Directors, had each adopted prearranged stock trading plans... Rule 10b5-1 permits officers and directors of public companies to adopt predetermined plans for selling specified amounts of stock. Once a plan is established, the insider retains no discretion over sales under the plan and the prearranged trades are executed through a broker in accordance with the plan."[4]

You are a little late. To me, that's an admission of guilt.

* * * *

November 4, 2010: Apollo was getting hit hard, down $2.35 to $36.05. It could see $30 by the end of the year. Another SEC filing made by the company this morning reported the ED was doing another program review. It seems to be a normal review. A client emailed me and was thinking about covering, but I suggested just the opposite. I would be inclined to *add* to the current short. We have the bulls on the run. There was nothing positive from the company; the wheels are coming off. Never cover!

It's right before Election Day though, but with the market up 1.5% that day and the for-profit education sector down 5% across the board, it was worth the risk to stay short through the election, which turned out to be the right play, as it came and went without incident.

---

4   "Form 8-K: Apollo Group, Inc.", *Securities and Exchange Commission,* http://www.sec.gov/Archives/edgar/data/929887/000095012310098528/p18276e8vk.htm, Nov. 1, 2010.

* * * *

Fortune magazine published an article titled "Did Steve Eisman unduly influence the Education Dept.?" It read, "After the U.S. Department of Education initiated a crackdown on for-profit colleges last spring, the industry began looking into evidence that the ED wasn't playing fair. It is now suggesting that the ED was in bed with famed short-seller Steven Eisman and is calling for an inquiry by the Secretary of Education."

In the world of short-selling, timing is everything—and that, according to the for-profits, is the issue. The ED confirms Eisman talked to two senior ED staffers to discuss a speech Eisman was giving. The highly publicized speech at the Ira Sohn Investment Research Conference in Manhattan on May 26 was titled "Subprime Goes to College." Eisman compared for-profit schools to the subprime mortgage industry and warned of $275 billion of defaults by students at for-profits over the next decade. Shares of for-profit education companies ITT Educational Services (ESI) and Corinthian Colleges (COCO) each declined 3% after his speech.

A month later, Eisman made the same remarks in testimony before the Senate education committee. The price of for-profit education stocks declined after his testimony. In an interview last month, Eisman declined to say whether his short positions benefited from the price declines after the two public events.

An ED spokesman said the Eisman meeting violated no department or federal rule, adding that they do not see any compliance problem in engaging with a broad a range of people, viewpoints, and as many perspectives as possible. Shireman and Bergeron "provided no information or reaction to Mr. Eisman," other than to point out factual errors in one slide. The ED staff met with many people from various perspectives and backgrounds about the for-profit industry.

* * * *

I interviewed a UOP enrollment counselor. If given a choice between being unemployed and being retrained to be a more responsible enrollment counselor, they are trying to choose the latter, although many enrollment counselors are so corrupt they can't be retrained. I heard there was a list of verbal—verbal only—things enrollment counselors are not supposed to say or even make reference to when talking to potential new enrollments. One enrollment counselor was nearly fired for questioning why quotas can't be discussed. Look for such Draconian measures to swing the pendulum in our favor. Currently, management was in the process of increasing salaries for enrollment counselors to be more competitive in the job market. This rise in expenses was obviously expected as that leads to lower earnings. These increases would be staggered over several quarters. A lot of high producers, making $75,000 to $125,000 are disgruntled under the new system, as they no longer have the opportunity of fast raises. UOP may have a couple rounds of layoffs as the company (and industry) shed enrollment counselors who are no longer able to survive or who no longer want to survive absent incentive compensation.

Management was desperately trying to change the corporate culture. Management was reportedly far less hostile toward the enrollment counselors, having seemingly figured out the advantages of using carrots over sticks. Students who had no business being put into classes in the first place are no longer being recruited. This culture shock was causing some confusion, especially for enrollment managers, over what can and can't be said, making for a difficult transition. Recall that many enrollment managers are nothing more than the most predatory recruiters in the company who have been promoted to a management job. Promotions are not based on education or merit but sustained high enrollment, no matter what was said to achieve it. That's going to come back to bite the company.

* * * *

I didn't think APOL management realized what they've done or cared to know how deep the corruption was among the enrollment counselors. Investors have just seen the beginning with the three-week trial program. What happens when they take action to not recruit Pell Runners? Hopefully, the regulators figure out that one. Or when they just plain stop recruiting people who have no business being in college? Further, if the mid-level management was made up of corrupt former enrollment counselors, they are going have to rip the guts out and replace those people.

In my spreadsheet, I took my new enrollments for the APOL quarter down from 92,200 last quarter to 42,700, down 49,000 this quarter, doing it my way. Management has a choice: they can deal with it as fast as they can or do so over several quarters. I am inclined to believe the former, based on down 40% guidance. They can't reliably throw a number like 40% around. They have no idea how much enrollments will decline. The important question was why am I crazy enough to think total revenue for associates could be down 16%? That's where it gets exciting. They recruited 92,200 students last quarter, probably more because of the Pell Runners.

* * * *

November 10, 2010: Bloomberg article by John Heckinger: "Executives Collect $2 Billion Running U.S. For-Profit Colleges.""Strayer Education, Inc., a chain of for-profit colleges that receives three-quarters of its revenue from U.S. taxpayers, paid Chairman and Chief Executive Officer Robert Silberman $41.9 million last year. That's 26 times the compensation of the highest-paid president of a traditional university."

Top executives at the 15 U.S. publicly traded for-profit colleges, led by APOL and EDMC, received $2 billion over the last seven years from selling company stock, SEC filings show. At the same time, the industry registered the worst Title IV default and four-year-college dropout rates in U.S. higher education. Since 2003, nine for-profit college insiders sold more than $45 million of stock apiece. Peter Sperling, vice chairman of Apollo's University of Phoenix, the largest for-profit college, collected $574.3 million.

* * * *

November 29, 2010: For-profit schools have 50% low-income students and 37% students who are African-American. A new report out from the liberal education policy group Education Trust says there was a disproportionate impact on the poor and people of color. It mirrors another financial debacle that the country should be in no rush to relive: the subprime mortgage crisis. The growth of the industry has been just as quick, the financial devastation similarly crushing. *In the last decade, enrollment at for-profit schools has jumped 236 percent*, even though public and not-for-profit private schools saw just 20 percent growth. The growth has come primarily from low-income students and students of color, which the industry proudly claims was a testament to their commitment to the nation's neediest and most disenfranchised.

I didn't really press the issue, but Cheddar Boy went out of his way to suggest that the statistics UOP quotes regarding the percentage of African-American students was a farce. In 2010, APOL claimed that 28% of its students were of African-American descent. Cheddar always believed it was much higher, especially in places like Atlanta. According to "IPEDs" the ED search engine, UOP Online had a 15% graduation rate for African-Americans and 26% for Caucasian students.

* * * *

November 30, 2010: Yesterday APOL announced 700 full-time personnel lay-offs, primarily enrollment counselors. That's just over 10% of the enrollment counselor sales force, with the vast majority of enrollment counselors in Phoenix and the remainder spread throughout the ground campuses. This was likely just the first round of lay-offs, and many more employees have already quit. Without incentive compensation, lower echelon enrollment counselors are barely making enough money to support themselves.

* * * *

November 30, 2010: "Criminal Trial of Former Dean Could Be a Preview of Fraud Case Against Kaplan."[5] This week's criminal trial of a former Kaplan University dean accused of sending threatening messages via the university's computer system could turn into a seamy preview of his billion-dollar whistleblower lawsuit against Kaplan.

---

5   Goldie Blumenstyk, "Criminal Trial of Former Dean Could Be a Preview of Fraud Case Against Kaplan," *Chronicle of Higher Education*, Nov. 30, 2010.

The former dean, Ben Wilcox, says Kaplan officials have framed him to undermine his allegations of widespread misconduct by Kaplan. So as part of his criminal defense, his lawyers plan to introduce testimony and reams of evidence that they say will show that the for-profit university inflated grades, misled prospective students, enrolled its own employees to fraudulently obtain federal student-aid funds, and falsified documents to obtain accreditation.

November 30, 2010: In the *Chicago Tribune* by Ameet Sachdev: "Wilcox, a former Kaplan dean, says company officials fabricated the e-mails to frame him and undermine his allegations of widespread fraud at the for-profit college. He has filed a federal whistleblower lawsuit in Florida."

"The e-mails were sent June 11, 2007, from addresses that belonged to another Kaplan employee at the time. Additional threatening messages were posted to a Kaplan online bulletin board later that month. Assistant U.S. Attorney Michael Ferrara said in his opening statement that the evidence will show that the e-mails and messages were sent by Wilcox because he was angry over being fired in 2006."

December 2010

December 7, 2010: Like other for-profit higher-education companies, Kaplan was under pressure from new government rules to reduce student-loan default rates. The division of Washington Post Co. has planned a program that will require certain students to enroll on a provisional basis, tuition-free, in an effort to weed out unqualified students before they take on hefty loans.[6]

Jeff Conlon, Kaplan Chief Executive, said the elimination of 770 positions stemmed from overall slowing enrollments and the company's decision to focus student selection on those "who are most likely to thrive in a rigorous academic environment and meet their financial obligations."

The Washington Post also published an article saying, "The Government Accountability Office has revised portions of a report it released last summer on recruiting practices in for-profit higher education, softening several

6   "Washington Post's Kaplan To Lay Off 5% On More Selective Enrollment," Dow Jones Newswire December 7, 2010

examples from an undercover investigation but standing by its central finding that colleges had encouraged fraud and misled potential applicants."[7]

* * * *

December 9, 2010: (Bloomberg—by John Lauerman)[8] "Twenty for-profit colleges reaped $521 million in U.S. taxpayer funds in 2010, seven times more than in 2006, by recruiting members of the military and veterans through misleading marketing, according to a Congressional report today."

"Getting the money from military personnel helped the companies circumvent a cap on the aid they can receive from the Education Department, their main source of income, according to the report from Iowa Democrat Tom Harkin, chairman of the Senate Health, Education, Labor and Pensions committee. Congress should protect veterans and taxpayers from documented abuses by those colleges, the report's authors said."

"Congress may have unintentionally subjected this new generation of veterans to the worst excesses of the for-profit industry: manipulative and misleading marketing campaigns, educational programs far more expensive than comparable public or non-profit programs, and a lack of needed services, according to the report."

"Rising numbers of veterans report that they've been aggressively recruited by for-profit colleges, said Donald Overton, executive director of Veterans of Modern Warfare, a service organization in Silver Spring, Maryland. The colleges have even tried to recruit veterans with disabilities or injuries that might hamper their chances for success in the classroom."[9]

* * * *

---

7   Nick Anderson, "GAO Revises Its Report Critical of Practices at For-Profit Schools," *Washington Post*, http://www.washingtonpost.com/wp-dyn/content/article/2010/12/07/AR2010120706803.html , Dec. 7, 2010.

8   John Lauerman, "For-Profit Colleges Scam Military for $521 Million, Report Says," *Bloomberg*, http://www.bloomberg.com/news/2010-12-09/for-profit-colleges-scam-military-for-521-million-senate-committee-says.html, Dec. 9, 2010.

9   "For-Profit Colleges Reaped $521 Million from Military," *Daily Herald*, http://www.dailyherald.com/article/20101209/business/101209495/print/, Dec. 9, 2010.

December 10, 2010: The HELP Committee report released this week about the military stated, "Between 2006 and 2010, Veterans Administration and Department of Defense Education benefits received by 20 for-profit education companies increased from *$66.6 million dollars in 2006 to a projected $521 million in 2010.* Between 2009 and 2010 alone, revenue from military education benefits at 20 for-profit education companies increased 211%. Revenue from DOD education programs at 18 for-profit education companies increased from $40 million in 2006 to an expected $175 million in 2010, a 337% increase. Four of the five for-profit schools receiving the most post-911 GI Bill funding in the first year have loan repayment rates of only 31-37%. The same 4-5 schools receiving the most GI funding have left at least one campus with student default rates about 24% over three years. The national rate was 7%.

In fact, during just the first year of availability of post-911 GI Bill benefits of the $1.75 billion in total benefits paid out, $640 million or 36.5% was paid to for-profit schools despite the fact that these schools enroll only 23% of military beneficiaries and $500 million in VA benefits was paid just to 30 schools that have received document requests from the Help Committee."

The 30 for-profit schools that received document requests from the Help Committee in August 2010 reported 23,766 students receiving military benefits of any type in 2006, but 109,167 students receiving benefits in 2009 and 100,702 students through approximately the first half of 2008. Several companies did not track students receiving benefits prior to the implementation of post-911 benefits and thus, the 2006 numbers may underestimate the number of service members attending the schools with service-related benefits. For 2010, eight of the companies provided full-year data. Thirteen companies provided partial year data and nine companies did not provide any data for 2010. Thus, 2010 beneficiary members are likely to be much higher than 100,702.

According to the committee's analysis of all students enrolling in the school's associate degree programs between August 1, 2008 and July 31, 2009, 47% had dropped out my mid-2010, as had 52% of the students enrolled in the school's bachelor degree program. Students who dropped out of these programs within the first year did so after an average of 180 days. The school also has an overall retention of just 33%.

A second school that received $2.02 billion in federal financial aid dollars in 2009 generated $488.8 million in profits and spent $120,000 in lobbying in the first quarter of 2010 and has not produced basic information about the company's revenues or student body requested by the Help Committee. Supplementing the $1.02 billion in revenue from federal financial aid dollars the company received in 2009, it was on pace to receive $101.4 million in federal military education benefits in 2010, the highest dollar figure for any for-profit school. For one company, the overall student outcomes for this particular school were poor for students entering between summer 2008 and summer 2009; 53.1% of associate degree students and 44.5% of bachelor students had dropped out by the summer of 2010 and had dropped out within a medium of 90 days, just over three months. The company has a loan repayment rate of 31% with two campuses and repayment rates of only 4%, and has 11 campuses with three-year default rates over 25%. Meanwhile, the company's revenues provided a 37.1% profit margin in 2009.

* * * *

December 13, 2010: Our story became even more bizarre. An organization called the Coalition for Educational Success filed a lawsuit against the U.S. Department of Education, seeking records from the ED related to communications between the ED and certain investors who may have "shorted the stock" of for-profit schools. Even rumors around the issue of gainful employment regulations that target just for-profit career colleges have caused a decline in such shares value and substantial capital loss in the stock market by companies owning career colleges.

In paragraph eight, it was alleged that, "…short sellers who bet against performance of the for-profit education sector have a significant financial stake in regulation that would harm that sector; for example in a few days following the release of the GAO report the market capitalization of the 15 publicly traded organizations that own and operate career colleges dropped by nearly $4.4 billion or about 14% drop in share price of the publicly traded for-profit colleges would financially benefit any individual or company that was shorting stocks for the for-profit schools."

* * * *

December 22, 2010: EDMC announced today that its subsidiary, Stauzenberger College Education Corporation ("Stauzenberger"), which owns Brown Mackie College locations in Louisville and Hopkinsville, Kentucky, received a subpoena from the Attorney General of Kentucky requesting documents and detailed information for the time period of January 1, 2008 through December 31, 2010. The Kentucky Attorney General previously announced an investigation of the business practices of for-profit post-secondary schools and that subpoenas had been issued to six proprietary colleges that do business in Kentucky in connection with the investigation.

* * * *

December 31, 2010: APOL at $39.40. I recommend a meaningful short position heading into APOL's January 10 earnings report. Last quarter, management indicated that new enrollments would be down 40%, although it's more likely to be around 60%. There are a couple of reasons why this was the case. It will be most important to note the drag on total enrollments created by the loss of new enrollments. If APOL was unable to replace the students who are dropping out intra-quarter, the Ponzi-like enrollment scheme falls apart, dragging down both total enrollments and revenue.

Management has turned paranoid, ruling enrollment counselors with an iron fist. Unsure of what they can and can't say to prospective students, enrollment counselors are saying nothing at all, for fear of losing their jobs, and having never been trained on what they should be saying. *Frontline, ABC,* and GAO hidden camera footage and print media have instilled paranoia in the industry, as they should!

UOP suspended its incentive compensation scheme for enrollment counselors on September 1 2010. The quarter that ended November 30 will be the first full quarter to reflect this change. Management already announced layoffs of around 700 ECs, and will likely announce another round. Now that ECs have no upside, no commission, no incentive to work hard, they become dead wood fast.

Again, in the absence of incentive compensation, UOP had a lot of deadwood. UOP's revenue in 2011 was still $4.7 billion down from $4.9 billion in 2010. From the fourth quarter of 2010 enrollment was 470,800 students, by the fourth quarter of 2011, they were at 380,000, while in 2012 they were at 328,000 students. So there was some delay in the decline, perhaps driven by the company begrudgingly dropping students in T-drop. It's hard to say. By August of 2013, total enrollment was 301,100 students down from 418,700 in 2011, while UOP revenue was down to $3.3 billion from $4.3 billion in 2011. That can't all be attributable to the lack of incentive compensation and the economy. The associate degree enrollments took the worst hit as that was where all the Pell runners were buried. For several quarters associate enrollments represented 40% of total enrollments. By the end of 2011, associate enrollments were negative 32% and bachelor enrollment wasn't far behind. I think the combo of dropping temporary drops from the enrollment and having no new students to make up the gap, pressured revenue and enrollment more than people expected. How long can they keep up the charade as I suspect they are not done yet?

The market still has not heard a single word about the academic counselor incentive compensation issue uncovered earlier in the year. In fact, according to one of my sources, almost the entire company is on incentive compensation. Source indicated, "Academic counselors, directors of enrollment, directors of student services, campus directors, financial aid counselors/directors—everyone is on a matrix and all are tied to enrollment whether it be new or retained (i.e. total enrollment). Moving away from a performance-based system isn't removing a tool from the organization; it would be upending the foundational base/culture that the entire organization is built on." Sounds like Amway to me.

AFTERWORD

For a hint of things to come, consider this interview with a former VP of Academic Affairs at Apollo Group back in 2011:

Me: "I have to repeat some of the things I've come across. I've had this one enrollment counselor who has been gone for a year, but he thinks nothing has changed [Cheddar]. He worked there for three years and only had one student graduate. Fifty to sixty percent of his enrollments dropped within the first three weeks. Only 15% finish the first year. He said all of the other enrollment counselors at the campus behave similarly. I said to him "maybe you are just an aggressive enrollment counselor." He said, "You will have to look at the graduation rate for the whole company," which as you know, depending on which numbers you are looking at, is around 19% and 25%."

"From that I deduced, from having talked to a former director of operations, that there are a lot of students on the back-end in the 438,000 current students who are in temporary drop status. And they should be moved to permanent drop status, and then if you suddenly have no new enrollments coming in because of the salary freeze, the incentive compensation freeze, the enrollments are going to attrite to zero. And then over a period of time as the weeks and months go by, the company is going to be forced to put more students floating around in temporary drop status into permanent drop status. And the total enrollments could suddenly drop at a much faster rate than anyone could possibly have imagined, and really without any explanation from the company. Is that plausible?"

Source: "I would say that is not an unreasonable scenario. Under the best of circumstances, the issues of retention are significant enough; the other issues are pervasive enough that, again, if there is a hiccup in any new enrollment it is very possible that it could begin to implode."

Me: "I just wonder what is going to allow them to *not* drop those students. Maybe they can find a reason why their enrollments might be down just a little but not a lot. So I am trying to gauge the timing of that kind of drop. Any thoughts on what might precipitate that kind of drop?"

Source: (heavy sigh) "On the ground level, we were in meetings to try to get some clarity on rather lengthy T-Drop lists. The standard for when a student will be changed to a 'Permanent Drop' or 'P-Drop' was a very high standard. The student had to say they would *never* attend UOP again in order to be placed in P-Drop. They had to say they never wanted to be contacted again. Short of that…unless one of the campus directors or I said this student needs to be a P-Drop because they moved or they hate us, chances are they would stay in T-Drop status…. So even if you had only a 3% chance of getting a certain group of those students back in, it didn't cost any more to have the ECs, say ok let's go with the 3% chance. That's not a very good way to run a railroad but that was the mentality."

Me: "So if you stopped showing up for class two or three times you would automatically be dropped from the class. The academic counselor called you to try to get you back in one week, two weeks, three weeks, four weeks and either they're not reaching a person or not getting a call back. All that time the student is in T-Drop. If I am hearing you correctly, unless they reach that student on the phone and the student says, "I quit, don't contact me again," they could potentially keep that student enrolled six, eight, nine, ten months?"

Source: "That is correct, that would be when I was involved in the process that was exactly right. In fact, I would say it would be longer than six, nine, ten months, it could be a year or more that the student would still be in T-Drop status."

In 2011, new associate degree enrollments were down greater than 50% four quarters in a row. New bachelor enrollments were down nearly

30% for all of 2011. I guess they stopped recruiting Pell Runners and the true fundamentals are showing themselves.

Management said in a July 1, 2011 company conference call, "As a result of the decline in new enrollments during 2011 coupled with a large number of students who are graduating or otherwise leaving the university, we continue to expect increasing declines in both total enrollment and revenue for the fourth quarter of 2011, and we expect that total enrollment and revenue growth rates will remain negative throughout 2012. We do expect new enrollments to grow again in 2012, and also expect to achieve higher retention rates for those new students." Good luck!

* * * *

Several of the schools have followed DV, ESI, and COCO by getting into the business of making loans directly to students or even giving them money and calling it scholarships. This is a good thing for the short, as it put the schools at risk of that student defaulting if there is a loan to be paid back. Maybe they won't recruit students who seem unlikely to repay a loan from the school. The grants get a little tricky because the schools are filling the gap between tuition and the student loan maximum award, thus allowing the schools to buy their revenue stream. That has enormous risks and conflicts of interests associated with it, which I discussed in the book. It's hard to say going forward whether or not the regulators will allow that business practice to continue. I suspect not if the CFPB is around. With COCO divulging the rate of default on those loans at 60% regulators are going to be focused on that source revenue.

The question is: whether UOP is continuing to commit fraud. I think the behavior has changed at UOP and in the industry since they stopped using incentive compensation for enrollment counselors. However, given the way they have behaved in the past as I discussed in the book, can the industry really be trusted? I think as long as there is an incentive compensation system, even if it is for non-enrollment counselors, then regulators have to keep an eye out for potential abuses. Theoretically, as revenue deteriorates, more and more people will be laid off, or perhaps simply have their salary cut. I still think UOP's stock price could decline over time as expenses increase to improve the quality of the teachers.

* * * *

In September of 2010 a qui tam lawsuit case was filed by Attorney Dan Bartley. It was sealed so no one even knew about it. A second amended complaint was filed in August of 2011, which was unsealed.[10] The author makes some serious allegations against UOP.

Hoggett elaborates, "Financial aid misrepresentation is under-reported to regulators and government agencies because many students drop out in the first class, before financial aid is certified, so the fees owed are transferred to the university's internal collection apparatus, and thus not included in the university's official default rate"[11] [Notice the date of this letter is all the way back to 2009]

"The university has improperly kept scholarship money belonging to a student that did not start class....[t]he student later received a tax form in the mail from the scholarship foundation, showing that her scholarship had been used. Upon investigation, it was discovered that the University had received the scholarship monies in April of 2008, and retained the funds after the student did not start."

"The campus is not in compliance with HLC requirements for faculty governance. There are no Area Chairs at the campus. We are required by accreditation to have Area Chairs covering 14 areas of content."

"We were told they [teachers] were not 'good team members' since they did not realize retention was the goal and would not do 'whatever was needed' to accomplish that goal. *This apparently included working after a course was completed with a failed student to allow for work to be done after the course to perhaps allow the student to pass.*"

"The University pressures thousands of students into enrolling before

---

10   *Derek Hoggett vs. University of Phoenix.* Case 2:10-cv-02478-MCE -KJN Document 21 Filed 08/05/11

11   Derek Hoggett letter to US Department of Education Office of Inspector General February 2009 OUS-11-00026 4-4 Page 2.

they are either ready or financially able or both. The result is that *more than half of all new University students drop before the beginning of their fifth class*, and many more drop long before graduating."

"The University of Phoenix's risk of its accreditation is heightened by the fact that many of the records documenting university activities and student advisement are incomplete. Many required conversations are never documented, including about financial aid and program requirements....[t]he University would have difficulty meeting many of its academic and regulatory requirements. A consistent theme in the campus audits that I have seen is that academic or faculty records were missing or were very incomplete."

"Enrollment counselors are told *not to include evidence of these unethical and illegal practices* in the conversation notes on the student's record [internal Galaxy software], or to put in the record any conversations that would alarm the regulators. Education regulators use student records to help evaluate the University."

The school policy reads, "Please avoid using words like EMOROCO or Emotional Roller-Coaster in the notes in Galaxy. Do not worry about old notes, but going forward please refrain from using these words in the comment section. This is a compliance issue especially since this could reflect negatively on us when students wish to see their file."

"The University encourages staff *not to fully document issues or conversations* with students that could prove embarrassing or non-compliant. Counselors and other staff are routinely warned about the content left in the official student records, as students have a right to see their files at any time."

"Staff is routinely told 'if it is not in Galaxy, it didn't happen.' Galaxy is the student record database where different departments have access to student's record. However, much of the documentation required in student files is absent. During the enrollment cycle, most conversations regarding financial aid, program outcomes, or academic progression are not documented. To my knowledge, a major investigation of these records has never been made."

"Enrollment staff is instructed to hide these sales practices from educational regulators during campus audits. Before a recent visit by [an] audit by education regulators, counselors were told to hide all posters relating to Drive Theory, and any enrollment awards for student recruitment, that are usually posted in the work cubes."

"Enrollment counselors are instructed to mislead students as to their courses contained in a specific degree program, or about the job prospects that relate to that degree."

"The university's lead contact policy states that the only way a student may not be contacted is if the students has specifically requested placement on the Do Not Call list. Statements by students that they are attending other schools, or have no interest in attending the University of Phoenix, is not regarded as sufficient reason to be removed from the contact lists."

"UOP continues to mislead consumers, shareholders (by repeatedly stating it has ended the following practices), and the Department of Education. University faculty is pressured to violate *academic policy* and government requirements in an effort to keep students in class, and therefore paying their tuition fees. Students are passed that by any standard should be failed."

"Faculty told us they felt *pressure from operational staff, as a matter of campus policy, to not fail students.*"

"I truly am enthused about establishing a goal for academics to have responsibility for 'student success' (and seeking words to do that), but as Bill said clearly in the meeting in December, we *do not want the accrediting body ever seeing a faculty goal of 'retaining' students; it is a conflict of academic rigor and will not fly.*" (Minutes of Director of Academic Affairs teleconference.)

When I talked to Hoggett, he said that he believes this occurred at several locations at the company. He would not say why he thought that. We have been told that in the below excerpt, "others in UOP management" refers to the Regional Director of Enrollments based out of Kansas City.

"UOP, since the time the institution has been eligible to receive funds from ED, has falsely certified each year that it is in compliance with regulations such as the incentive compensation ban, while intentionally and knowingly violating such regulations in order to receive the Title IV and Higher Education Act funds. (b) The subject fraud is blatant and systemic, and is a direct result of the institution's business plan. (c) This conduct was not deterred or altered by the *Hendow* settlement. (d) UOP has continued to violate the incentive compensation ban from December 12, 2009, to the present. (e) To hide UOP's conduct, *in early August 2010, UOP Compliance Manager Ryan Stanley and others in UOP management publicly ordered all enrollment counselors at the South Austin UOP campus to print, and then destroy, any files or documents on their desktop computers that related to training, and sales scripts.* (f) Management then confiscated all of the printed documents. (g) Recruiters were not told to stop using these scripts; they were just not to keep any evidence of them. (h) The failed tactics used by UOP recruiters trying to make their numbers were not changed."

In the summer of 2014, the Hoggett case was dismissed, for the moment; however, I still believe the quotes from the suit are relevant.

EPILOGUE

I promised at the beginning of this book that I could offer up a possible way to slow down the sector's bad behavior. Publicly traded companies have to be treated differently. The problem with Gainful Employment was its difficulty to enforce. It was a nightmare from the start trying to tie IRS income data to FAFSA applications, which was just one of the things they talked about doing.

The industry really hates the 90/10 rule. If schools receive near the 90% of their revenue from Title IV; the other 10% has to come from somewhere else, out of pocket or GI Bill money. By now the large for-profit schools are all banging up against that ceiling, limiting their ability to grow because so few of their students have any money. For awhile the GI Bill money lowered the ratio because it was part of the 10%, thus allowing the industry to recruit more students in the 90% pool. Fifteen years ago, that ratio was 85/15.[1] Through heavy lobbying efforts the sector pushed for 90/10. I've been told by investigators at the ED they add 5% for fudge factor to what the schools are already reporting anyway. And this was data the ED already has at its disposal. If that number was rolled back to 70/30 or even lower, it would clip their wings. It wouldn't put the for-profits out of business, but it would severely limit their ability to steal from the student loan program. It would force them to recruit more students who have a better chance of success. The Pell Runner issues would be partially solved, and the recruiting of low-income inner city youths into worthless associate

---

1   Mark Kantrowitz, "Consequence of the 90/10 Rule" http://www.edvisors.com/down-loads/student-aid-policy/20130819-90-10-rule.pdf

degree programs would be cut back. That ratio was the one thing that still intimidates the industry, for good reason. It would solve a lot of problems really hard and really fast. The only thing needed was the political will to implement it. And unfortunately, that's not going to happen until the student loan bubble explodes en masse and Congress figures out it was caused by for-profit education companies.

I also think the publicly traded for-profit schools should have their access to Pell grants limited. Why not set up a ratio similar to 90/10, but have it be for Pell grants, too? For example, if UOP was generating $4 billion of revenue annually and $1 billion of it was coming from Pell, which has revenue recognition issues. So we are already at 25% of revenue. Perhaps rolling that number back to 15% would be prudent, as it would limit any leftover nefarious recruiting tactics at the low end of the economic spectrum. If the for-profit schools are legitimate, prove it by cutting back the access to Pell funds. I know Congress talked about limiting marketing dollars, but I think there would be too many ways around any limitation.

* * * *

Just looking at the advertising that's out there, it certainly appears the for-profit sector was trying hard to look similar to traditional schools, hoping that if they can improve their image through advertising, maybe they can drive their retention higher, reducing pressure on the enrollment growth (decline) caused by recruiting low-quality students. It's hard to know whether the industry was successful in this endeavor. I have doubts. If graduation rates rise and default rates fall, maybe the schools are more legitimate.

One thing we haven't heard much of, however, and I think it's around the corner, is the trend in tuitions. The education industry has been able to raise tuitions 5% per year or more right through the recession. People know how important it is to have a college education system. But with the kids coming out of school with so much debt relative to their earnings, students are having a much harder time supporting their debt levels. There's a bottleneck the college industry has enjoyed. However, outside of the top tier and second tier schools, we have started to see small non-for-profit actually lower tuition, which would decimate the for-profit education model over time. In fact, even with the advantage of using federal dollars to buy advertising, a small price war at the lower echelons of the college system would decimate the for-profit schools. Several of those types of schools already have tuition 50% below for-profit education companies. That channel should prevent price increases.

Cheddar Boy had it right. The regulators definitely need metrics that measure aptitude for colleges in general, not just for-profit schools. One of those should be graduation rates. The national graduation rate is around 58%. UOP's graduation rates remain in the 30s for both associate and bachelor students.[2] I would mandate a certain rate and suspend Title IV if a school fell under a threshold.

---

2   University of Phoenix, "Press Release: University of Phoenix Releases 2011 Academic Annual Report," *Securities and Exchange Commission,* http://www.sec.gov/Archives/edgar/data/929887/000119312512035909/d291857dex991.htm, Feb. 2, 2012. "Bachelor's degree modified graduation rates declined from the 2010 Academic Annual Report to 31 percent for students who graduate within six years and 33 percent within eight years, both down by 3 percentage points in 2011."

APPENDIX 1[1]

Ray Dirks and the Equity Funding Scandal
Brian Trumbore
President/Editor, StocksandNews.com

Over 30 years ago, a scandal broke involving a large insurance company, Equity Funding Corporation based out of Los Angeles. The central figure ended up being a securities analyst at Delafield, Childs, Inc., Raymond L. Dirks, who one day in March 1973 received a call from a disgruntled employee at Equity Funding, Ronald Secrist. Secrist was upset over his small Christmas bonus and he had a story to tell. As you read what follows, you'll be reminded of today's headline grabbing cases, ranging from Enron and Parmalat to Martha Stewart. Yes, we've been here before, and we'll just keep repeating the same mistakes, over and over again until the end of time.

Equity Funding had been creating false insurance policies for years, which the company then turned around and packaged to reinsurers, pocketing the cash. Incredibly, the fraud was known by as many as a thousand employees. As reporter Robert Cole wrote for the New York Times back on April 15, 1973, "Those closest to (the scam) were believed to have cleverly concealed their tracks through intimidation, subterfuge, threats of violence and the use of doctored computer tapes."

Equity Funding would use the fake profits to maintain the share price

---

1   Reprinted with permission from the original author, Brian Trumbore, "Ray Dirks and the Equity Funding Scandal"

and the hope was that one day it would be able to buy a major life insurance company and then "go straight." Equity Funding's books were loaded with fake bonds and CDs, but when questions arose, the accountants trusted the explanations of company officials. Remember, it was 1973 and computers weren't in use anywhere near what they are today, so at times the auditors accepted handwritten lists as proof various positions existed. Employees involved in the scam also created computer printouts and paper files during late-night parties after receiving a specific auditor request. And all this time that Equity Funding deceived the auditors, the analysts on Wall Street and various insurance industry watchdogs were taken in as well.

For example, one month before it all unraveled, Cowen & Co. issued a report where the analyst recommended purchase of Equity Funding "for aggressive accounts." Burnham & Co., Inc. said on January 30 "We regard the stock, selling at 9.9 times estimated 1973 earnings, an excellent value and rate it a Buy."

On March 26, the day before the NYSE halted trading, the analyst for Hayden, Stone, Inc. wrote a memo addressing the fact that "several rumors have been circulating which have affected Equity Funding's stock; we have checked these rumors, and there appears to be no substance to any of them." This particular analyst had checked with insurance regulators in various states and each one said they had no present intention of conducting any inquiries.

As for Ray Dirks, he told his favored institutional clients of the scam and alerted the SEC. There was a mad dash to get out, and those who didn't act quickly enough, or who didn't have the knowledge, lost everything. Overall, the fraud exceeded $300 million.

Dirks ended up being censured by the SEC for his actions and over the next ten years he fought the decision, all the way up to the U.S. Supreme Court. Following is an extensive excerpt from a brief filed by the Justice Department, in defense of Dirks, before the Supreme Court, October 1982. It's as good a description of the issues in the case as you'll find anywhere.[2]

---

2   In order to make this read a bit easier, I have substituted "Dirks" for "Petitioner." Some of the quotes noted in the brief refer to the original SEC case, as well as the Appeals Court ruling.

"Dirks is a securities analyst, 'well-known for his investigative talents,' who researched insurance company securities. In March 1973, Dirks applied those investigative talents to uncover a major fraud perpetrated by the officers of a publicly-owned insurance company. As the court of appeals observed,' in two weeks of concerted effort, at times resembling something from detective fiction, Dirks investigated and confirmed rumors of massive fraud by the Equity Funding Corporation of America, an insurance holding company whose stock traded on the New York Stock Exchange. Largely thanks to Dirks one of the most infamous frauds in recent memory was uncovered and exposed. Despite his efforts to uncover and expose the criminal scheme at Equity Funding, the Securities and Exchange Commission charged Dirks with 'tipping' material inside information in violation of Section 10(b) of the Securities Exchange Act of 1934.

"Dirks first learned of the fraud at Equity Funding from a former officer of the company, Ronald Secrist, who met with him for several hours on March 7, 1973.'Secrist made a series of detailed but nearly incredible allegations about Equity Funding,' including allegations that the company had produced large numbers of spurious insurance policies to inflate its sales revenues and that 'its top officers had Mafia connections which they used to threaten the lives of employees who objected to the fabrications.' Secrist urged Dirks to verify the existence of the fraud and then expose it. He expected Dirks to transmit evidence of the fraud to 'his firm's customers' and 'clients,' thereby triggering large-volume securities sales that would lead to a full investigation: 'by jarring the stock, he would jar the corporation - this was my plan - he would jar the corporate officers and would also rattle the Wall Street financial community to the extent that someone would take action very quickly.' Secrist believed that selling pressure would cause the price of Equity Funding stock to 'drop close to zero very quickly,' and thus 'reveal the fraud to the world' and 'prevent its continuation.'

"During their initial meeting, Dirks sought and obtained Secrist's permission to convey evidence of the fraud to the *Wall Street Journal*. Secrist warned, however, that merely presenting the information to regulatory authorities, including the SEC, would be abortive. Secrist stated that employees who attempted to do this in the past had been 'brushed aside with a comment that that's a ridiculous story;' those employees also found that the information was sometimes relayed back to Equity Funding and that 'they were placed in personal jeopardy as a result of having gone there.'?..

"In addition to interviewing former employees of Equity Funding, Dirks also met with Equity Funding's present and former auditors in an attempt to spread word of the fraud and bring it to a halt. As the Commission explained:

'Dirks also learned that Equity Funding's auditors were about to release certified financial statements for the company on March 26. He immediately contacted them and apprised them of the fraud allegations, hoping that they would withhold release of their report and seek a halt in the trading of Equity Funding securities. Instead, the auditors merely reported Dirks' allegations to management.'

"As early as March 12, 1973, Dirks also attempted to communicate his evidence to the *Wall Street Journal.* 'Dirks expected that a highly respected publication like the (Journal) could be effective in helping him investigate the Secrist allegations and to expose the fraud if it proved to exist.' Those efforts also were unavailing.

'During the entire week that Dirks was in Los Angeles investigating Equity Funding, he was also in touch regularly with William Blundell, the *Wall Street Journal*'s Los Angeles bureau chief. Dirks kept Blundell up to date on the progress of the investigation and badgered him to write a story for the Journal on the allegations of fraud at Equity Funding. Blundell, however, was afraid that publishing such damaging rumors supported only by hearsay from former employees might be libelous, so he declined to write the story.'

"Dirks provided Blundell with 'the substance of all he knew,' including his 'notes' and the 'names' of all witnesses. Nevertheless, given the 'scope of the fraud,' Blundell doubted that it could have been 'missed by an honest auditor' and discounted the entire allegation.

"Increasing circulation of rumors about the fraud led Dirks to believe that it was 'unlikely that Equity Funding stock would open for trading on Monday, March 26, because trading would be halted by the NYSE.' This did not occur, however, and Dirks again spoke to William Blundell of the *Wall*

Street Journal and urged him to publish a story exposing the fraud. Blundell refused to do so but stated that he intended to discuss the matter with the SEC's Los Angeles Regional Office. Blundell secured Dirks' permission to propose a meeting with the SEC that would include himself and two other key witnesses. Dirks then contacted the SEC and voluntarily presented all of his information at the SEC's regional office beginning on March 27 and continuing throughout the next three days.

"During the two-week period in which Dirks pursued his investigation and spread word of Secrist's charges, the price of Equity Funding stock fell precipitously from $26 per share to less than $15. This led the NYSE to halt trading in the stock on March 27. Shortly thereafter, Illinois and California insurance authorities impounded Equity Funding's records and uncovered evidence of the fraud. Only then did the SEC file a complaint against Equity Funding and only then did the *Wall Street Journal* publish 'a front page story written by Blundell but based largely on information assembled by Dirks.' Three days later, Equity Funding filed a petition (for bankruptcy).

"While Dirks' investigative activities succeeded in revealing in a few days that 'one of the darlings of Wall Street, a company that had managed to produce continued high earnings growth for a decade, was, instead, a gigantic fraud,' government authorities with jurisdiction over Equity Funding did not move so quickly. As early as 1971, the SEC had received allegations of fraudulent accounting practices at Equity Funding. Moreover, on March 9, 1973, an official of the California Insurance Department informed the SEC's regional office in Los Angeles of Secrist's charges of fraud. The SEC's staff attorney 'stated that similar allegations had been made about Equity Funding before by disgruntled employees.' He nonetheless recommended 'delaying any type of inspection of the Equity Funding operations until next year absent further corroboration. Equity Funding's Chairman - one of the principal architects of the fraud - testified that, prior to March 1973, he received no questions from auditors, state regulatory authorities, or federal regulatory authorities that suggested 'they suspected there was a fraud at Equity Funding.' When asked whether Dirks was 'personally responsible for having uncovered the events at Equity Funding,' he candidly stated: 'I think Mr. Dirks is entitled to personal credit for that.'

"Following public revelation of the Equity Funding scandal, a federal grand jury in Los Angeles returned a 105 count indictment against 22 persons, including many of Equity Funding's officers and directors?[Guilty pleas or convictions were obtained on all 22. Chairman Stanley Goldblum received an 8-year prison sentence and a substantial fine.]

"While the *Wall Street Journal*'s reporter, William Blundell, was 'nominated for a Pulitzer Prize for his coverage of the Equity Funding scandal,' Dirks was charged by the SEC with violating the antifraud provisions of the federal securities laws based on his selective revelation of information about Equity Funding prior to general public disclosure. Following an administrative hearing, the Commission found that Dirks had 'tipped' nonpublic information concerning Equity Funding in violation of those provisions. It observed that 'Dirks received the information from inside corporate sources. From the nature of the information, the inference must have been obvious that his sources had received it during the course of their corporate duties, and that the company intended that it should be kept in confidence.'

"Despite its finding of a violation, the Commission imposed only a censure - its mildest sanction - on Dirks. It observed that 'it is clear that Dirks played an important role in bringing Equity Funding's massive fraud to light, and that he reported the fraud allegations to Equity Funding's auditors and sought to have the information published in the *Wall Street Journal*."

In a 6-3 decision, the Supreme Court overruled prior judgments and Dirks was finally cleared, ten years later. Essentially, the Court ruled that for a recipient of a tip to be guilty of insider trading, the insider who provided the tip must have been seeking to profit from the tip. There never was any evidence Ray Dirks personally made a dime off of his actions.

Today, Dirks is head of his own research / investment banking shop, specializing in small companies steeped in controversy. I'll leave it at that.

But I do have to note a comment Dirks made during the above proceedings concerning the New York Stock Exchange and its internal procedures.

"There is the question of the NYSE, a venerated American institution which advertises the safety and security of investing in its listed companies, but which, in fact is an antique, costly and dangerous system perpetuated for the convenience of its members." [Charles Geisst]

A little ahead of his time, don't you think?[3]

\---

The Commission's decision in this case (to suspend Dirks) threatens to undermine, rather than enhance, investor confidence. If administrative rulings strip away the incentive of security analysts to investigate frauds, there will be more frauds in the future and they will persist for longer periods of time. By contrast, if investors may continue to expect that competent analysts, acting in their own economic interest, will assist the government in policing the securities markets, their reliance on the integrity of the marketplace will be strengthened.

It was inevitable that the Equity Funding fraud would have victims. Because of Dirks' actions leading to the discovery of the fraud, there were fewer victims than there otherwise would have been. And to the extent that private parties retain an incentive to act as Dirks acted there are likely to be fewer victims of such frauds in the future.

Respectfully submitted,

Rex E. Lee, Solicitor General
DI Lowell Jensen, Assistant Attorney General
Stephen M. Sharpiro, Special Assistant to the Solicitor General
Roger M. Olsen, Deputy Assistant Attorney General
October, 1982

Note: As part of the investigation into the fraud, it was discovered that of more than $3 billion worth of life insurance ostensibly issued by Equity Funding between 1964 and 1973, more than $2 billion proved to be fictitious.

Sources: Brian Trumbore President/Editor, StocksandNews.com[4]

---

3   U.S. Department of Justice archives; Robert J. Cole / New York Times (1973) ; Linda Greenhouse / New York Times (1983) "The New York Times Century of Business" Floyd Norris and Christine Bockelmann "Wall Street: A History" Charles R. Geisst
4   This last section is actually taken from a follow-up article which I elected not to publish in its entirety. However, I wanted to share the Solicitor General's thoughts.